Vision, Instruction, and Action

Vision, Instruction, and Action

David Chapman

The MIT Press
Cambridge, Massachusetts
London, England

This book was printed and bound in the United States of America.

Library of Congress Cataloging-in-Publication Data

Chapman, David.
   Vision, instruction, and action / David Chapman.
      p.   cm. — (Artificial intelligence)
   Includes bibliographical references (p.   ) and index.
   ISBN 0-262-03181-7
   1. Artificial intelligence. 2. Cognition. 3. Visual perception.
4. Computer vision. 5. Sonja. I. Title. II. Series: Artificial intelligence
(Cambridge, Mass.)
Q335.C4829 1991
006.3—dc20   91-13739
                                                      CIP

Contents

Series Foreword

Artificial intelligence is the study of intelligence using the ideas and methods of computation. Unfortunately a definition of intelligence seems impossible at the moment because intelligence appears to be an amalgam of so many information-processing and information-representation abilities.

Of course psychology, philosophy, linguistics, and related disciplines offer various perspectives and methodologies for studying intelligence. For the most part, however, the theories proposed in these fields are too incomplete and too vaguely stated to be realized in computational terms. Something more is needed, even though valuable ideas, relationships, and constraints can be gleaned from traditional studies of what are, after all, impressive existence proofs that intelligence is in fact possible.

Artificial intelligence offers a new perspective and a new methodology. Its central goal is to make computers intelligent, both to make them more useful and to understand the principles that make intelligence possible. That intelligent computers will be extremely useful is obvious. The more profound point is that artificial intelligence aims to understand intelligence using the ideas and methods of computation, thus offering a radically new and different basis for theory formation. Most of the people doing work in artificial intelligence believe that these theories will apply to any intelligent information processor, whether biological or solid state.

There are side effects that deserve attention, too. Any program that will successfully model even a small part of intelligence will be inherently massive and complex. Consequently artificial intelligence continually confronts the limits of computer-science technology. The problems encountered have been hard enough and interesting enough to seduce artificial intelligence people into working on them with enthusiasm. It is natural, then, that there has been a steady flow of ideas from artificial intelligence to computer science, and the flow shows no signs of abating.

The purpose of this series in artificial intelligence is to provide people in many areas, both professionals and students, with timely, detailed information about what is happening on the frontiers in research centers all over the world.

J. Michael Brady
Daniel G. Bobrow
Randall Davis

Acknowledgments

Phil Lesh once said that the Grateful Dead's success could be attributed to the fact that "despite working together for so long we retain the ability to surprise each other." This accurately describes my relationship with my collaborator Phil Agre, to whom my first thanks go.

Rod Brooks supervised this thesis. I couldn't have asked for a better advisor. He knew when to leave me alone and when to twist my arm for text. His advice on difficult problems, technical and political, was unerring.

Barbara Grosz and Tomás Lozano Pérez formed the other two thirds of my committee. Their expertise in fields about which I initially knew nothing was invaluable. Their insistence that I get some of my facts and references straight has improved the thesis greatly.

In addition to these people, John Batali, Brad Blumenthal, Jon Connell, Jim Davis, Gary Drescher, Ian Horswill, Leslie Kaelbling, Beth Preston, Jeff Shrager, Penni Sibun, Orca Starbuck, Lambert Wixson, and Ramin Zabih commented on drafts of the thesis. Christina Allen, Jerry Feldman, Ken Forbus, several members of the Interaction Analysis Laboratory, Jim Mahoney, Stan Rosenschein, Eric Saund, Candy Sidner, Susan Stucky, Shimon Ullman, Dan Weld, and many other friends and colleagues have provided useful comments in conversation and by email.

Thanks to all of you.

Vision, Instruction, and Action

1 Introduction

This book describes Sonja, a system which uses instructions in the course of visually-guided activity. The book explores an integration of research in vision, activity, and natural language pragmatics. Integrated systems are uncommon in AI research, but they provide otherwise unobtainable insights into the relationships between AI problems and techniques.

Sonja engages in sensible activity in a domain characterized by complexity, uncertainty, immediacy, and continual change. It has access to this domain only via the domain's primitive actions and via a simulated but realistic visual system.

Although Sonja can play autonomously, it can also make use of instructions provided by a human advisor. The system interprets instructions in terms of the situation in which they are given, including the physical configuration of the environment and the system's current and projected activities. It uses instructions flexibly; it does work to figure out what they mean, can interleave instruction use with other goal-directed activity, and rejects instructions that make no sense.

1.1 What Sonja does

In this section I will describe a short scenario which demonstrates some of Sonja's abilities.

Sonja plays a video game called Amazon. An Amazon scene appears in figure 1.1. A player of Amazon (a person or Sonja) controls an icon on the screen representing a woman warrior: the amazon. The amazon can move about in a dungeon. In the dungeon there are walls and various enemies and tools. In this scene, some walls form a room, there are a ghost and a demon that will attack the amazon, and there are three amulets (on chains) that will give the amazon magical powers when they are picked up. The player can cause the amazon to shoot at the monsters and kill them.

Sonja plays a competent beginner's game of Amazon autonomously. It knows how to kill off monsters, how to pick up and use tools, and how to get about in the dungeon maze. Sonja doesn't always know how to choose the right thing to do when there are several plausible courses of action available. In these circumstances, instructions from an advisor can be useful. The scene of figure 1.1 is one in which Sonja would do fine without instructions; I will, however, micromanage the system to

Figure 1.1
An Amazon scene. The amazon is in the center of the picture; one amulet is
directly to her right. The frog-like thing with ears is a demon; a ghost is directly
below it. In the room there are two more amulets.

demonstrate how Sonja can use them.

In this scene, an advisor might suggest to Sonja "Go in and get the amulet." To use this instruction, Sonja first has to figure out what "the amulet" refers to. Because Sonja's access to Amazon is mediated by perception, it must perform a visual search of the scene to find the amulet referred to. Sonja's visual system models in detail facts about human visual search. I'll argue that it is important that Sonja and its human advisor have similar visual processes, because communication depends on a shared understanding of the world.

"Go in and get the amulet" doesn't refer to just any amulet; the amulet must be one that is in the room the amazon will go into. The amulet to the amazon's right is not satisfactory, for example; it wouldn't count as carrying out "Go in and get the amulet" to go into the room and then come out and pick up the amulet outside. Sonja's ability to find the right amulet depends on its ability to see whether an amulet is in a room. The ability to recognize rooms and containment relationships is also needed for getting about in the dungeon; to get the amulet, Sonja will have to go through the doorway, which entails finding it.

Sonja identifies the bottom left amulet as the one most likely to have been referred to by the instruction and starts the amazon heading for the doorway. Its passage, however, is blocked by the ghost. Sonja has to kill the ghost to make progress; it does so by shooting shuriken (throwing stars) at it (figure 1.2). Because Sonja lives in a dynamic world in which events are not entirely under its control, it can not treat instructions as though they were programs or subroutine calls. Sonja may have to carry out arbitrary amounts and kinds of work before completing an instruction. Its use of instructions must be intelligent and flexible in order to combine and interleave the use of several instructions.

Having dispatched the ghost, Sonja starts to shoot at the demon (figure 1.3) which also blocks passage through the doorway. At this point the human advisor recommends "Use a knife." Knives in Amazon have several functions; they can be used to jimmy the locks on doors and they can be thrown at monsters and other things to destroy them. While it takes three shuriken and a couple of seconds to kill a monster, a single knife will do the job quickly. On the other hand, knives can only be used once, whereas the supply of shuriken is unlimited.

The instruction "Use the knife" can only be carried out after it has been made sense of and interpreted in terms of the situation at hand.

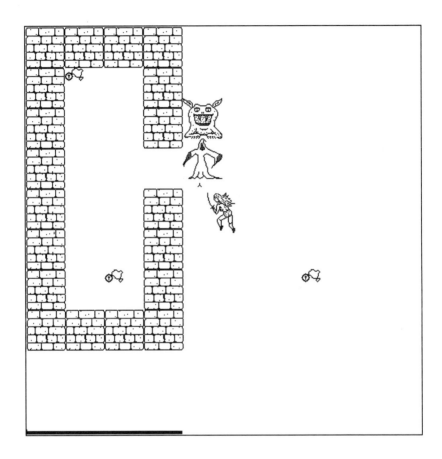

Figure 1.2
Sonja kills the ghost by shooting shuriken at it. A shuriken is visible as a small
three-pointed star between the amazon and the ghost.

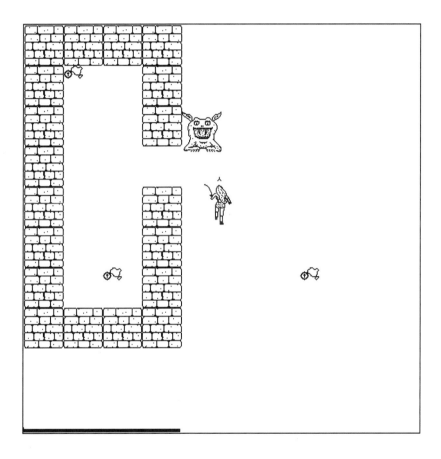

Figure 1.3
Sonja shoots at the demon.

Figuring out what the advisor meant involves looking at the scene for opportunities to use a knife in one of the various ways possible. In this instance, there are no doors to open. On the other hand, throwing a knife at the demon would make sense. Whereas ghosts must touch the amazon to hurt it, demons breathe rapidly-moving fireballs, and so are more dangerous. It is often worth using up a knife to kill one quickly. Sonja accordingly throws a knife at the demon (figure 1.4). This example shows that Sonja can not only carry out several courses of action at once, but can also use several instructions at once; it used the knife *in the course of* going into the room to get the amulet.

Sonja proceeds through the doorway (figure 1.5) and turns to head toward the amulet it has identified as that which the instruction-giver intended (figure 1.6). It turns out, however, that the instruction-giver actually intended Sonja to get the top amulet. That Sonja misunderstood only becomes apparent to the instruction-giver once Sonja is through the door and has turned to head downward. At this point, the instruction-giver says "No, the other one!" to repair the misunderstanding. Sonja finds an alternative referent for "the amulet," namely the top one, heads toward it (figure 1.7), and picks it up (figure 1.8).

1.2 Contributions

This book contributes to at least three fields: the theory of activity, computational linguistics, and machine vision.

1.2.1 Contributions to activity theory

A theory of activity is concerned with how agents *do* things. Agre and I have been developing a new theory of activity over the past five years [3, 4, 5, 6, 7, 36, 37, 38].

This theory proposes that activity arises from the interaction of an agent with its environment. The agent can participate in ongoing events by taking continual account of environmental conditions. The theory includes a new, participatory theory of representation. The theory requires and includes a realistic, detailed model of perception.

The theory is motivated by issues of computational and neurophysiological plausibility. We demand that a theory of activity explain how an agent can usually decide what to do before it is too late to do it. We

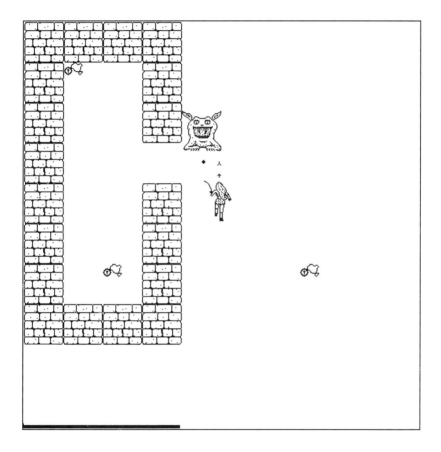

Figure 1.4
The amazon throws a knife at the demon based on the instruction "Use a knife".
The knife appears as a small arrow directly above the amazon.

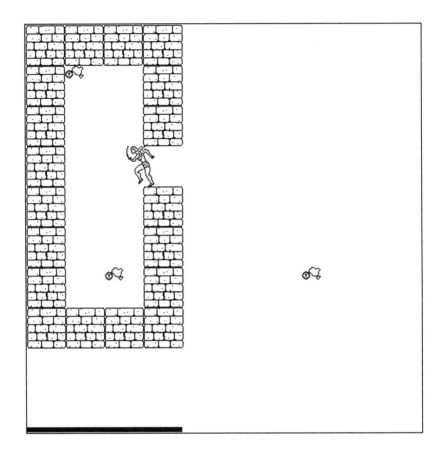

Figure 1.5
Sonja passes through the doorway of the room.

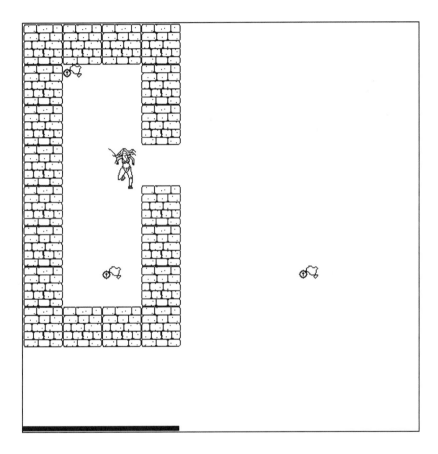

Figure 1.6
Sonja turns downward to get the bottom amulet.

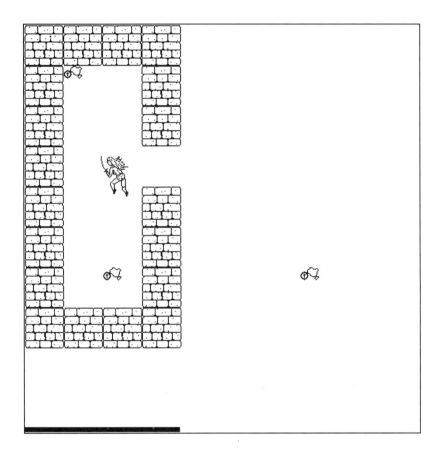

Figure 1.7
Sonja has been told "No, the other one!" and heads for the top amulet instead.

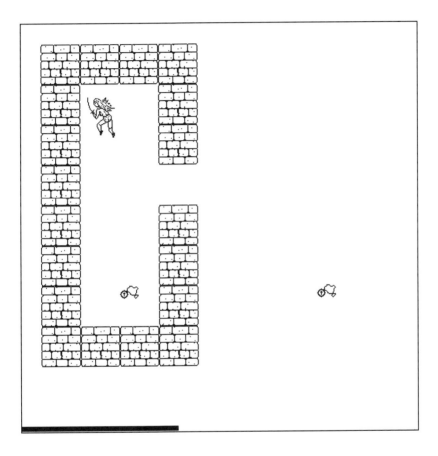

Figure 1.8
Sonja has just picked up the amulet, causing it to disappear from the screen.

also demand that the theory not contradict established facts about how the brain works.

Sonja is the most recent of a series of implementations of parts of this theory. It extends previous work by addressing linguistic issues. This connection allows and requires that the use of instructions be flexible and sensible, taking account of current goals and circumstances. Sonja also extends our understanding of the architecture underlying activity and incorporates many technical improvements.

1.2.2 Contributions to computational linguistics

The principal linguistic tenet of this book is that language use must be grounded in concrete activity. Although I believe this is a universal phenomenon, it is particularly clear in video game instruction use. The ability to understand instructions is inseparable from the ability to use them: that is, to engage in the activity they recommend.

This book concentrates, among linguistic phenomena, on reference. Most previous computational work on reference has concentrated on specification: finding a mental representation which refers to the same thing as a given linguistic representation. Sonja is concerned instead with external reference, the ability of representations to designate objects in the world. Sonja implements external reference causally, by grounding reference in language users' interaction with the objects and activities to which their speech refers.

Sonja models several pragmatic issues in addition to reference, in particular linguistic repair processes and the use of temporal and spatial expressions.

Sonja also extends existing work by connecting language use with more detailed and realistic theories of vision and activity.

There are many linguistic phenomena that Sonja does not model; for example, it does almost no syntactic processing.

1.2.3 Contributions to vision research

Sonja integrates and extends several bodies of work in intermediate vision. The book presents an implementation of a unified visual architecture and demonstrates that this architecture can support a serious theory of activity.

Sonja demonstrates for the first time that various visual mechanisms previously proposed on psychophysical, neurophysiological, and speculative computational grounds are in fact useful by connecting them with a natural task domain. The implementation fleshes out many aspects of these theories which have previously been left unspecified. For example, it includes a detailed interface between intermediate vision and central processing.

Sonja does not incorporate a realistic model of early vision. The book suggests ways it could.

1.3   Guide to the book

This book is long and in places dense with technical detail. You may not want to read all or most of it. Here are some suggestions for how to proceed if you only intend to read part of it, or to see if you are interested in more.

- To get more of an idea of what Sonja can do, read the introduction to chapter 8 and then skim sections 8.3 through 8.7, looking particularly at the pictures.
- If you are interested in how Sonja does it, you can start with chapter 3, which describes Sonja's architecture in general terms.
- If you are interested in particular in Sonja's approach to vision, skim chapter 3 and then read chapter 6, which explains Sonja's visual system in detail.
- If you are interested in Sonja's instruction use, read chapter 5.
- If you are interested in Sonja's approach to activity, read chapter 2 for philosophical underpinnings, skim chapter 3 on the architecture, chapter 8 on how Sonja plays Amazon, chapter 9, which analyzes the implementation, and appendix B on skill acquisition.

After skipping around, you may want to read the chapters in order. At any rate, I'll describe them in order in some more detail.

Chapter 2 describes the theory of activity underlying Sonja. You should read this chapter through if you are going to read much of the rest of the book, as it introduces terms that are used throughout. Together with chapter 3, it explains why I wrote Sonja the way I did and why that's interesting; Sonja may seem trivial, bizarre, and unmotivated without this explanation.

Chapter 3 describes the theory of cognitive architecture Sonja implements. This theory is principally motivated by arguments from neurophysiology and from vision research. It puts strong constraints on cognitive theory. For example, it would not be easy, and probably would not
be possible, to implement most current cognitive models in this architecture. I present some basic facts about the brain and argue that they imply that the human cognitive machinery makes traditional programming
techniques like pointers, variables, datastructures, virtual machines, and
dynamic storage allocation expensive, and suggest finding ways to design agents which do not depend on these devices. I argue for a division
between peripheral systems (sensory and motor systems) and a central
system. I argue for a particular sort of architecture for the visual system based on learnability criteria. This architecture consists of a set of
relatively high-level visual building blocks which can be assembled into
visual routines by the central system. I propose a particular provisional
model of the central system which is intended to allow an agent to act
flexibly in realistic domains.

Chapter 4 is about Amazon. You definitely want to read section 4.2,
which explains the domain in detail. The rest of the chapter explains
why Amazon is and isn't a good domain to explore the issues this book is
about. It describes the criteria I used in choosing the domain, considers
its realism, and discusses some shortcomings of it which became apparent
only late in the implementation.

Chapter 5 describes instruction use in Sonja. I describe a framework
for grounding reference in concrete activity. I show that naturally occur-
ring instructions must be made sense of in terms of the current situation
before they can be used. Making sense of video game instructions involves reorienting attention and requires understanding instructions in
terms of activities their user is capable of carrying out autonomously.
This chapter describes various sorts of instructions Sonja can use and
explains how Sonja uses them.

Chapter 6 describes Sonja's sensory and motor systems, particularly
its vision system. The vision system addresses the fundamental visual
problems of selectively applying visual processing to subsets of the image, finding regions of the image with task-relevant properties, and es-
tablishing spatial relationships among parts of the image. It models
a variety of relatively well-understood but previously unimplemented

psychophysical phenomena. I discuss visual attention and visual search, their psychophysics and their implementation in Sonja. Finally, I discuss visual operators—the building blocks of visual processing—and the visual routines assembled out of them. Visual routines perform the spatial reasoning Sonja needs to get about in Amazon.

Chapter 7 describes the implementation technology of Sonja's central system. This system is implemented as a digital circuit. I document the two languages used to design this circuit: a circuit description language and a higher-level arbitration language used to express a three-phase central system architecture. This chapter also documents debugging facilities I implemented to help design Sonja.

Chapter 8 describes the specific digital circuit which is Sonja's central system and explains how it and the peripheral systems together allow Sonja to play Amazon and to take instructions.

Chapter 9 concludes by evaluating the implementation and analyzing its relationship with the theory. I discuss ways in which the implementation technology worked well and ways in which it needs work. I consider whether Sonja demonstrates the points I set out to make.

Two appendices are concerned with future work. Appendix A proposes an extension to Sonja that would allow it to play collaboratively. Appendix B discusses skill acquisition. Much of the theory underlying Sonja makes sense only if it can be made compatible with some theory of skill acquisition. I analyze various existing of skill acquisition in terms of Sonja's architectural constraints, concluding that some popular approaches are impractical or inadequate. The chapter then describes an implementation of an approach to skill acquisition that is compatible with the book's approach to activity. Unfortunately this implementation didn't work. I analyze the failure and suggest future directions.

2 The concrete-situated approach

This book is part of an on-going study of concrete activity: that is, of actively doing something in the world, as opposed to cogitating. I've been conducting this research in collaboration with Agre. Much of our work to date is summarized in our joint papers [5, 6, 7, 38] and in his thesis [4]. Because of the volume and complexity of this work, because most of the central insights are due to Agre, and because they are well documented in his thesis, this chapter is only a summary.

The approach[1] to activity I will present here is quite unlike that currently prevalent in cognitive science. However, in this exposition, I will not explicitly contrast it with the traditional alternatives. The theory is also not without antecedents; in fact, most parts of it have been proposed in literatures other than AI. The principal contribution of our work is in giving these ideas computational grounding. Our paper "What are plans for?" [7] and Agre's thesis discuss the relationship of the concrete-situated approach to previous work in AI; Agre's thesis in addition sketches some of its intellectual history in other fields.

The sections of this chapter explain how the concrete-situated approach

- is principally concerned with *routine* activity (2.1);
- takes an agent's concrete *situation* to be its principal resource in acting (2.2);
- stresses that activity involves *interaction* with an external environment whose influence on activity is equal to the influence of the agent (2.3);
- seeks to describe the *dynamics* of such interaction (2.4);
- in particular seeks to characterize the *routines* an agent falls into (2.5);
- proposes that activity arises from continual *improvisation*, or recomputing what to do (2.6); and
- incorporates a new theory of representation called *deictic* representation (2.7).

These aspects of the theory cohere and reinforce each other. They do not stand alone: the theory of deictic representation, for instance, only makes sense for agents that are interacting with their environments in

---

[1]I'll talk more about what I mean by an "approach" in section 9.1.1.

the course of practical activity. The routineness of activity and dependence on the situation make improvisation feasible. Deictic representation is the principal computational support for improvisation. And so on.

2.1   Routineness

All research begins with simplifying assumptions or idealizations. Most research in AI starts by restricting attention to particular capacities such as vision, language, or planning and studies them largely in isolation. We start instead with a *routineness idealization*. The routineness idealization holds that most activity is *routine*. Routine activity is the regular, practiced, unproblematic activity that makes up most of everyday life. Routine activity does not require that you think new thoughts. (I'll make the notion of a "new thought" more precise in section 3.1.2.) The routineness idealization holds that we can and should study routine activity first, making only occasional reference to the novel elements that are introduced from time to time into in the course of routine activity.

Extensive existing studies of routine activity in several fields demonstrate that it is indeed practical and useful to study routine cases before novel ones. Most of these studies are not computational, but are based in philosophy, psychology, sociology, and anthropology. (For a review, see Agre's thesis [4].) Heidegger [118], for instance, presents a phenomenology of routine activity and argues that this analysis should be the basis of an understanding of what we would call cognitive phenomena, rather than the other way around. (For discussions of the implications of this argument for AI, see Dreyfus [61], Preston [221, 222], and Winograd and Flores [296].) Ethnomethodological sociologists, as another example, study the nature of the routine interpersonal interactions that make up much of everyday life [120]. They are able to reveal much about cognition by studying the ways people say "hello" on the phone or nod their heads in conversation or pay the check in a restaurant.

Computational studies of routine activity begin with Agre's running arguments system [3, 4] and with a system I implemented called Pengi [5]. Pengi illustrated many of the themes I will develop in this chapter; by implementing only the routine case of a particular sort of complex activity, it demonstrated that it was possible to avoid the enormous

computational and explanatory overhead required by the then-existing
approaches to activity in AI.

There are four reasons to think that it is important to understand
routine activity before trying to understand novel activity.

- Routine activity is by far more common. We spend most of our lives
engaged in activities like making breakfast, driving to work, reading the
paper, typing forms, giving the kids a bath, and grocery shopping; these
rarely involve novel elements. Even creative work is mainly routine: it's
rewording sentences or painting the background of the scene or playing
another gig at the Rat.[2]

- Because most activity is routine, the processes which are responsible
for novel activity must accommodate and depend on those which are
responsible for routine activity. Novel activity is possible only against
a background of routine competence. In fact it typically proceeds by
assembling routine pieces in novel patterns.

- Routine activity is evolutionarily prior. The activity of animals up
to the level of lower vertebrates is wholly routine. For instance, Gallistel [93] argues that learning in animals up through amphibians proceeds
only by selective facilitation or inhibition of innate motor patterns. This
demonstrates that it is possible to isolate routine activity altogether. It
also suggests that if there is distinct neural machinery responsible for
novel activity, it must depend on the stable, previously evolved machinery for routine activity.[3]

- As a practical matter, many of the most useful applications of artificial intelligence may be in automating routine activities in order to free
people for more interesting pursuits.

These issues are further explored in papers by Agre and myself [4, 38].

Any idealization falsifies the phenomena in certain ways. This is
inevitable; we can't do research without one idealization or another.
The routineness idealization marginalizes questions about where new
thoughts come from and how they connect with the existing machin-

---

[2]These observations are an appeal to your own experience of everyday life. I don't
know how to quantify routineness, nor do I know of any careful studies of how much
of life is routine.

[3]I take no stand on the question of whether machinery specific to novel activity
is necessary, desirable, or to be found in the human brain.

ery for routine activity. Appendix B sketches some starting points for studying these questions.

I believe that the idealization of routineness falsifies the nature of activity less than some other idealizations have. Whether or not this is the case will depend on considerable further research, as computational studies depending on this idealization have only just begun. However, even if not, the idealization may still be useful, because it exposes issues more familiar idealizations hide.

2.2 Situatedness

The concrete-situated approach holds that an agent's most important resource in computing what to do is its concrete situation. In driving, you are responsive to other cars, to road signs, and to the geometry of the road. Pouring milk over your breakfast cereal, your hand constantly adjusts the flow to prevent milk from splashing off the irregular flakes and spilling out of the bowl. There are, of course, other resources available (internal and external memory, for example), but concrete action without perception is virtually impossible.

Use of the immediate presence of the world makes some hard problems easy.

- If you want to find out something about the world that will affect how you should act, you can usually just look and see.[4] Concrete activity is principally concerned with the here-and-now. You mostly don't need to worry about things that have gone before, are much in the future, or are not physically present. You don't need to maintain a world model; the world is its own best representation. (We'll explore this idea further in section 2.7, on deictic representation.)

- If you want to know what action to take, you can often just look and see that as well. In a great many situations, it's obvious what to do next given the configuration of materials at hand. And once you've done that the next thing to do is likely to be obvious too. Complex sequences of actions result, without needing a complex control structure to decide for

---

[4]This doesn't imply that knowledge is free; as we'll see in section 3.3.3, looking is an active process which requires computation and sometimes external work such as head motion or removal of occluding objects. Looking is, however, usually computationally cheaper than alternatives such as deduction and is to be preferred in such cases.

you what to do. (See section 2.6.)

• If you want to know what the effect of an action will be, or whether a particular approach to a task will work, and if you can't tell just by looking, you can usually safely try it and find out. You rarely need to perform simulations. (See section 2.7.)

• If you want to become expert at a task, you can learn it gradually by practice, rather than solving the general case all at once. The world benignly falls into useful regularities, so you can trust your accumulated experience. (See appendix B.) You aren't playing a game against the world; your breakfast is not out to get you. Doing the wrong thing is rarely fatal.[5]

• The world has people in it as well as things. You aren't on your own; someone else has probably had to do what you want to do before and can help and give advice. (See chapter 5.) After a few rounds of collaboration, you'll become expert yourself. (See section B.3.1.) Many tasks are socially organized as involving division of labor, so that you can participate in activities in which you *never* learn all the roles. Medical activities provide many examples; Hutchins [126] has studied in detail other examples in the domain of learning to navigate naval ships.

The nature of concrete situations makes some traditional approaches to activity unworkable.

• Situations change continually. Algorithms which formally solve your problem are no use if they terminate after the problem has changed or solved itself or turned into a disaster.

• Real situations are immensely messy, always more complicated than any representation of them can be.

• Real situations, in particular, make it hard to know exactly what the outcome of your actions will be.

• Perception is your only access to the situation around you. You can only see and hear things that happen nearby. Some things that matter to you will always be unknown and unknowable. Algorithms which require complete information are no use.

---

[5]The *natural* world is dangerous. Fortunately, people do not live in a state of nature, but in an embedding culture which eliminates most natural dangers. This fact is depended on extensively by human cognition.

The concrete-situated approach addresses these four difficulties by suggesting that agents

- Intimately interact with the changing situation (section 2.3);
- Represent only relevant aspects of the situation (section 2.7);
- Continually improvise and try out alternative ways of doing things (section 2.6); and
- Ground representation and action in perception (sections 2.7, 3.3.3, and 3.3.5).

2.3 Interactivity

The concrete-situated approach is *interactionist*. It holds that the organization of activity is emergent from interactions between an agent and its environment, rather than being a property of an agent (as in *mentalism*) or of the environment (as in *behaviorism*). Causality rapidly loops in and out of the agent, rather than looping around inside the agent's head and occasionally emerging to affect the world (figure 2.1).

The complexity of activity arises not principally from the complexity of the agent or of the world, but from the complexity of their interaction. Simon's parable of the ant [259] argues that a simple system can engage in complex activity if it is put in a complex environment. But Simon's ant is virtually programmed by its environment; its activity will not be much more complex than the environment is. The complexity of an interaction can be much greater (or much less) than the sum of the complexities of the agent and its environment. A small finite state machine, for instance, can compute any recursive function when placed in the environment of two counters [183]. On the other hand, a photocopier is a complicated machine which does something simple. Like a person and unlike Simon's ant, Sonja is a complex system. However, it is designed so that the complexity of its activity is much greater than the sum of the complexity of its machinery and the complexity of its domain.

An agent that accepts the world as an equal partner in organizing its activity does not continually try to force interactions to conform to a

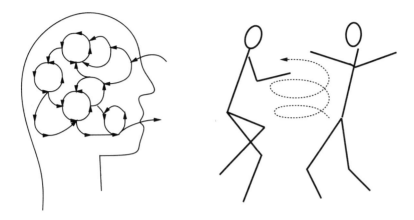

Figure 2.1
Mentalist and interactionist causal loops. In mentalist theories, causality mostly
loops around inside an agent's head, occasionally passing from module to module
and relatively rarely crossing the borders of the skull. Playing chess is a mentalist
prototype of activity. In interactionist theories, causality constantly passes between
the agent and the world. Dancing is an interactionist prototype of activity. It
emphasizes that people are not disembodied heads, but whole agents interacting
with others via sensors and effectors in a social context.

preconceived idea of how things should go. That's futile; other processes
and agents in the world would constantly force you off track. On the
other hand, taking the world as a *merely* equal partner implies that
you can not just react to situations as they arise. Sensible interaction
requires forethought.

Locating the determination of activity in interaction implies viewing
life as a series of opportunities and contingencies: openings to participate
in particular sorts of activities and events that arise as you do so. Life
is not a series of problems, each handed to you as a unit and requiring
a unitary solution. Life is constantly ongoing. The concrete-situated
approach takes dancing and hanging out, rather than solving the eight
puzzle or designing a circuit, as prototypical activities. These activities
involve other people, who are likely to make it hard to impose your
solutions. On the other hand, in these situations the other people will
share the work of making interaction simple.

2.4 Dynamics

A *dynamic* is a pattern in the interaction between an agent and its
world. What sort of dynamics an agent participates in depends on the
machinery that composes it and on its world. What sort of machinery an
agent must have depends on what sort of dynamics it needs to participate
in and what sort of world it will be situated in. The concrete situated
approach prescribes interleaving study of machinery and dynamics.

Here is an example dynamic. If you live in a graduate student house-
hold, you probably have in your kitchen cupboard a stack of bowls, not
many of which match. When you use a bowl, you put it back at the top
of the stack. Over time, the bowls that aren't used often tend to sink to
the bottom of the stack. This example illustrates several points about
dynamics generally.

• Dynamics are not causal agents. Bowls don't end up at the bottom
of the stack *because* of a sinking dynamic; they end up at the bottom
because other bowls are taken out from under them.

• A dynamic operates only *ceteris paribus*, when an unbounded set of
conditions hold. If you have a big dinner party, you may use all your
bowls and they'll end up back in the cupboard scrambled and then will
slowly sort themselves out again over the course of the next few weeks.

• Dynamics are not processes in the agent's head. They are patterns of interaction which may be noticed by a theorist. Dynamics are typically not represented by the agent (though some are). Most people with such a stack of bowls probably have never noticed this dynamic. Activity has a coherence and orderliness which is not a product of any representation of it. Other people may have noticed this dynamic, but typically that doesn't make any difference to the operation of the dynamic. Even when dynamics are represented, typically they do not occur in virtue of their representation (though some do).

• A dynamic typically operates in many different domains. For example, if you do not deliberately sort your records and always return them to one end of your shelf, the same dynamic that sorts bowls will ensure that the records you listen to most often will be closest to the end.

• Beneficial dynamics often arise without their having been intended by the agents involved. This is not just an accident, but depends on subtle facts about the structure of activity which are beyond the scope of this discussion; see Agre's thesis [4] for some starting points. The bowl-sorting dynamic is a small example; it often saves you work because the bowl you want is more often at the top of the stack than chance would predict. More important examples come from the dynamics of apprenticeship, in which skills are often transferred by means neither intended nor understood by the expert or apprentice. For example, in any collaborative activity, it is sensible to divide up labor in such a way that the more experienced actor does the hard bits (which she's more likely to get right) and the less experienced actor does the easier bits. This allocation of tasks is sensible independent of any intention to transfer skills, but it has the effect that the more experienced participant demonstrates competent performance of skills that are just beyond the less experienced participant's ability. This dynamic of unintended demonstration is centrally important in the transfer of skills to preverbal children [148], is a principal mode of skill transfer in many nonindustrial cultures [161], and plays an important role even in situations in which the actors understand themselves to be transferring skills via explicit teaching [30].

The concrete-situated approach shifts explanatory focus from things in the head to dynamics. We postulate new pieces of machinery only as a last resort; this is the principle of *machinery parsimony*. Machinery parsimony is simply good engineering. A well-designed radio is not one that includes every flashy new kind of circuit, it is one that gets the job done with the fewest components. Simple, elegant radio designs usually require a deeper understanding of the physical principles underlying radio operation than do brute force, kitchen-sink designs.

As I will show, powerful dynamics enabling efficient performance of difficult tasks can arise from some simple kinds of machinery. This can be hard to accept at first: in AI, we are trained to find complex machinery impressive, not to find complex explanations of patterns of interaction impressive. It is an easy mistake to dismiss Sonja as trivial because its machinery is uninteresting. What is interesting is the *relationship between* the machinery and its environment.

In studying a particular capability of an agent, AI research has usually begun by asking "What knowledge does the agent need to solve this problem? What machinery does the agent need to manipulate this knowledge?" Frequently, the answer is to propose a new module in the agent's head which gives the capability to the agent. Concrete-situated research asks "what patterns of interaction between the whole agent and its environment will allow it to engage in this sort of activity?" We have found that the deeper your dynamic understanding, the less machinery you need. Bits of machinery, when postulated, do not subserve particular capabilities; the entire agent is applied to every task. Dynamics and bits of machinery do not correspond one-to-one, as they often do in theories based on modularity assumptions. An engineering analogy may again be helpful: while in a crude bridge particular members may be responsible for supporting particular bits of the platform, in a sophisticated truss design the forces are so distributed and combined that every member contributes to supporting every section.

2.5 Routines

A *routine* is a regular, practiced pattern of interaction. Routines are what get work done. You may engage in routines of getting into your car, checking for new email, taking a shower, going for a run, typing your name, saying "hello" to someone you've just been introduced to, scratching your nose, choosing which sandwich to have for lunch, feeding your cat, or making a ski turn.

Routines can have arbitrary temporal extent; you may participate in a yearly academic routine and in a routine of writing your section number on the blackboard. One routine may be made up of other routines: that is, you may routinely engage in one routine after another. This does not mean, however, that one routine "calls" another. Routines, like other dynamics, are not causal agents. The actions that make up a routine are not the *result* of routine; the agent performs actions for specific reasons which make sense at the time. For instance, you don't put bowls on the top of your pile because that will sort them, you put them there because that's where it's easiest to put them. Routines are not programs, are not bits of machinery, and are typically not represented by their agents.

The routine is the concrete-situated approach's unit of activity. This contrasts with stimulus-response theories, in which the unit of activity is an atomic response to a stimulus or perhaps a fixed action pattern, and also contrasts with mentalism, in which the unit of activity is a plan or other thing-in-the-head that controls activity. Routines are a better way of describing activity than stimulus-response pairs because atomic actions rarely make sense in isolation. Routines extend over time and involve many cycles of interaction with the world; a routine is often useful only because of its eventual outcome. Routines are a better way of describing activity than plans or other things-in-the-head because activity is interactive and does not typically conform in detail to representations the acting agents have of it. Useful explanations of activity must be dynamic, explaining patterns of interaction; explanations of what is in an agent's head are useful only if they relate what's inside to the world outside.

For us, the big question in designing an agent is, what sort of machinery will engage in the sorts of routines we want? The architecture we propose is not the only one that will engage in routines; in fact almost any system interacting with an environment will, because routines typically arise from physical determinism. If you put the same agent into the same situation twice, it will do the same thing. Even though real situations and real agents are never exactly the same twice, people and places change only slowly. Your desires, your daily routine, the arrangement of your office and kitchen, your route to work, and your relationship with your office mate are all relatively constant. An agent's activity can be mainly routine because the world is mainly routine. [6]

If any architecture will engage in routines, then, why make a fuss about them? Because we wish to examine rigorously the relationship between an agent's routines and its machinery. In many theories of activity, an agent engages in a routine in virtue of having a representation of it such as a plan or program or script. This is indeed one way to bring about routines; for reasons discussed at length in papers by Agre and myself [4, 7] we prefer other ones.

Because a routine is an pattern of interactive activity, one cannot literally *implement* a routine; one can only implement a device which will *participate in* a routine when put in a particular kind of environment. However, I will often speak loosely of implementing routines, meaning implementing such a device.

Because life is on-going and mainly routine, because trouble is rarely fatal, and because there are social and cultural supports for skill acquisition, routines can gradually *evolve* over a period of development. An agent rarely *has* to solve a problem that is beyond its routine capacities. It's almost always true that

- You've done much the same thing before.
- You don't need the best solution.
- You can do it the obvious brute-force way the first time and worry about optimizations later.
- You can cut corners.
- You can keep trying till you get it right.
- You can work around it.
- You can put it off.
- You can take another tack.
- You can get help.
- You can watch someone else do it.
- You can always just give up.
- You get to *choose* when to try the hard cases.
- So you get to choose when to learn new tricks.

---

[6]This means that the approach we advocate is inapplicable to worlds that are not mainly routine. We hypothesize that people would not have evolved as they did in such worlds.

2.6   Improvisation

An embodied agent must always be doing something, even if it is just
resting. One way to continually act is to continually compute what is
the most sensible thing to do at each instant. We call this approach
improvisation.[7]

The alternative to improvisation is to spread computing what to do
out over time. This approach entails keeping *control state*, which tells
you where you are in the process and which computation to perform
next. (The paradigm of control state is a program counter.) Control
state is frequently also used to tell you what to *do* next, as when executing a plan. The concrete-situated approach advocates minimizing
control state. Control state depends by definition on out-of-date information about the world. Out-of-date information about the world may
not longer be correct. Steering your car to the left because the value of
your program counter is 457 is risky; it's much better to steer your car
to the left because there's a car in the lane to your right.

If you have enough computational power to improvise—that is, to
avoid maintaining control state—it is better to do so. Our empirical studies of human routine activity convince us that improvisation
is usually possible for people. Sonja demonstrates technically that goal-
directed activity in at least one complex domain can also be improvised.

Sonja has no control structure. We will see that in spite of this
Sonja can abort a routine when conditions change so it no longer makes
sense, repeatedly try an action until it succeeds or some other alternative makes more sense, temporarily suspend one routine to engage
in another, interleave two or more routines, and combine several routines to achieve multiple goals simultaneously. Such abilities are at
the horizon of the state of the art of research on execution architectures (e. g. [84, 95, 165, 180, 210, 294]), which use elaborate control
machinery to achieve them. These architectures need a lot of machinery
to selectively break out of a basically sequential architecture, in which
what you do at each moment depends principally on what your program counter reads. In Sonja all these abilities emerge automatically

---

[7]Not all the connotations of this word are intended: in particular, "improvisation"
suggests novelty, and we are principally concerned with routine activity. We haven't
found a better term, though. The intended connotation is that of spontaneity and
responsiveness.

from computing what to do at each moment without maintaining control state. Sonja's architecture starts without sequentiality, so it needs no machinery to compute when to overrule a program counter based on sensory information.[8]

Improvisation demands that the computations subserving activity keep close to perception. If you are going to recompute what to do at every instant, you probably don't have enough time to build elaborate abstractions from your sensory input. You don't have enough time to do search or theorem proving or problem solving. You want your representation of your situation to be causally grounded in that situation.

2.7 Deictic representation

The demands of improvisation lead the concrete-situated approach to posit an unfamiliar form of representation. The sorts of representations we are used to are *objective*: they represent the world without reference to the representing agent. *Deictic* representations represent things in terms of their relationship with the agent.[9] The units of deictic representation are *entities*, which are things in a particular relationship to the agent, and relational *aspects* of these entities. For example, *the-cup-I-am-drinking-from* is the name of an entity, and *the-cup-I-am-drinking-from-is-almost-empty* is the name of an aspect of it. *The-cup-I-am-drinking-from* is defined *indexically* [23] in terms of an agent and the time the aspect is used. The same representation refers to different cups depending on whose representation it is and when it is used. It is defined *functionally*, in terms of the agent's purpose: drinking.

Deictic representations are defined in terms of a *causal* connection to the thing they represent. The literal *the-cup-I-am-drinking-from* is just a text string and of no use to concrete activity. The representation this string names is practically useful only if it plays a role in actually drinking from the cup.

The indexical, functional, and causal properties of deictic representa-

---

[8]Production systems [196] are also motivated in part by the intuition that dependence on control state is the exception rather than the rule. However, most production system architectures end up with more seriality—and more complex machinery—than Sonja because of conflict resolution and working memory.

[9]Agre originally used the phrase "indexical-functional representation" for this concept, and it appears that way in several of our joint papers. He switched to "deictic representation" in his thesis, and I am following his usage.

tions are what make them useful for concrete activity. The part of the world that is relevant to activity is that which is causally connected to the agent (indexicality). Representing things that are irrelevant to the task at hand would be inefficient (functionality). Causal connection with the things represented gives the agent the access needed to manipulate them.

We hyphenate the names of deictic representations because they are typically *noncompositional.* The implementation of *the-cup-I-am-drinking-from* will almost certainly *not* depend on a token representing "I" or on general representations for cups or drinking. These names are a theorist's names, not the agent's names. In particular, they are not linguistic or symbolic entities in the agent's head.

We say that an agent *registers* an entity or aspect with which it has entered into the appropriate causal relationship. An agent will not register most of its entities and aspects most of the time; since I am typing, not driving, I am not registering *the-car-I-am-overtaking.*

Deictic representations are interactive: a deictic representation is not a thing in the agent's head, but a pattern of activity, possibly involving external actions, which allows the agent to get at things in the world which are relevant to its purposes.[10] The causal connection between deictic representations and the things they represent typically goes in both directions. Perception is the most common causal grounding in one direction: you can register an entity if you can see or feel it.[11] This makes questions about the nature of perception central to questions about the nature of representation. Consequently, much of the rest of this book will be about perception, particularly vision. Manipulation of the thing represented is the most common grounding in the other direction. Together these imply that rather than *modeling* the world, an agent can be *part* of it, letting signals flow through it. The agent uses the world directly as a source of information about the world.

Any theory of representation must provide an account of *abstraction*: how a representation which originally applied in one situation can apply in another. Familiar forms of representation provide abstraction by means of variables which can be bound to constants. You may have a

---

[10]It is, in fact, unclear whether or not deictic representations should be called "representations" at all. They have some but not all the properties traditionally attributed to representations. Since there is no generally accepted technical definition of "representation" the question admits no definite answer.

[11]Another common way is via mechanical connection (as in *the-keys-in-my-pocket*).

representation that says that for all times t, cars c, and agents a, if at time t car c is coming directly at a, it is rational for a to head orthogonal to the vector from c to a at time $t+1$. You may also know that at time 34558, (which happens to be *now*), car C0786 is coming directly at agent A7787 (which happens to be you). Then by binding c to C0786, a to A7787, and t to 34558, you can deduce that it is rational for A7787 to move in a direction orthogonal to the vector from C0786 to A7787 at time 34559. Then some (necessarily) non-representational machinery can actually cause A7787 to make the appropriate movement.

Deictic representations provide a very different means for abstraction: they don't represent identity, only relationships. A sensible agent is wired up so that when it registers that *there's-a-car-coming-directly-at-me*, it will register *the-direction-to-the-car-coming-directly-at-me* and use that directly to get out of the way. In a situation like this, you don't care what time it is, you already know who you are, and you don't care which car *the-car-coming-directly-at-me* is, you just want to get out of the way. This *passive* account of abstraction requires no computation beyond that already needed for registration. Passive abstraction is a good example of a deeper understanding of dynamics leading to simplified machinery. Having understood that the interactions involved in concrete activity rarely require you to represent the identity of objects, but only your relationship to them, you can eliminate the machinery for unification and instantiation which any system using objective representations requires.[12] Rather than offering new machinery for controlling universal instantiation (which is usually combinatorially explosive), deictic representation offers a dynamic understanding which allows us to eliminate instantiation altogether: the machinery that registers *the-car-coming-at-me* never knows which car it is.

Because a deictic representation must be causally connected with its referent, part of its responsibility is to *constitute* an object. The real world is not neatly divided into discrete objects with identity labels on them. What *counts as* an object depends on the task. Is a window frame part of the window? It is when you are the carpenter nailing the window into the wall; it isn't when you are the cleaner squeegeeing it off. *The-*

---

[12]In rare circumstances, it is important to distinguish perceptually indistinguishable objects. In these cases, more complex schemes are required; some of these are compatible with the current theory, which only suggests that it is better to avoid representing identity when possible.

window-I'm-nailing-into-the-wall and *the-window-I'm-squeegeeing* have to do the work of separating their referents out from the surrounding world.

Some of the aspects of a situation that a sensible agent must register live in the future. In order to choose what to do, you must know what is likely to happen next, or what would happen if you took a particular course of action. We call determining probable futures *projection*.

One way to project futures is by *simulation*: you can build a model of the current situation and apply rules that transform it according to your expectations. Many theories of action privilege simulation as the sole method of projection and make machinery for simulation a central part of the architecture. However, simulation is generally expensive (and, as we'll see in section 3.1, incompatible with neurally plausible hardware). Luckily, there are several alternatives. It seems unwise, then, to make simulation the only means of projection.

Sonja projects by *visualization*, using visual machinery to literally *look to see* what will happen next. The detailed mechanisms of this are discussed in chapter 8. Still other means of projection are possible; a more sophisticated agent ought to incorporate several.

We will see in section 3.3.5 that deictic representations can be efficiently implemented in neurally plausible hardware. We'll see in section 3.1.2 that there are reasons to doubt that objective representation can be so implemented.

Deictic representation is not the only sort of representation people use, nor is it intended as a *general* theory of representation. The instructions given to Sonja, for example, are not deictic representations. There are many propositions that can not be stated in a deictic representation scheme. There are purposes for which a photograph, a visual image, a shopping list, or an equation is the appropriate sorts of representation.

3 Hardware and architecture

This chapter discusses the theories of *hardware* and *architecture* that
motivate Sonja's design. I use these terms as they are used by computer designers: hardware is the stuff out of which machinery is made;
architecture is the way it is organized. I argue that some simple and
well-established facts about the brain put strong constraints on cognitive architecture. These constraints are violated by much current work
in AI. If one's interest in AI is the engineering of intelligent systems by
whatever means, this may not be cause for concern. Sonja, however, is
intended to illustrate a *biologically plausible* theory of activity, and its
design is based on neuroscientific and psychological evidence.

Section 3.1 describes "essential connectionism," a set of facts about
neural hardware that are well established, constrain architecture, and are
obeyed by Sonja but not by some other cognitive models. These facts
suggest avoiding the use of pointers, variables, inspectable data structures, interpreters, and dynamic storage allocation. Section 3.2 argues
for a particular top-level modularity for the brain, dividing peripheral
systems from a central system, and argues that the central system itself
is not modular. It proposes a particular provisional non-modular central
system architecture. Section 3.3 concerns the architecture of the visual
system. It argues for a particular model of visual processing, the visual
routines theory. This theory too puts strong constraints on cognitive
theories; it would be difficult and perhaps impossible to interface most
current cognitive theories of central systems processing with this model
of vision, because it delivers different sorts of representations than they
require as inputs. I propose a particular interface between the visual
and central systems.

3.1 Essential connectionism

The kind of hardware an agent is built out of puts engineering constraints
on its architecture. If computation is cheap and communication between
computational units is expensive, for instance, a Von Neumann architecture makes sense. If computation is expensive and communication is
cheap, other architectures make more sense.

Much of the architecture of the human brain is still mysterious, but
some basic facts about human brain hardware are certain. These facts
are playing an increasingly large role in AI with the increasing popular-

ity of connectionism. I believe that these facts and their implications, which together I will term *essential connectionism*, ought to be of central importance in cognitive science, because they put strong, surprising constraints on cognitive architecture. Sonja respects these constraints.

3.1.1   The essential connectionist commitments

The essential connectionist facts[1] are that the brain

- is made up of a great many components (about 10^{11} neurons)
- each of which is connected to many other components (about 10^4)
- and each of which performs some relatively simple computation (whose nature is unclear)
- slowly (less than a kHz)
- and based mainly on the information it receives from its local connections.[2]

This organization is strikingly different from that of a Von Neumann computer and also from cognitive models such as inference engines-with-databases. It implies that computations that operate in a second or less must involve no more than about a hundred sequential steps [80]: each step must involve a neuron firing, which takes a few milliseconds. Almost all perceptual computations operate in under a second. So do many action choices: video game players routinely respond in less than a second to changing circumstances; conversational interactions involve coordination processes which also operate in under a second. These are complex computations which must involve much more than a hundred neuron-like computations, implying that massive parallelism must be used [80].

These facts make most of the software technologies AI systems have mainly been built out of prohibitively expense and suggest that alternative techniques must be found. In particular, we must find ways to avoid using pointers, variables, inspectable data structures, interpreters, and dynamic storage allocation. I'll explain why in the next section.

3.1.2   The essential connectionist constraints

---

[1] These facts are reviewed in any introductory neuroscience text, for example that of Kandel and Schwartz [143].

[2] There are also global interactions based on chemical diffusion. The role of these interactions in neural computation is uncertain; I ignore them in this book.

Pointers are expensive Any computation involves computational units (data items, for example) that must talk to each other. Any computational architecture must provide a communication scheme, or router, that allows them to.

One way to allow computational units to talk to each other is via connections. If two units need to talk to each other, you literally wire them together. It is possible to implement many sorts of computation this way; many of the purposes to which semantic networks have been put can be implemented with connections, for instance [78, 79, 252].

Most AI programs use a more flexible means of communication: pointers. Pointers are more general than connections; they allow *selective* communication between arbitrary computational units. To implement pointers, a communication scheme must allow a piece of hardware to talk to different other pieces of hardware at different times. Pointers are, by definition, side-effectable.

Pointers can be implemented easily on a Von Neumann machine. The computational units are arranged in a star configuration, with the ALU at the hub and memory locations on the rim. Most units don't directly talk to each other, they talk to the ALU, which combines two at a time. This has a high cost, however. Only a tiny fraction of the hardware in the machine does anything at any given time: the ALU and whichever memory locations are being accessed. (Pipelining and memory hierarchy improve this situation only by a constant factor.) Almost all of the hardware is devoted to memory, which just sits there, and to addressing logic and memory management, which just connect memory locations to the ALU, rather to than computing anything useful [122].

If your hardware computes slowly, as does the brain's, this approach won't work. You've *got* to get millions of computational units doing useful work at any given time because individually they are useless. But this makes the communication problem much harder. If you have n computational units that can point to each other, you have to implement n^2 communication paths. Some sort of crossbar or router is needed. It's not clear how many computational units are needed for human intelligence, but a million seems like a lower bound [122]. We don't *know* that the brain doesn't include an n^2 crossbar of this size, but the neuroanatomical evidence is generally against it [49]. As an engineering matter, building a trillion-connection crossbar seems hard; if it is a prerequisite for intelligence, it will be a long time before we'll see progress in AI. We would do well to look for alternatives, both for practical reasons and because it is likely that if there is a way to avoid this quadratic overhead, evolution would incorporate it into the human cognitive architecture.

Finding an efficient implementation for pointers has been termed the *variable binding problem* in the connectionist literature [200]. All the approaches I know of require at least n^2 hardware.[3] This is an area of active current research, and a better solution may be found, but it seems likely to me that we need instead to find architectures that use pointers as little as possible. The architecture proposed in this chapter and implemented in Sonja is one. Such an architecture is evidence that those who dismiss connectionism on the grounds that it does not support pointers and so can not implement cognition [90] may be mistaken.

Having given up the full generality of pointers, which allow anything to talk to anything else, we might go to the opposite extreme and adopt an architecture in which each processing element can only talk to a small fixed set of neighbors. Although I think this is worth exploring (as it has been by connectionists and others, for instance Brooks [27]), I think a middle ground is possible. We may want to build small special-purpose routers when the number of things that need to communicate form a small subset of whole system. Sonja, for instance, uses addressing logic to access its retina; see section 6.1.

An architecture in which pointers are expensive requires deeply re-thinking AI engineering issues. Without pointers, you can't bind variables to symbolic values, so you can't implement unification, so you can't use objective representation schemes which require universal instantiation. Without pointers, you can't have inspectable, compositional data structures that can be passed around freely and taken apart and put together in different places. Without pointers, you can't build or traverse graphs. Most well-understood AI technologies depend on one or more of these abilities. We need to find alternatives; Sonja provides some.

Dynamic storage allocation is expensive   Dynamic storage allocation, or "consing," is the ability to find unused computational unit and connect it to a given one. Dynamic storage allocation is extensively used in AI systems to create new representations in the course of activity.

---

[3]Touretzky and Hinton [272, 273, 274] have described an elegant approach that (as I've argued elsewhere [34]) seems to require n^3 hardware. Drescher [60] provides a straightforward solution that is n^2. There are many more in the literature.

Standard dynamic storage allocation techniques require pointers. There are alternatives that are better suited to essential connectionist architectures. In an essential connectionist architecture, finding an unused computational unit is easy; since all computational units can be computing all the time, one thing they can do is to keep track of whether they are in use. The hard part is creating new connections. Feldman [75, 76] describes *recruitment* schemes for doing so. These schemes would not be a good way to implement pointers, because they are slow and allow only a relatively small number of units to ever communicate with a given one. They are unlikely, therefore, to support creating large numbers of new representations in the course of routine activity. They are plausible candidates for the basis of long-term changes, as might be required by learning, for example.

I can now make precise the hypothesis of section 2.1 that routine activity is that which does not require "new thoughts." The hypothesis, technically, is that all routine activity can be engaged in by an architecture with a fixed, limited connection pattern. By fixed I mean that no new connections are formed and that limited I mean that the architecture does not make extensive use of pointers. Sonja is an existence proof that at least *some* complex routine activity can be implemented in such an architecture. Appendix B talks about thinking new thoughts and making new connections.

Virtual machines are expensive   Virtual machines, or interpreters, are a staple AI implementation technique. They allow an architecture of one sort to act like an architecture of another sort. This simulation ability has been used as the basis of arguments that facts about the brain can be ignored by cognitive scientists because however the brain works at a low level, it can simulate the architecture of your choice at a high level. I think such arguments are wrong. The fastest RISC machines, for instance, have a gate depth of ten; executing an instruction takes ten times as long as the basic gate delay. These machines are optimized for gate depth; most virtual machines have a simulation cost much greater than ten. If neurons compute at less than 1 kHz, any virtual machine would compute at well under 100 Hz. While such a machine might be used to implement slow processes such as conscious thought, it couldn't run fast enough to serve as the basis of concrete activities such as video game playing. Such activities must be implemented directly; computation must stay "close to the hardware" rather than involving layers of abstraction.

3.1.3   Advantages of essential connectionist hardware

Thus far I have described essential connectionist hardware as a liability. Yet it has many advantages. Later in this chapter, I'll show that this sort of hardware naturally and efficiently implements the kinds of dynamics—highly interactive routines and deictic representations—which I believe for other reasons must underlie concrete activity. The massive parallelism it provides is required to sustain the massive signal bandwidth which must pass through a situated agent. Von Neumann machines simply can't keep up with the demands of real-time vision. Similarly, they don't have time to take into account the countless factors that are relevant to computing, in each instant, what to do. The sections of this chapter starting with 3.2 are devoted to showing that essential connectionist hardware can.

3.1.4   Alternative implementations of essential connectionism

Most connectionists, in additional to the essential connectionist commitments, hold some variant of a particular model of the computation performed by the individual neurons. This model supposes that

- neurons are connected randomly or uniformly
- all neurons perform the same computation[4]
- each connection has associated with it a numerical *weight*
- each neuron's output is a single numerical *activity*
- activity is computed as a monotonic function of the sum of the products of the activities of the input neurons with their corresponding connection weights.

Unfortunately, these propositions are not neurophysiologically plausible in detail (see Crick [48] and Crick and Asanuma [49] for a discussion of the relevant neurobiology and an evaluation of the faithfulness of connectionist models).

I have adopted an alternative essential connectionist implementation medium, *depth-bounded digital circuits*. Like neurons and connectionist

---

[4]These first two assumptions are rejected by increasingly many connectionists; Feldman [79] discusses of some of the relevant issues.

units, a digital circuit is made up of many components (gates), which
perform simple computations based on information derived from the
components they are connected to. A depth-limited digital circuit is
one in which paths between the inputs and the outputs are limited in
length. Depth-limited circuits must use broad parallelism to compute
anything interesting, because individual paths through them are too
short to do much work. Such circuits can do useful work even with large
gate delays (corresponding to slow neural computation).

Depth-limited circuits are not a plausible model of neural functioning
in detail, but they do reflect the essential connectionist constraints, so
that a designer working with such circuits has to work around most of
the same problems a designer working with other connectionist hardware has to work around. In fact, they are equivalent within a constant
factor to any other essential connectionist hardware technology in which
each component does limited computation. For example, a standard
connectionist unit can be simulated by a small digital circuit (assuming limited-precision arithmetic) and standard connectionist units can
similarly simulate gates.

The advantages of digital circuits are that they are well understood,
have existing design methodology to draw on, and can be simulated
more cheaply than real-valued connectionist units. Adopting them is,
however, an engineering move only, and not a theoretical commitment.
I have, in fact, used real-valued components in some parts of Sonja
where they seemed useful. My circuit simulator does not distinguish
analog and digital components, so these can be thought of as having
been implemented either way.

3.2   The central system

3.2.1   Modularity

It is common in cognitive science to make a first division of the mind
and brain into *peripheral systems* and *central systems*. The peripheral
systems are concerned with sensory and motor processing. The central
systems are concerned with cognitive processes such as learning, reasoning, and planning. This division is almost universally accepted (an
interesting dissent being that of Brooks [25, 26, 27]). I will adopt a version here also. This version is similar to that proposed by Fodor [89],

and I will make use of his arguments for it here.

The reason to believe in the central/peripheral split is that much evidence (some of it reviewed later in this chapter) shows that perceptual and motor processes are in large part innate, immutable, localized to specific brain areas, and task- and domain-independent. There are, moreover, good engineering reasons for these facts. On the other hand, people and other intelligent agents learn, so there must be some other part of the brain that is the locus of learning, development, and storage of task- and domain-dependent skills.

The modularity of the peripheral systems (that is, how many and which ones there are) is becoming clearer as a result of neurophysiological and psychophysical studies. The modularity of the central systems is less clear. Fodor argues that the central systems are *not* modular; that, in fact, there is a single homogeneous central system. His main argument (much simplified) is that anything you know can potentially be brought to bear on any cognitive task, so there's nowhere to draw modularity boundaries.

I've come to the same conclusion in a different way.[5] In a previous attempt to build an integrated agent, combining planning, acting, learning, and reasoning [31, 32], I found that research from these AI subareas each saw their job as transforming representations in one format into representations in another format, but that the interfaces didn't match up. Natural language would produce a "semantic" representation of an English string, but no other module wanted that representation as input. Planning wanted "goals" as inputs, but no one else supplied them.[6] Planning thought that perception was supposed to deliver a different sort of representation than perception was willing to deliver. Every theory of learning had different ideas about what learning's inputs and outputs were supposed to be. In sum, connecting together the modules most frequently proposed in cognitive science research is hard. (It may be, however, that a different modularity is possible, or that further research on connecting together modules will succeed.)

Another reason to avoid modularity is that much of the work required by the modules seems to result from the modularity boundaries them-

---

[5] Brooks's work is motivated by similar observations [27].

[6] Some natural language understanding systems (e. g. Allen's [10]) transform requests or commands into goals, but this is not enough to keep an autonomous agent going; most goals must be generated internally.

selves. Each module, since it has no access to the workings of other modules, has to solve problems in the general case, which is usually much harder than solving specific concrete problems. Each modularity boundary implies representations that are passed across it; these representations typically require pointers, which are expensive. A good example of these difficulties is provided by the modularity boundary between planning and execution. This boundary requires that a planner solve problems without access to ongoing circumstances. It implies a representational interface, plans. Agre and I have argued that eliminating this modularity boundary makes sensible action much easier [7]. An agent without this modularity doesn't have to solve the provably intractable problems a planner does. Plans, which require pointers to represent, can be eliminated.

These considerations argue for a single, homogeneous, nonmodular central system, which is what Sonja has.

3.2.2   A three-phase central system architecture

I don't have a good theory of how the central system works. I've adopted a scheme, described in this section, which is adequate for Sonja and will probably generalize some. I make no theoretical claims for it.

In concrete activity, the job of the central system is to compute what to do. Routine activity, according to the hypothesis of section 3.1.2, involves no allocation of new processing elements or connections. This suggests statically allocating hardware for each task. Since these bits of machinery are permanently allocated to specific tasks, there's no issue of freeing up hardware to allocate to the current task, so it makes sense for all these bits of machinery to keep thinking all the time; otherwise they will simply be idle.

Sonja's central system, then, is composed in part of *proposers*, bits of circuitry which each continually figure out whether it would be sensible to do some particular thing right now. (There are many similar schemes in the literature, perhaps most famously Minsky's Society of Mind [185].) Proposers make *proposals* for action. Since proposals are domain- and task-specific, there are as many proposers as things you might do. Proposers thus effectively exploit essential connectionist hardware by keeping most of the hardware working most of the time. This parallelism, I argued earlier, is a requirement on any cognitive architecture that respects the constraints of essential connectionism. Because proposers are allocated statically, the architecture scales well: each new ability the agent acquires requires new proposers only in proportion to the complexity of that ability.

A proposer often proposes actions which are incompatible with those suggested by other proposers. *Arbiters*, another kind of central system component, choose among suggested actions (figure 3.1). Collectively the arbiters form an *arbitration network*.[7]

Arbiters and proposers typically both take into account the situation at hand, information about which comes from the sensory systems. However, the information coming from the sensory systems is in sensory terms, not in terms of the current task. *Registrars*, the final sort of central system component, interpret sensory inputs in terms of relevant aspects of the situation. Registrars and arbiters, like proposers, are small circuits that all operate continuously and in parallel.

Is this three-phase architecture right? What is the internal structure of the components? How are they organized? Not enough is known about either activity or brain structure to answer these questions. Lacking such answers, I've fallen back on engineering intuition. Ultimately, I believe that criteria of learnability will provide most of the constraint on the nature of the central system. Agre's thesis [4] uses this constraint to argue for a particular sort of additive construction of the central circuitry. Neither Pengi nor Sonja is constructed in this way, because it is not a very strong constraint, and because Agre leaves open the question of what adds the circuitry and how. I believe that the central system must incorporate a statistical induction engine, and the nature of this engine probably will provide strong constraints when we understand it. (This point is taken up again in appendix B.)

Even apart from these questions, it is clear that this model of the central system leaves many things out. There is no model of memory, for example. I've resisted the temptation to add one because I don't think enough is known about memory to choose between incompatible competing models and because the best models are so complex that im-

---

[7]The function of this arbitration network is superficially similar to that of the conflict resolution phase of a production system [177], but is actually quite different. Production systems are intended to model slow, serial cognitive processes [196]. The job of the conflict resolution phase is to enforce seriality by choosing just one of the applicable productions to fire on each cycle. Sonja's central system architecture is intended to model fast parallel subconscious processing. Typically many proposals for action are adopted simultaneously; by default there is no conflict. Arbitration is required only when two proposers suggest incompatible courses of action.

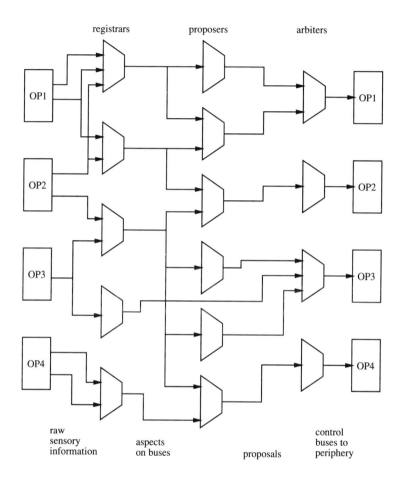

registrars proposers arbiters

raw
sensory
information

aspects
on buses

proposals

control
buses to
periphery

Figure 3.1
The three-phase architecture. In this diagram, trapezoids represent small circuits
and lines represent buses connecting them. Registrars compute aspects of the
situation based on inputs from sensory operators. Proposers suggest actions based
on these aspects. Arbiters choose between conflicting actions, often based on
information provided by registrars (as in the case of the third arbiter from the top).
The outputs of arbiters are vectors of control signals that go to effector operators.
Registrars, proposers, and arbiters are distinguished only by their role in computing
what to do; there are no restrictions on what form the circuits that implement them
may take.

plementing them would have been a major work in itself. This does *not* mean that Sonja's central system does not maintain state; only rather that such state is not used in a principled way.

3.3   Architectures for vision

This section argues for a particular theory of vision, the visual routines theory. Section 3.3.1 argues that vision must be task-specific in part. Section 3.3.2 argues that task-specificity is not by itself a sufficient constraint on vision for creatures much more complex than insects. Section 3.3.3 describes and argues for visual routines; section 3.3.4 describes the implications of the visual routines theory for the central system and explains the nature of the interface between the visual and central systems. Finally, section 3.3.5 explains how visual routines can implement deictic representations.

3.3.1   The purpose of vision

Much of the vision literature supposes that the purpose of vision is to deliver a complete model of a scene. This model, similar to those used in CAD systems, would identify all of the objects visible in the scene and specify their shapes, locations, and orientations. Most AI literature concerned with cognition also supposes that vision delivers complete scene models, though of a somewhat different sort, one that describes properties of objects and relationships between them in an expressional representation such as predicate calculus ground terms. (This project is sometimes termed "pixels to predicates" [211].)

I think that scene models such as these are neither necessary nor generally very useful, and that they are much harder to generate than the information that vision actually needs to extract. I will propose a different model, after arguing against these alternatives. Most of these arguments have been made earlier and at greater length by Ballard [21], Edelman and Poggio [65], and Horswill [129].

• The models these theories propose are constructed independently of the specific purposes to which the seeing agent will put them. In the concrete-situated approach to activity, you are almost always engaged in some specific activity, and the purpose of vision is to support that activity. Different sorts of objects are important in different sorts of activity; most of the things you see at any given time are irrelevant to whatever you are doing, and recognizing and locating them would be wasteful.

• As we saw in section 2.7, what counts as an object, and the boundaries of objects, depend on your purposes. As another example, the top of a paint can should be considered part of the can when you are carrying paint around, but a separate object when you are dipping a brush in it. This too suggests that objects cannot be recognized in a domain-independent way, and that the viewer's goals must be taken into account by object recognition.

• Extracting precise metrical information and surface descriptions from images is a principal concern in machine vision. It seems to be a very hard problem, in principle as well as in practice; it is numerically unstable, computationally expensive, and depends on finding "constraints" which seem to be hard to come by [129]. It seems likely that going to such trouble is not necessary. It's rare for activity to depend on precise metrical information; work in robotics [173] shows how compliance (sliding) can achieve precise positioning without precise measurements.

• Specific concrete activities demand that you know particular aspects of a given situation. For example, in playing Amazon, you'd like to know which monster is nearest to you, roughly how far away it is, and whether you've got a clear line of fire at it. These aspects are *relational* in character, and they would not be made explicit by the sort of CAD model that most vision research proposes. Such a model *cannot* make relational properties explicit, because there are too many (vastly more than there are properties of individual objects), and a model would have to make *all* of them explicit because it is constructed without reference to the seer's purposes. Although relational properties *are* made explicit in the sorts of representations cognitive AI researchers hope to get from vision, the same combinatoric arguments apply. In practice, since cognitive AI almost never connects with vision, the researcher selects the relational properties needed for the task.

• Computing the relevant relational aspects would require much additional work beyond that of constructing the model. It is, furthermore, not clear that the model would be much help in computing these aspects; it is not clear that some other representation wouldn't be much more useful.

• The constant terms involved in an expressional representation (such

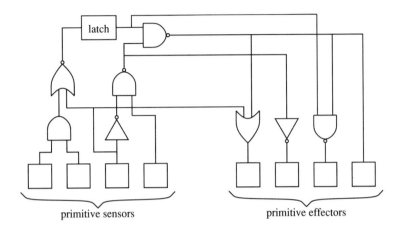

Figure 3.2
An agent wired up to do the right thing. In this approach, the agent consists of
some unstructured circuitry interposed between sensors and effectors.

as `block-7691`) refer to specific, objectively given individuals. A visual
system which generates such representations must determine the identi-
ties, as well as the types, of objects. This is usually difficult and often
impossible. The visual system would have to provide a different constant symbol for every corn flake in your bowl and keep track of which
is which. The world is full of indistinguishable things, and we clearly
don't distinguish as many things as we could.

3.3.2   Insect vision

Why do we need vision, if not to produce a model of the world? We need
vision because we want to act, and action must be responsive to environmental conditions. The considerations of section 3.3.1 suggest that vision
must be *task-specific*, at least in part. One approach to visual system
design is to posit that the doctrine of visual task specificity, when added
to engineering intuition and the constraints of essential connectionism,
is sufficiently constraining. This approach does not mandate a division
between visual and non-visual processing, or the central/peripheral split.
The way to go about building creatures, on this view, is to just "wire
them up to do the right thing" (figure 3.2) This is roughly the position taken by Brooks [25], though he adds an additional architectural

principle of layered design.

Perhaps the most interesting example of this approach is Connell's mobile robot Herbert [45, 46]. Herbert navigates about an office environment collecting Coke cans. This task requires several different sorts of visual perception and corresponding sorts of spatial reasoning, for navigation, can recognition, arm motion, and grasping. These sorts of perception and reasoning are implemented in Herbert by independent task-specific modules. The architecture has no central/peripheral split; individual modules or small clusters of modules are each responsible for both certain forms of perception and related forms of action.

This is an approach for which I have a great deal of sympathy. I believe, in fact, that it is entirely appropriate for insects. Insects have a fixed wired-in repertory of activities they can engage in. I don't think it will work for modeling people and other more sophisticated animals who can learn new skills, and I have not adopted it in Sonja. I'll explain why in section 3.3.3.

3.3.3   Visual routines

People regularly learn new skills. Since vision is task-specific, this means that learning to pilot a glider or play a new video game or make pancakes involves building new visual machinery. Unless some strong constraints are put on the architecture of the visual system, I believe this is a very hard problem. If vision were made up of completely independent task-specific modules, as in the insect vision model, learning a new task would require building a whole new pathway between the primitive sensors and effectors. As well as contradicting neuroanatomical evidence, this seems like an impossibly difficult learning task. More generally, the learning task of building new visual hardware seems difficult, and I believe that ameliorating this problem should be considered one of the most important constraints on visual architecture.

I believe that this constraint must be satisfied by including in the visual system a clean set of relatively high-level primitives which can act as a tinkertoy-like kit from which new visual machinery can be built. Making the primitives high-level means that the learning combinatorics are much reduced, and making the set "clean" makes it easier to discover useful combinations of primitives. (The lesson here is similar to that of Eurisko [162]: learning is easy if you have a set of primitives which generate a space in which useful combinations are relatively dense [163].)

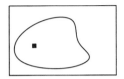 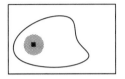 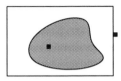

Figure 3.3
A visual routine for computing containment. Starting from a point marked with a
solid square (first picture), a wave of "activation" is spread (second picture). The
wave stops when it hits a boundary. Then, a "point at infinity" is tested to see
whether it is activated (third picture). In this case, the point at infinity is marked
with another square; it is not activated, and so the first square must have been
inside a boundary.

A model of this sort, the *visual routines model*, has been proposed by
Ullman [283]. This model posits a small, innate set of *visual operators*
which perform particular sorts of visual work. These operators collectively constitute a *visual routines processor (VRP)*. The VRP is not the
only visual system (I'll discuss some others in section 6.6), but it is the
one most involved in acquiring new visual skills.

The visual routines theory posits *visual routines*, patterns of activation
of different visual operators over time. Many visual properties, particularly topological properties such as connectedness and containment, are
difficult or impossible to compute using a single type of processing. Different sorts of processing must be applied in sequence. Ullman proposes
that patterns of visual processing be thought of as programs, or routines,
whose primitive operations are parameterized types of visual processing.
The strength of this idea is that a small set of visual primitives can be
recombined into an infinite number of types of visual processing. The
demands of visual analysis are very diverse; yet given the right set of
operations, it may be possible to assemble visual routines capable of
performing whatever sort of visual work is necessary for a new task. A
vision system can thus be thought of as a sort of programming language.

As an example, Ullman describes a visual routine for computing
whether or not a particular point is contained within a closed curve
in the image. This routine involves applying two primitive operations.
First, a "wave of activation" is propagated in the image, starting from
the point of interest, and expanding in parallel in all directions, but stopping when a boundary is reached. (See figure 3.3.) This computation

can be performed efficiently on a parallel two-dimensional grid machine. Second, a "point at infinity"—any point that is for some reason guaranteed to lie outside any curve—is tested to see whether it has been activated. If it has, we know that the activation has "leaked out" of any surrounding curve, and that the original point is not in fact contained in a closed loop. If it hasn't, we know that there is a containing curve.

This example is rather abstract. You might also have visual routines for checking your speedometer, for glancing at your keyboard to align your fingers in home position, for checking a pancake to see if it is ready to flip, or for finding safe footing when walking in the mountains. Chapter 8 will explain Sonja's visual routines in detail.

Ullman's containment routine makes use of two visual operators, spreading activation and testing a point to see if it is activated. Discussion of other visual operators will be deferred until chapter 6. It will be useful, however, to discuss some of their general characteristics and their role in vision as a whole.

I will distinguish *early, intermediate*, and *late* visual processing. Although these terms are current in the literature, and "early" vision is well-defined, different researchers use the terms "intermediate" and "late" vision differently.[8] I will give these terms fairly precise meanings which roughly align with current practice and which express distinctions important in the design of Sonja.

The retina is a two-dimensional array of light sensors. Neuroscientific study shows that the parts of the brain to which it is immediately connected preserve this retinal topology [174]. This *retinotopic* neural processing comprises *early vision*. We also know that the body's effectors are controlled by small non-retinotopic nerve bundles. So there must be some point at which retinotopic processing stops and some other representation begins. The evidence suggests that this transition occurs fairly early on in processing, well before the level of motor control. It seems plausible that the later representation consists, at least in part, of *compact encodings*, consisting of small groups of neurons which together represent a particular non-local property of the image. This is corroborated by neurophysiological evidence; for example Perrett *et al.* describe experiments that suggest that individual monkey neurons respond selec-

---

[8]The term "early" vision originates with Marr [171]. The terms "low-level" and "high-level" are also commonly used to express similar concepts.

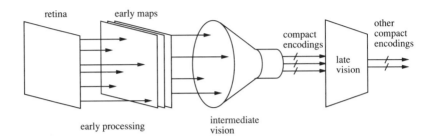

Figure 3.4
Early, intermediate, and late vision. Early processing computes, point by point,
retinotopic maps from the retinal image; intermediate vision crunches these maps
down into compact encodings; late vision computes with compact encodings.

tively to faces [213].[9] Feldman [79] presents engineering arguments and
neurophysiological evidence that encoding is probably predominantly in
terms of small groups of neurons, rather than individual ones. Let us
therefore term visual processing which uses these compact encodings
late vision, and processes that reduce retinotopic to compact encodings
intermediate vision (figure 3.4).

Early vision is coming to be quite well understood [124, 172, 174].
In addition to being retinotopic, early vision is bottom-up and applies
uniformly and in parallel over the image. *Bottom-up* visual processing is
that which depends only on the retinal image. A process is bottom-up
if and only if the same computation occurs whenever the same image
is presented. Bottom-up processing, thus, cannot depend on any non-
visual contextual factors, on memories or other state, or on the agent's
intentions. Early vision produces "unarticulated" output representations, typically a single continuously variable or boolean value at each
point in the image. Early visual processing is performed by a set of
fixed, innate, retinotopically organized machines called *early maps*. The
identity and function of some of these maps are known; new maps are
still being discovered and the functional properties of some remain to
be determined. There appear to be roughly fifteen maps; among them
are ones that compute color, edge orientation, stereoscopic depth, and

---

[9]The interpretation of these and related experiments is still controversial; Maunsell and Newsome [174] provide a review.

various properties of motion such as speed, direction, and size change.[10]
Visual operators are intended to model aspects of intermediate vision,
and visual routines aspects of late vision. Intermediate and late vision
are less well understood than early vision. There is little applicable
neuroscientific evidence and the computational constraints are less clear.
The approach taken to them in this book is, accordingly, exploratory and
speculative in some respects.

3.3.4   Implications for the central system

Ullman says little about what is responsible for causing the right visual
operations to happen at the right times. He writes about visual routines
as programs which are executed in the usual way. He talks briefly about
a process of compilation which synthesizes new routines from specifications, and suggests that these routines are stored for later use. He seems
to suggest that this compiler is in the visual system, and so presumably
specific to vision. This compilation process is in fact akin to classical
planning: it produces programs (plans) from specifications (goals) and
stores them for reuse. In section B.1.2 I'll argue that this is a bad model
for skill acquisition in general; the same considerations apply to visual
activity.

Agre has suggested reinterpreting the notion of visual "routines" in
terms of his use of the word "routine" rather than the use as "program
fragment." In this model, visual routines are not programs to be executed, but rather patterns of activation of visual operators, just as routines more generally are patterns of activity. Agre has further suggested
that rather than having special machinery for executing and synthesizing visual routines, that visual operators could be activated directly by
the central system.

These suggestions amount to some strong claims:

• The interface between the central and visual systems consists of a
fixed set of buses, with visual information running from the VRP to the
central system and visual commands running from the central system to
the VRP. It seems plausible to generalize this model to other peripheral
systems.

---

[10]Early work by Zeki [299, 300] suggested a one-to-one correspondence between
retinotopic maps and types of visual information. It is now known that the correspondence is many-to-many [174]. I will ignore this observation for simplicity.

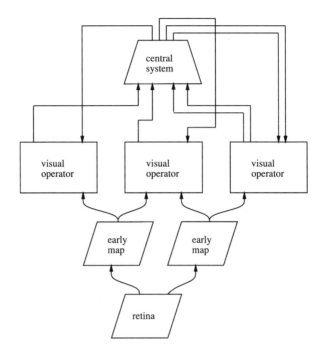

Figure 3.5
Overall modularity. The central system takes inputs from the visual operators and
produces control outputs for them.

• Late vision is not distinct from cognition, and is supported by the
same central machinery. Accordingly, I draw the line between peripheral
and central systems rather differently than most researchers; I put more
of the responsibility for perception into the central system than is usual.
• The central system must be able to provide new control outputs for
the sensory systems within tens of milliseconds after getting new inputs
from the sensory systems, because visual routines may involve several
cycles of interaction and operate in well under a second. Sonja's central
system architecture satisfies this constraint; others do not.

For purposes of vision, the central system's job is to get the right
arguments to the right visual operators at the right times. The architecture of figure 3.5 is in many respects similar to that of a horizontally

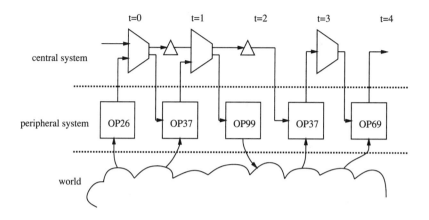

Figure 3.6
A generic visual routine. This diagram multiplexes time and space along the x axis;
it shows how the central system, on successive ticks, produces control inputs for
visual operators based on their outputs on the previous tick. The trapezoids
represent the central system as a whole; of course it has more inputs and outputs
than are illustrated. The triangles represent delay elements that store information
within the central system from tick to tick. The squares represent peripheral
operators, which also take time to compute.

microcoded computer. The central system plays the role of the control
logic and the peripheral systems play the role of the datapaths. The central system has narrow, mostly one-bit buses; the peripheral systems, like
datapaths, operates on wide data values. Like some current horizontally
microcoded architectures, termed *very long instruction word* machines
[86], there are many datapaths all of which operate in parallel on every
cycle (though some of them may not do anything useful, if there is no
computation of their sort to be performed on that cycle). Thus visual
routines are strictly *patterns* rather than simply sequences of visual operations: several operations may occur simultaneously. The job of the
central system is to compute on each tick the values of the parameters
controlling the peripheral operators; the vector of the values is analogous
to the vector of control bits provided by a horizontal microinstruction.

Now we can put the pieces together. Figure 3.6 illustrates a generic
visual routine. This figure is somewhat confusing in that it multiplexes
both time and space along the x axis. In this diagram, causality weaves
in and out between the central system, the peripheral system, and at

times the world. That is the major difference between this architecture and a horizontally microcoded architecture: visual routines are interactional patterns, not programs. Along the top is pictured the central system, as a circuit, at several moments in time. Each trapezoid represents an instantaneous snapshot of the whole central system. The middle row represents various visual operators at particular moments in time; it suppresses from view all but the relevant operators.

The routine starts with the world presenting inputs that cause the bottom-up operator OP26 to produce a new input to the central system. This corresponds to *noticing* something unexpected. Based on this input, and possibly also on state information from within the central system, the central system directs OP37 to report on some aspect of the visual input. Based on this result, the central system directs OP99 to take some action, an eye movement perhaps, and also gives directions to OP37 (perhaps new directions but possibly the same ones; the central system has to give every operator inputs on every tick). Based on this result, the central system gives directions to OP69, which delivers another value, and so the process continues.

This visual routine actually incorporates some motor work. More generally, the notion of a "visual" routine is an abstraction. Late visual processing is usually in service of some specific perceptual-motor task, and as there is no separate hardware for late and as the task will typically involve tight feedback between vision and action, late is inextricably tied up with everything else.

3.3.5   Visual routines implement deictic representations

In section 2.7, we saw that deictic representations are indexical, functional, and grounded causally, particularly in perception. Deictic representations in Sonja are implemented with visual routines which discover particular aspects of the visual scene. A visual routine is task-specific and performed only when it is useful; this gives deictic representations their functional character.[11] Visual routines discover properties of the specific circumstances that surround the agent that engages in them; this makes deictic representations inherently egocentric and thereby indexical. Your visual routine that implements *the-cup-I'm-drinking-from*

---

[11] This is analogous to Ballard's hypothesis that "the internal representation of the image is minimal with respect to the goals" [20].

is relative to *you* because you are always looking in front of your face and that's where the cup will be. Additional indexicality is introduced by visual routines making explicit *relational* properties of the scene. An Amazon player may have a visual routine which finds *the-monster-closest-to-the-amazon*, an entity that is defined indexically, in terms of *the-amazon*.

4 Amazon

This chapter describes the video game Amazon, Sonja's domain. Section 4.1 explains how I chose this domain, drawing on earlier experience with writing a similar system for a similar domain. Section 4.2 explains Amazon in detail: what sorts of things are in the domain and how they interact. Section 4.3 describes some modifications I made to Amazon to make it easier to implement Sonja. I argue that these modifications do not vitiate the points the book makes. Section 4.4 considers whether or not Amazon is a realistic domain; I conclude that it is, though it is in some ways an atypical one.

4.1 Criteria for a domain

Sonja descends from an earlier system called Pengi [5] which I wrote to illustrate the concrete-situated ideas discussed in chapter 2. Pengi's domain was a video game called Pengo. My reasons for choosing Pengo as a domain for Pengi were different from my criteria for choosing Amazon as a domain for Sonja, but I'll explain them because they affected the choice of Amazon.

Pengi was intended to illustrate the point that the then-standard "planning" view of activity was inadequate for domains that are complex, uncertain, or real-time. Thus, I wanted a complex, uncertain, real-time domain. Pengi was also designed to demonstrate concrete-situated ideas about activity. These ideas emphasize perceptual connection with the world, so I wanted a domain which required substantial perceptual interaction, but which would not require that I spend years solving known difficult problems in vision research.

Video games have just these properties. A snapshot of a Pengo game appears in figure 4.1. In this game the player controls a penguin, which appears near the upper left corner, which is fighting against some bees in a maze made of ice cubes. The penguin and the bees can both kick ice cubes, so that they go skidding across the underlying ice surface until they run into something. If the something is a penguin or bee, it dies. Bees hatch from larvae inside ice cubes.

This scene has about two hundred and fifty objects in it. Simply representing the coordinates of all these objects would take at least as many propositions. To encode some basic information about their spatial relationships (what's next to what, where there are regions of freespace,

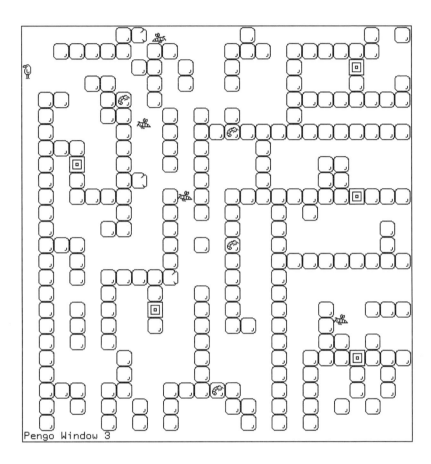

Figure 4.1
A Pengo game in progress. This scene has several hundred objects in it (it is
complex); it changes several times per second (it is real-time); and in it bees act
partly at random (it is uncertain)

where there are connected blobs of cubes and what their shapes are) would require a few thousand propositions. The game, therefore, is more *complex* in terms of sheer size than typical AI domains. Pengo is *uncertain* because the bees' behavior has a random component. It is *real-time*, with the penguin and the bees moving around at about twenty Hertz. Although a player might not have to track the game at this rate, surprising things happen quickly enough that a player's response time has to be well under a second; maintaining a complete and consistent model of the screen would require updating hundreds of propositions per second.

These properties together ensure that planning and problem solving techniques, which depend on exponential search and theorem proving, would be swamped by Pengo. This was one major point of our paper on the subject.

On the other hand, Pengo was in many ways an easier domain than some others. For one thing, it didn't require building an actual robot. I believe that studies involving actual robots are vitally important [26], but I didn't want to take one on. Pengo also didn't require building a complex simulation, just implementing a video game, which took about a month.

Video game playing is a strongly perceptual activity for humans; I incorporated into Pengi the best available theories of human vision. Because video games are two-dimensional and because the images involved are generated by a computer, I could bypass hard problems in early vision such as noise tolerance, stereo, and shape-from. This made it possible to implement Pengi in a few months.

I based Sonja's design on that of Pengi in many ways, and I took it as given that Sonja's domain would be another video game. However, I wanted to make different points in this book, and I needed a different sort of video game.

- The game had to be amenable to being played by a system similar to Pengi.
- For advice to be useful, it had to be the case that the player should often have several plausible mutually exclusive alternative courses of action available. Each of these things should be relatively easy to do; deciding which thing to do should be relatively hard. This is not generally the case in playing Pengo, in which there are few strategic choices

to make.

- For there to be enough to talk about, the game had to be be ontologically complex. In Pengo, ice cubes, bees, and larvae are all there is; and few of each of these have any interesting properties at any given time.

- In Pengo, almost all the relevant aspects of a situation change from second to second. I wanted the game to be one in which some things change more slowly, so that longer-term intentions would be useful. This would allow instructions to talk about events in the future, and would require that a player project probable futures.

- Ideally, I wanted the game to be non-violent. I was bothered by the violence of most video games on political grounds, and also felt that it actively distorted the design of Pengi.

Gauntlet, a popular Dungeons and Dragons-like arcade game, immediately came to mind. It met all the criteria except the last one. I spent a few days trying to design a non-violent game that met the other criteria and failed. So I gave up and implemented a game modeled fairly closely after Gauntlet: Amazon.[1]

4.2   Amazon

Sonja plays Amazon from the same perspective a human does: looking at the screen, which is to say as if looking down on the dungeon from above. It does *not* play it from the point of view of the amazon icon. I emphasize this because many people have been confused about Pengi in this way.

Figure 4.2 displays a scene in which all of the sorts of things in the Amazon domain appear. This diagram is a snapshot of the Amazon window as it appears to the player. This window actually provides a view into a small part of a larger underlying dungeon. The window tracks the *amazon*, which, as described in section 1.1, is the player icon. When the amazon gets close to the edge of the screen, the window smoothly moves over the underlying scene to keep the amazon within

---

[1]It appears that Gauntlet was modeled after a game called Dandy, which was implemented as a thesis by Palevich, then a student at MIT [205]. Though Dandy is a violent game, Palevich designed it to foster cooperation as opposed to conflict among video game players. Gauntlet and Amazon retain these cooperative characteristics; I'll discuss them further in chapter 5 and in appendix A.

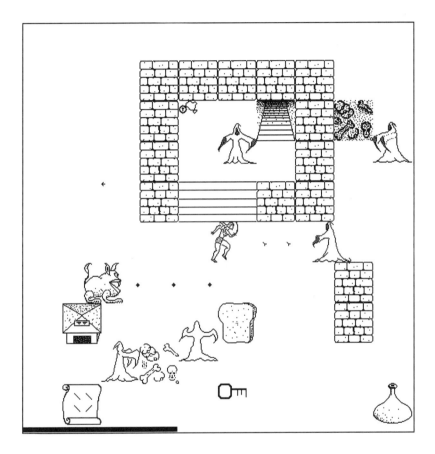

Figure 4.2
An illustrative Amazon scene. All of the sorts of things that can appear in an
Amazon game appear in this scene.

bounds, revealing new parts of the dungeon as it goes.

The amazon can move in the eight king's-move directions only; motion is continuous (actually a pixel at a time and fast enough that there is no noticeable flicker). The dungeon is broken up by *walls*. The motion of monsters and the amazon is *compliant* against walls: that is, if one runs into a wall on a diagonal, it will slide along it. Walls frequently form *rooms*, such as that directly above the amazon.

Ghosts and *demon bunnies* also inhabit the dungeon. (I tried to draw demon toads, but they just wouldn't cooperate.) The monsters can also move only on king's-move axes, but always head as nearly as possible toward the amazon within that constraint. (There are eight different icons for each monster type, corresponding to their headings.) The player has a continuously variable *health*, which is represented by the black bar of varying width at the bottom of the screen. When a monster runs into the amazon, it continuously saps your health. When your health runs out, you die. The demon bunnies also breathe *fireballs* at the amazon; several are visible in the figure as a line of small lozenges. Fireballs take a certain amount of health when they hit the amazon. You can fight back by making the amazon hurl *shuriken* at the monsters; these are the small three-pointed icons to the right of the amazon. It takes three shuriken hits to kill a monster. After the amazon fires a shuriken, she is exhausted by the effort, and can not move or shoot again for a fraction of a second. Shuriken and fireballs mutually annihilate when they collide. The amazon has an inexhausible supply of shuriken.

Monsters are intermittently produced by *monster generators*. *Piles of bones* produce ghosts and *bunny hutches* produce demons. You can destroy a pile of bones with ten shuriken hits, but hutches are invulnerable. Just when and where next to a generator a new monster will appear is random. Piles of bones also unpredictably have a *dark shadow* fall upon them, which renders them invulnerable until it passes. (The dark shadow is visible on the upper right and not on the lower left pile of bones in the figure.)

There are several types of *goodies* you can pick up by running into them: amulets, scrolls, keys, knives, potions, and pieces of bread.

If you pick up a magic *amulet*, it grants you one of five magic powers at random: your shuriken may bounce off of walls (rather than being absorbed by them), you may repel monsters (instead of attracting them), you may find that you are able to recover from throwing shuriken much faster (so that you can effectively fire a denser stream of them), your speed may increase by a factor of five (so you go zooming about, easily outmaneuvering monsters), or you may be given a magic shield (so that monsters sap your strength more slowly). (An amulet, with its chain, is visible in the room in the figure.) These effects wear off after a minute or two. Magic *scrolls* work similarly, except that the effects are permanent. (A scroll appears near the bottom left corner of the figure.) Scrolls have four *characters* on them, which are diagonal strokes. A scroll is *ready* when all four characters point inward. You can only pick up a scroll when it is ready; otherwise it acts just like a wall. The characters on a scroll slowly mystically change themselves around.

Keys are needed for opening *doors*. (The horizontal striped area in the figure represents the door to the room.) *Knives*, once picked up, can be thrown against monsters, killing them instantly, or they can be used to jimmy the lock on a door. (Knives appear as small arrow-shaped icons; one is to the left of the room in the sample scene.) You must be facing a door and right up against it to jimmy it, and knives are used up once they are used for either purpose. Knives, unlike shuriken, are conserved; you can only use one once.

A *potion* (appearing as a bottle in the figure) can be picked up and saved for future use. When activated, a potion kills every monster on the screen.

Pieces of *bread*, when picked up, increase your health, counteracting the damage done by the monsters.

The *stairwell* leads down to the next level of the dungeon: a whole new space to explore.

4.3   Modifications

I wrote Amazon before I had more than vague ideas about what Sonja was going to do. This, together with its similarity to Gauntlet, made it seem "real" to some degree. I was for this reason not very happy to have to modify it for Sonja's sake.

I made two modifications. The first was that the game as I originally wrote it was not ontologically complex enough. Some of the complexity I described in the last section I introduced later in order for there to be interesting things to give advice about. Since this was an *addition* to the game, it did not seem serious.

More seriously, I found I had to redesign the layout of the dungeon. It turned out that getting about in the dungeon was a hard task for Sonja, and I had to restrict the allowable configurations of walls to make it easier. The reason for this is recounted in section 8.7. This was disappointing, but as getting about the dungeon was not a focus of the work, it did not seem like a real cheat.

Late in the implementation of Sonja, I realized that Amazon was a bad domain in ways I hadn't anticipated, because I hadn't articulated some domain properties that Amazon lacks but that turn out to be important. Lack of these properties result in limited opportunities for certain types of visual work and certain sorts of natural language reference which I would have liked to explore further. I'll discuss these properties in sections 9.4.2 and 9.6.4. I discovered these problems too late to correct them by changing domain.

4.4   Realism

People often say of Pengo as a domain that it is as much a simulation as any other AI domain, and that this undercuts my arguments about the importance of using real world domains. Although I think there is a lot of truth in this, it is not literally correct: Pengo and Amazon are real, not simulated domains. Playing video games is a real human activity which people pay money to engage in.

There are two ways in which this criticism is valid, however. The first is that although the *domains* of Pengi and Sonja are real, their *visual systems* are in fact simulated. I don't use a TV camera; Sonja and Amazon coexist in the same computer and communicate not through light rays and joystick motion but via Lisp datastructures. This, I think, would be quite easy to rectify, and probably not much would be learned in the process, because Sonja's visual system, though simulated, is realistic; for discussion, see section 9.5.1.

The second, more serious issue is that playing Amazon, though a real human activity, is in some ways atypical.

The vision problem in Amazon is both easier and harder than in most other domains. It is easier in that the visual scene is two-dimensional, without occlusion, with uniform "illumination," with clearly delineated, brightly colored objects moving about in it. It is harder because in you often have to keep track of many monsters trying to attack you at once; this stretches one particular ability of the human visual system (tracking) to its utmost. (This, I imagine, is one reason video games are fun.)

The extreme time pressure of video games, though shared with some other human activities, is atypical. You don't generally have to make split-second decisions while making breakfast. (On the other hand, you do have to do some things on time: you can't go catatonic proving theorems while you've got eggs on the stove.) Extreme time pressure makes it difficult to engage in cognition. More typical activities do permit somewhat more explicit, articulated thought about what you are doing (though probably a lot less than has usually been posited).

In most domains, not everything relevant to your activity is perceptually accessible. This is true of Amazon also: the screen displays only a small part of the underlying universe. Further, we'll see that Sonja's visual system allows it to access only a small portion of the screen at any time. However, most of what is off the screen is irrelevant to most play. Amazon is atypical in that almost everything you need in order to decide how to act is perceptually accessible with minimal work. This makes it possible to make do with almost no state; activity in many other domains will require greater use of memory.

The notion of goals serves in AI both to individuate activities and as an account of motivation. Goals and activities are more clearly defined in video games than in most other domains. Video game activity is strictly instrumental and has an objective measure of success (a numerical score). Most activity is less easily described in terms of determinate goals. The rich structure of dinner conversation, for instance, is hard to account for in these terms. Understanding activity in such domains will require better theories of the structure of activity and of motivation.

Most human activities do not involve hostile agents (such as the monsters in Amazon). Cooperation is far more characteristic, but has been studied much less. I'll have more to say about this in appendix A and section B.3.1.

5 Instruction use

This chapter explains how Sonja uses instructions. Although instruction use is an interesting phenomenon in its own right, the issues discussed in this chapter are interesting principally for their implications for language use more generally. Sonja provides a framework for grounding instruction use in concrete activity. Such a framework can be an implementation medium for theories of pragmatic issues such as reference.

Section 5.1 begins by describing human video game instruction use. Video game instruction use is a form of language use with many special characteristics which are exploited by Sonja. I'll argue, though, that some characteristics of video game instruction use show up in language use more generally. In particular, video game instruction use highlights the problem of reference, discussed in section 5.2. In that section, I present alternative theories of reference and adopt a causal theory. A main contribution of Sonja is showing in detail how reference can be causally grounded in activity, particularly perception. I discuss the issues of indexicality and reflexivity, which are simultaneously problems in and resources for resolving references. Section 5.3 explains how you give Sonja instructions and how Sonja keeps track of the instructions you've given it. An instruction buffer mechanism provides for compositionality of processing. The section provides a table of all the instructions Sonja can use. Section 5.4 explains how instructions affect Sonja's activity. Instructions act by redirecting Sonja's attention and by managing its routines. Section 5.4.4 describes various specific linguistic constructs Sonja uses, and section 5.4.6 describes various linguistic issues that Sonja does not address at all. Finally, section 5.5 describes previous computational research on instruction use and on reference.

5.1 Video game instruction use

I was inspired to implement Sonja by observation of human video game instruction use. I spent time in video arcades watching video game players giving and using instructions. I video taped and transcribed some of these interactions. Video game instruction use differs from other forms of language use, and from other forms of instruction use, in many ways. These are largely determined by the social and physical context of video game playing, and are reflected in Sonja's instruction use.

Video game playing is a *social* activity for many practitioners. People go to arcades with their friends and play together or watch each other play. Video games are most quickly learned by collaboration, imitation, and from explicit instruction. (I'll talk more about these sorts of learning in section B.3.1.)

Video game instruction use is *situated*: the instruction giver and taker are right next to each other and have the same perceptual access to the situation. Many video games are in fact collaborative (two players cooperate in fighting off simulated enemies), in which case the instruction giver may be an involved participant and not merely a kibbitzer. This contrasts with written instructions and those given over the phone. Video game instruction givers and takers depend heavily on this shared access (see section 5.2.4), as does Sonja.

Some instructions are *immediate*: intended to apply only to the current situation. "Pick up that item" is an example. "Immediate" does not mean *instantaneous*, though; carrying out "Pick up that item" may take a second or two. Other instructions are intended to convey *general* rules which will apply in many situations. An example in my video corpus is "Turn your perspective before you go around the corner." This is *always* good advice in playing Xybot, and the instruction taker probably understood that he should permanently change his going-around-a-corner routine accordingly. Sonja models only immediate instruction use: you say something like "Use the knife!," it figures out, based on what's currently going on, what you must mean by that, uses the knife in the appropriate way as soon as feasible, and then forgets all about the suggestion. Sonja does not learn from advice it is given. (Appendix B suggests ways it might be extended to do so.)

Video game players understand that learning to play a video game involves learning a series of game-specific skills in a characteristic order that varies little from player to player. Thus players understand that individuals can be ranked in a nearly total order with respect to their understanding of a particular game. There is relatively little room for difference of opinion about how to play. This ranking makes instruction-giving a natural, useful, and in fact common function. Players understand that instructions given them by a more expert player are probably correct, and are therefore are willing to take them partly on trust. Sonja, likewise, tries to make sense of instructions when it can, and rejects instructions that obviously make no sense, but must take others on trust.

Video game instructions are typically accepted without any response.

This contrasts with instruction use in many other domains, in which it is common for instruction users to acknowledge instructions, to report success or failure, and to negotiate their meanings with the instruction giver by asking for elaborations of them and engaging in conversation about their application to the situation at hand [41]. These phenomena are rare in video game instruction use, probably because there isn't time for them; by the time you could have negotiated the meaning of an instruction, the situation to which it is relevant is often long gone. Sonja, accordingly, is not equipped to engage in extended conversation about individual situations or objects.

Probably again because of the time pressure of video game playing, immediate video game instructions are brief. The mean length of utterance in my transcripts is around five words. There are many one and two and three word utterances ("Danger!" "Other way," "We're losing energy.") The longest utterances are about three simple sentences. Video game instructions are also syntactically simple. For example, there are *no* subordinate clauses in my transcripts, which represent about an hour of interaction and about three hundred utterances. As we'll see in section 5.3, Sonja does not make much use of the syntactic structure of the instructions given it.

5.2   Reference

"Get the ghost" can be used in a particular Amazon-playing situation to *refer* to a particular ghost. How? In this section I'll review theories of reference and discuss the problem of indexicality. I won't propose a general theory of reference, but rather will adopt a version of the *causal* theory, which grounds reference in physical causality. The contribution of this book to the theory of reference is to show in greater detail than has previously been given how such a grounding is possible.

5.2.1   Theories of reference

Most theories of reference explicitly or implicitly divide the problem in two by positing that there are, in addition to natural language representations, "mentalese" representations. The first part of the problem, which following Sidner [256] I'll call *specification*, is figuring out how natural language expressions correspond to mentalese representations;

the second part, *external reference*, is figuring out how mentalese representations correspond to external objects. For example, the name "Jerry Fodor" is taken to specify a particular mentalese representation, which in turn refers externally to a particular person. The problem of specification is considered a problem for linguistics, and one on which progress might be made relatively straightforwardly, because it is only a matter of transforming one sort of representation into another. External reference is usually taken to be a harder problem, and one for philosophy rather than linguistics.

There are, loosely speaking, two approaches to the problem of reference: *correspondence* theories and *causal* theories. (Some theories fit in neither category; Millikan's [182], for example.) Correspondence theories (such as those of Davidson [53], Montague [56, 208], and Tarski [269]) seek to explain compositionality of reference. For example, the meaning of "snow is white" is said to be that snow is white, and we know this because we know that the meaning of "snow" is snow and that the meaning of "white" is white. Such theories only address the specification problem, because they do not explain how atomic representations (such as "snow") correspond to their referents. Correspondence theories of reference in linguistics are concerned mainly with finding the canonical mentalese representation specified by a linguistic one. For example, it might be useful to discover that "The US President in 1990" specifies $GEORGE-BUSH.

Causal theories, such as those of Evans [71] and Kripke [154] ground reference in physical causality. For instance, it seems that a tachometer needle represents engine speed in virtue of its connection to the engine via cables and wires; that a computer vision system represents a scene in virtue of its connection to them via light rays and a TV camera; and that a shopping list represents the food items it lists in virtue of your ability to recognize them on a shelf when you see them. On the other hand, causal theories are unable to explain reference to abstractions, because abstractions do not participate in physical causality. What causal paths connect "3" or "Rudolph the Red-nosed Reindeer" to their referents?

5.2.2 Grounding reference in activity

This book proposes no general solution to the problem of reference. Causal grounding seems to explain nicely reference in the case of video game instruction use, and so I have adopted it. On the other hand, this

book is not concerned with specification, because Sonja has no mentalese. (Sonja forms an existence proof that an agent can make sensible,
complex use of external representations without addressing specification.)

A causal theory of reference must specify *which* causal connections
constitute references. This is relatively easier for immediate, situated
instruction use than for some other cases, because reference can be
grounded in activity. The causal connections that constitute the reference of the instruction "Pick up that item" are among those that let
the instruction taker carry the instruction out: the perceptual processes
that let the instruction taker find the referent of "that item." More
generally, resolving reference may require physical action as well: for
example to enable perception by moving your head or by pulling aside
an occluding obstacle.

Elucidating the grounding of reference in activity has implications for
linguistics more generally. Fillmore [82, 83], Herskovits [121], Jackendoff [131], Lakoff [160], Miller and Johnson-Laird [181], Stucky [263], and
Talmy [268], among others, argue for grounding pragmatics, semantics
and some syntactic phenomena in perception, bodily space, and activity.
They propose, for instance, that the meanings of many words and perhaps some syntactic constructions ground out in spatial reasoning and
representation. Some but not all of this work explicitly supposes that
this spatial reasoning is related to vision: either that it actually uses the
innate visual hardware, or that it has the form it has because it is the
result of the internalization of visual activity. Although these linguistic
studies are inspiring starting points, they are limited by lack of a connection to serious theories of activity and perception. Their theories of
vision are schematic and much of the time are theories of Cartesian space
rather than of vision per se. That is, meanings are taken as depending on
Cartesian spatial models, without reference to visual processing. As I've
argued earlier, the sorts of representations that vision actually delivers
may be quite unlike Cartesian models.

This book suggests only a *framework* for grounding linguistic theories in activity. The specific "linguistic theory" implemented in Sonja,
composed of routines that interpret specific instructions, is crude. Implementing a serious linguistic theory in this framework would be an
enormous project, but Sonja suggests it is possible.

5.2.3   Indexicality

Indexicality is the dependence of the reference of a representation on its situation of use. Modeling indexical reference was one of the main motivations for implementing Sonja.

Indexicality is a pervasive phenomenon which manifests in many ways. (Fillmore [82] provides a review of categories of indexicality.) The classical cases are words such as "now," "here," and "I," whose referents depend solely on the situation of use.[1] Sonja doesn't use this sort of indexicality (though it easily could, as will become evident).

Another class of cases is concerned with the dependence of reference on the *linguistic context*: that is, on what has already been said. Here is an example of this phenomenon (adapted from Grosz [104]):

A: I'm going camping next weekend. Do you have a tent I could borrow?

B: Sure. I have a two-person backpacking tent.

A: The last trip I was on there was a huge storm. **The tent** collapsed and I got soaked.

B: What kind of tent was it?

A: A tube tent.

B: Tube tents don't stand up well in a real storm.

A: Uh huh.

B: OK, I'll bring in **the tent** tomorrow.

Here, the two instances of **the tent** refer to *different* tents due to their distinct linguistic contexts. Considerable attention has been given to this phenomenon within pragmatics and computational linguistics, particularly under the rubric of *anaphora* [104, 103, 109, 113, 132, 256, 291]. Since Sonja maintains little linguistic history, it rarely uses the linguistic context to ground indexical references. Sonja can get away with this because video game instruction use also makes little use of the linguistic context. This is probably because in video game discourse it is usually easier to refer to objects in terms of their their appearance on the screen. Sonja does make use of the linguistic context in resolving indexicality

---

[1] *Situation semantics* [23] is a compositional semantics devised particularly to address this class of indexicals.

in one case, the directive "No, the other one!", which can refer to another monster or amulet or pile of bones depending on what instructions have previously been given. It would be interesting to extend Sonja to keep track of more of the linguistic context and to make more use of it in grounding indexical references. I think that existing techniques for doing this could be incorporated straightforwardly; it would be more interesting to try to find mechanisms that accurately model human memory for linguistic context.

The phenomenon of indexicality is broader than either of these forms. It is not restricted to a particular subset of words; the meanings of almost all words depend on context. For example, Enç [67] argues from examples involving tense scoping that all nouns and verbs must be treated as indexicals whose denotations can only be determined pragmatically. For example, in "All virgins will go to heaven," "virgins" denotes all those people who are virgins when they die, not, as it would in other contexts, all those who are virgin at some particular moment. Other arguments to the same end are proposed by Fillmore [83], Nunberg [203], and others.

What counts as "context" can be arbitrarily broad. Besides the linguistic context, it includes the physical, social, and cultural circumstances of the instance of use, and it includes the purposes, memories, and histories of the interlocutors. A nice example is provided by Winograd and Flores' analysis of "Is there any water in the refrigerator?" [296].

A: Is there any water in the refrigerator?

B: Yes.

A: Where? I don't see it.

B: In the cells of the eggplant.

If A intends to drink the water, this is an unhelpful answer. On the other hand, it is "literally correct," and if A intends to clean the inside of the refrigerator with a chemical that reacts violently with trace amounts of water, it might also be a useful warning. It's easy to construct examples like this in which, depending on almost arbitrary factors, words can be made to mean almost arbitrary things.

In the end, as Katz and Fodor [144] and Nunberg [201, 202] have argued, we shouldn't expect a theory of reference that is both general and detailed, because reference is inescapably domain- and task-specific.

Reference is, moreover, *locally organized*, in the ethnomethodological sense: it's an ongoing collaborative achievement of the participants, who can and will make use of arbitrary aspects of the situation [41, 114, 120].

Sonja is not able to use all the sorts of context I've described. However, it is able to use its understanding of the ongoing Amazon situation and its own purposes in interpreting utterances. Sonja can find the referents of instructions such as "Get the demon," which in context often picks out a unique monster that it currently *makes sense* to get, though several may be visible. Schematically, making sense of such references is simple: referents are found by engaging in visual activity. Although it is widely acknowledged that perception is important in determining reference, few specific theories have previously been offered. On the other hand, there is a large linguistic and computational literature on the semantics and pragmatics of noun phrases [23, 109, 125, 155, 258] describing many phenomena that are not reflected in Sonja. For example, Sonja interprets all noun phrases *referentially,* rather than *attributively* [155], and *specifically*, rather than *generically* [258]. Sonja does not process determiners, quantifiers, or demonstratives, and so does not distinguish between "the stairs," "a stairwell," "any stairwell," and "those stairs."

The utterances in my video corpus are highly indexical. Here are some examples. They are quite typical and not chosen for extreme indexicality.

- "Hey, that's mine." This is said with no conversational context. It refers to an object ("that") on the screen. Both players know which object must be meant; only one makes sense.
- "Forty percent energy." In context, this is understood as "You have forty percent of your energy left." In a different context, it would mean "I have forty percent of my energy left." Which is meant turns on whose energy level is relevant in jointly deciding what to do next. For instance, I may be pointing out that I have more than you do, so I should be the one to deal with the next batch of monsters, or I may be warning you that you are losing energy quickly and had better retreat.
- "Are we gonna go through the time warp again?" "We" is traditionally an indexical; it's trivially understandable in this context, though. Definite noun phrases have often been analyzed as non-indexical, but in fact here determining the referent of "the time warp" is much more complicated than that of "we". Both players know which time warp is

meant, though it is not visible and though it is a *different* time warp than the one they went through last time ("again"). It's the time warp that it might *make sense* to go through this time.

5.2.4 Reflexivity

Instruction use, like other language use, is organized *reflexively*,[2] meaning that the speaker can depend on the hearer to understand the situation in the same way the speaker does, and to understand that the two share an understanding, and so on recursively. For example, an instruction giver can only expect "No!" to communicate if the instruction taker understands herself to be engaged in the particular activity "No!" recommends against; the taker can only make sense of the instruction if she imagines that the advisor considers her to be engaged in that activity; the giver must further be able to count on the taker imagining this; and so on. Likewise, in video game instruction use, both participants must reflexively understand that "Get that guy" picks out a mutually-agreed-upon enemy.

Video game players depend on instruction givers and users seeing the evolving game the same way, despite its many shifting issues. They *must* make this assumption. If they didn't the instruction giver could never finish specifying everything that would be necessary to relate an instruction to the evolving game situation. I'm sure the players couldn't list their shared understandings if they had to. In my video tapes of collaborative play, most coordination *goes without saying* [232]. For the most part, talk is required only when there are minute differences in understanding, and it depends extensively on the shared background of understanding. Communication doesn't pick up a "meaning" from my head and set it down in yours. Instead, communication is part of the work of maintaining a common reality. The instruction giver and taker share a common reality because they are competent players and because they use language to keep the shared reality in good repair.[3]

---

[2]I am using this term as it is used in ethnomethodology [120]. This is unrelated to the use of "reflexive" to refer to situations in which the subject and object of a verb have identical referents.

[3]This point is central in the ethnomethodological conversation analysis literature [120]. It has also been recognized by some computational researchers, for instance Grosz [105].

The phenomenon of reflexivity has been accounted for by several authors [24, 40, 109, 111, 153, 212, 217] under the rubric of *mutual knowledge*. In this framework, the interlocutors have beliefs about each other's beliefs, and about each other's beliefs about each other's beliefs, and so on. Not all the authors I have cited have specified how these beliefs are to be implemented; the most obvious way, which has been adopted by many of them, is that beliefs are *mental representations*. I don't think this account can be right in general; it requires more representations than there is time to reason with.

In Sonja, I take an alternative, *passive* approach to reflexivity.[4] Sonja and a human interlocutor can make sense of each other because they have a similar enough understanding of the ongoing Amazon game. When you tell Sonja "Get the ghost" it will probably know which monster you mean because it is competent at finding the most important ghost to clobber at any given time. Sonja doesn't, and doesn't need to, reason about your beliefs, because they are almost all shared.

Passive reflexivity depends not only on the interlocutors sharing an understanding of the specific domain of discourse, but also on their having homologous computational machinery. We'll see that advice such as "Get the amulet" is useful to Sonja not only because it supports one activity (getting the amulet) over others, but because it tells Sonja how to allocate a scarce computational resource, namely visual attention. Advisors would not give such advice if they did not reflexively understand that players have limited visual attention. Exactly what sorts of structural homology between conversational participants are required probably depends on specifics of the conversation and its context. Section 9.4.1 proposes an experiment to see whether Sonja has adequate homology for its task.

Passive reflexivity is more efficient than representational reflexivity, so we should see how far we can get with it. It is not hard to find situations in which people *do* reason about each other's beliefs and the effect differences in beliefs will have on communication. The same principle suggests that we should seek minimally representational (and so maximally efficient) accounts for such situations. I have not done this in Sonja; it is an interesting problem for future research.

As in human communication, differences in understanding can lead

---

[4] A similar approach is taken by the linguist Rommetveit [232].

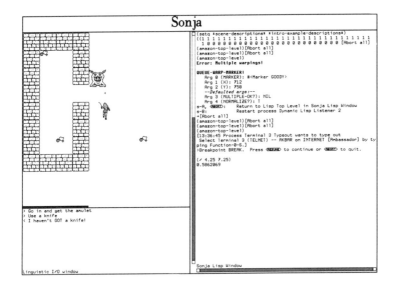

Figure 5.1
The lisp machine screen as it appears to an advice giver. The Amazon window is
on the left. Below it is a linguistic interaction window. The advisor's input appears
in this window after a greater-than sign prompt. Sonja's linguistic output appears
with a less-than sign prepended. The window on the right is a lisp interaction
window which is used in debugging the system. The top window is just a title.

to miscommunication; as in human communication, Sonja can participate in *repair* of misunderstandings. This is an instance of the situated,
interactive, improvisational organization of activity doing work in the
concrete-situated approach that requires representation and reasoning
in other approaches. Common situatedness makes it highly probable
that interlocutors share an understanding; interactivity allows them to
repair miscommunications; improvisational organization means that repair processes are not disruptive. I'll discuss repair further in section
5.4.4.

5.3 Giving Sonja instructions

Figure 5.1 shows the screen as it appears to you as an advisor of Sonja.
You can watch Sonja play Amazon in one window. When it seems that
an instruction would be useful, you hit the **suspend** key, which stops the

action and gives you a prompt in another window devoted to linguistic interaction. You type your instruction in this window, hit end, and Amazon starts running again.

Few instructions can be carried out instantaneously. Accordingly, Sonja must store instructions in some way, so that they effectively hang around until the activities they suggest are completed. Since I have little idea how people do this, I adopted the simplest mechanism I could think of for Sonja. *Instruction buffers* to keep track of which instructions have been given. (A complete table of Sonja's instruction buffers appears in figure 5.2.) Whenever an instruction is given, one or more instruction buffers are set.

Each instruction buffer has a *valid bit*, which tells whether a corresponding instruction has been given. A buffer remains valid until it is explicitly cleared by the central system. Each buffer has a *clear line* input; when it is set high the valid bit is cleared. The central system does this when it has succeeded or failed in carrying out the instruction, or when it rejects it.

In addition to its valid bit, an instruction buffer may have named *fields*, which are registers holding data values extracted from instructions. In Sonja, no buffer has more than one field, and few have any.

Compositionality of processing is provided in three ways. Several instructions may set the same buffer; for example, both "Get the potion" and "Get the amulet" set the buffer pick-up-the-goody. Buffer fields also contribute: the instructions "Head right" and "Head left," for example, set the same instruction buffer, suggested-go, but set its direction field differently. Further compositionality is provided by the organization of the central system, in that the same piece of machinery may take input from several instruction buffers. For example, the instruction buffers register-the-amulet and register-the-potion are used by the same visual search routine. These mechanisms for compositionality are effectively equivalent; it would, for instance, involve changing about five lines of code to make "Head down those stairs" and "Don't go down yet" share a single instruction buffer with a boolean negated? field, rather than having their own buffers go-down-the-stairwell and dont-go-down-the-stairwell. Since instruction buffers are not intended as a real theory of memory for instructions, I've made arbitrary choices between these mechanisms in the implementation.

Instruction buffers can be *chained* to store instructions involving a temporal sequence (for instance "Get the potion and set it off"). A chained instruction buffer has a *next pointer* to another buffer that represents the next activity in the sequence. When the buffer is cleared, indicating that the first activity has been completed, the valid bit on the next buffer is set high. Next pointers, like instruction buffers themselves, are not intended to be plausible as cognitive models, which is why it doesn't bother me that, as pointers, they violate essential connectionism. A real account of how instructions are buffered would be part of a real account of memory more generally, and such an account should respect the constraints of essential connectionism.

Figure 5.2 shows how instruction buffers are set based on an advisor's input string. From it we can see that, roughly speaking, Sonja does little syntactic processing. (I say "roughly" because it's not really clear how in Sonja to draw the line between syntax and semantics.) The system can accept only few dozen instructions; the natural language input window could be replaced with a mouse menu. The system does not incorporate a parser; a single Lisp procedure implements the table of figure 5.2. Depending on how "semantics" is defined, Sonja also does no semantic processing; certainly it constructs no semantic representation of its input.

On the other hand, the compositionality of Sonja's instruction use makes me believe that it would be straightforward to add to the system as it stands a parser that would set instruction buffers. Such a parser would currently be limited by the relatively small number of sorts of activities Sonja can engage in and consequently the relatively small number of sorts of advice Sonja could make use of. A deeper linguistic project is to determine how instructions are in fact buffered and what sort of processing connects linguistic input with specific proposals for action.

5.4   How Sonja uses instructions

Intelligent use of advice requires that you *make sense* of it. (Video game instructions are in this way unlike computer program instructions, which can be simply executed.) Making sense can in general require unbounded types and amounts of work. Sonja's sense-making is largely perceptual; it understands instructions by relating them to the current Amazon-playing situation. When Sonja is given an instruction, it reg-

Instruction	Instruction buffer(s) set	Field
Get the monster/ghost/demon	`kill-the-monster`	`type`
Don't bother with that guy	`dont-kill-the-monster`	
Head down those stairs	`go-down-the-stairwell`	
Don't go down yet	`dont-go-down-the-stairwell`	
Get the bones	`kill-the-bones`	
Ignore the bones for now	`dont-kill-the-bones`	
Get the *goody*	`pick-up-the-goody`	
	`register-the-`*goody*	
Don't pick up the *goody*	`dont-pick-up-the-goody`	
	`register-the-`*goody*	
Head *direction*	`suggested-go`	`direction`
Don't go *direction*	`suggested-not-go`	`direction`
Go around to the left/right	`go-around`	`direction`
Go around the top/bottom	`go-around`	`direction`
Go on in	`go-in`	
OK, head out now	`go-out`	
Go on in and down the stairs	`in-the-room`	
	`go-down-the-stairwell`	
Go on in and get the bones	`in-the-room`	
	`kill-the-bones`	
Go in and get the *goody*	`register-the-`*goody*	
	`in-the-room`	
	`pick-up-the-goody`	
Get the potion and set it off	`register-the-potion`	
	`pick-up-the-goody`	
	`use-a-potion` (chained)	
Scroll's ready	`scroll-is-ready`	
On your left! *and similar*	`look-out-relative`	`rotation`
On the left! *and similar*	`look-out-absolute`	`direction`
Use a knife	`use-a-knife`	
Hit it with a knife		
when it goes light	`hit-it-with-a-knife-when-it-goes-light`	
Use a potion	`use-a-potion`	
No, the other one	`no-the-other-one`	

Figure 5.2
Sonja's instruction buffers and the instructions that set them. Some instructions
have variant forms. `pick-up-the-goody` and `use-a-potion` are chained together
when the instruction "Get the potion and set it off" is given.

isters the entities the instruction refers to and uses the instruction to choose between courses of action that themselves make sense in the current situation. An instruction can fail to make sense if it refers to entities that are not present in the situation in which it is given, or if the activity it recommends is implausible in its own right.

5.4.1 Instructions reorient attention

Interpreting a noun phrase typically requires and permits new registrations. For example, if you are told "Use a knife" and you don't have one, you can look in likely places and do whatever it takes to recognize something as a knife. You might also remember where relevant knives are, or ask, or engage in an open-ended collection of other ways of finding one. Once you have found *the-knife*, you can register aspects like *the-knife-is-easily-accessible*, and this immediately suggests the proposal *pick-up-the-knife*. Similarly, the processing of verb phrases permits and requires new projections. If I say to you (as someone does in my video corpus) "Don't throw the barrel that way—throw it this way," you will project what would happen if you throw it "this way," which you might not have otherwise done. Then you'll see (if I'm right) that that makes better sense than throwing it "that way."

To summarize, *as part of taking an instruction you register aspects of the situation you weren't previously aware of, and project new possibilities. Based on these new registrations you engage in new activities.* Advice, to put it another way, serves to reorient attention; it tells you not only *what to do* but *what to look at*. This point has been made by Cohen [42]. An analogous one is made by Grosz and Sidner [105, 110], who stress the importance of attentional state in discourse. Grosz and Sidner's point is broader; visual attention is only one part of attention more generally, and the only part modeled by Sonja.

5.4.2 Instructions manage autonomous routines

Instructions recommend courses of action; Sonja's arbitration network takes account of such recommendations. Proposers (described in section 3.2.2) are each responsible for deciding, at every moment, whether the sort of activity they propose makes sense. The arbitration network is responsible for choosing among competing plausible proposals; instructions are taken into account. Because instructions can only influence arbitration when they make sense in terms of activities Sonja could engage in autonomously, their role in Sonja is one of *management* only.

In my video corpus, there are many instances of someone being told "Turn left!" when doing so would run him right into a wall. In this case, the player will turn left when he gets to the upcoming junction. But the instruction is not merely a syntactic ellipsis for "Turn left at the junction coming up"; I have examples of someone ignoring the instruction for a while longer, because when he gets to the junction an enemy starts shooting at him, and turning left would be suicidal. "Turn left" here 'means' "Turn left when it *makes sense* to do so." This isn't a matter of syntactic ellipsis; the same qualification applies to every instruction. It's not a matter of semantic amplification, either; what *makes sense* means depends on all the particulars of the specific situation. Relevance cannot be determined *a priori*; the use of "Turn left" is a matter for indefinite amounts and types of situation-specific interpretation.

This non-literality of instructions, combined with their management role, supports the notion using the outputs of instruction buffers as inputs exclusively to the arbitration network. An instruction can't force you to do something or tell you what's so; it helps you decide among competing alternatives.

A suggestion like "Get the amulet" does not tell Sonja what to do in the sense that a program would. Getting the amulet can take a lot of work; Sonja may have to navigate about the dungeon and fight off monsters along the way. Sonja is autonomously competent at getting amulets and many other routine Amazon activities; and you can no more tell it to perform the available primitive actions than you can tell me to send a particular sequence of neural impulses to my arm muscles. Instructions do not act like calls on high-level subroutines, either; getting the amulet may have to be interleaved with almost every other activity Sonja is capable of. "Get the amulet" is useful because it tells Sonja that getting the amulet, rather than (for example) going down the nearby stairwell, is the right thing to be doing at the moment.

The contents of the instruction buffers are inputs to the arbitration network (along with suggested activities from proposers and registrations of aspects from registrars). How, specifically, are instructions taken into account in choosing what to do? An instruction buffer's valid bit will typically *support* a particular proposal. This support, described technically in section 7.2.5, allows the system to resolve several types of arbitration decisions that are otherwise difficult:

- Before an instruction is given, there may not have been either any support for the proposal nor any objection to it. In this case the proposal is not taken. The instruction constitutes support for the proposal, so it can be taken.
- There may be several mutually exclusive proposals on the table, among which Sonja has no way to choose. The arbitration network must choose arbitrarily in such a case. If an instruction supports one rather than the others, Sonja can choose it.
- There may be several mutually exclusive proposals on the table, none of which is unambiguously preferable, but one of which is weakly preferred by default. If an instruction supports one of the others, minimal trust (of the sort video game instruction takers routinely extend to instruction givers) leads Sonja to take the supported proposal.
- An instruction may suggest an activity at a higher level of abstraction than any currently active. For example, at one point in my video corpus someone says "Try to get to the third level," when the hearer had just been wandering around aimlessly. Such a suggestion, if taken, can organize other activity.

Sonja implements instances of all these ways an instruction can affect arbitration except the last, which I haven't gotten to. Section 7.2.5 explains in more detail the arbitration machinery that allows instructions to manage activity.

5.4.3   Clearing instruction buffers

If I say to you "Stop shooting," you may be counted as following the direction even if you start shooting again later. For example, I may have said it because you were in danger of shooting something valuable; as soon as it is out of your line of fire, the instruction is void. Suggestions have temporal extent, which is rarely explicitly demarcated. You can ignore my suggestion as soon as it no longer makes sense. The instruction buffer clear lines (section 5.3) implement this: Sonja must explicitly clear its instruction buffers once a suggestion is no longer relevant. How can it tell when that is?

We shouldn't expect a general answer to this question, any more than to any other concerning real human activity. There are many specific cases in which the answer is clear. (All the instructions illustrating these cases are from my video corpus.)

- Some instructions suggest activities that have an inherent endpoint: "Turn left!" Having turned left once (even were that a durative activity) you would not continue by turning left again.
- Some instructions make sense for a good reason which stops being true: the "Stop shooting" example, for instance.
- Some suggestions become obviously nonsensical at some point. "You want to head, ahm, straight down" will eventually run you into a wall, at which point you'd better turn.
- Some suggestions may be explicitly countermanded. A complex example is " 'Kay, now go ba—keep going—take—left! left! Now go left again, now go down that, that alleyway... Turn—straight!—the way you are going now. Now take a right—take the first right."

I've implemented instances of all of these except the last.

5.4.4   Some kinds of instructions Sonja can use

This section describes some sorts of advice Sonja can use and reviews literature on these sorts of advice. This taxonomy of advice types is intended for expositional purposes only, not as any sort of linguistic theory. The classes are *indexical reference to objects, indexical reference to activities, negations, temporal expressions, spatial expressions, indirect speech acts*, and *repairs*.

I have implemented only one to a few examples of each of these classes. As Sonja is a pilot study of a new architecture, the intention is to demonstrate that constructs like these are possible and to suggest some mechanisms, rather than to achieve full coverage of particular phenomena. These mechanisms are explained in greater detail in chapter 8.

Indexical reference to objects   Typically, instructions support both proposals to take action in the world and proposals to do visual work. For instance, "Head down those stairs" supports both going to a stairwell and performing a visual search to find a stairwell if Sonja is not already registering one. This implements *indexical reference to objects*. Section 6.2 describes the mechanisms of visual search in more detail.

Indexical reference to activities   Not only the objects used in an activity but the activity itself suggested by an instruction can depend on context. For instance, in Amazon, "Use a knife" can suggest throwing one at an enemy or using one to jimmy a door, and Sonja can figure out which is meant. (Section 8.6 explains how.) I know of only one previous study of this phenomenon, due to Robinson [229], who extended Grosz's focusing algorithm [106], intended originally for nominal anaphora understanding, to disambiguate indexical references to activities.

Negation Most of the instructions Sonja can use have corresponding *negated* forms: "Don't go in there," "Don't pick up the amulet." The interpretation of these instructions shares machinery with the positive forms. Specifically, the instruction buffer for a negated instruction objects to the same outward activities the buffer for the positive form supports. On the other hand, both instruction buffers support registering the relevant entities if they are not already registered. Thus a negated instruction draws attention to the same entities as the corresponding positive instruction.

Temporal expressions Temporal expressions in my video corpus include "Turn it *now*—there you go," "When you come back, make sure you take the first right," "Keep goin', straight, then take the right at the end of the hall," and "That dude should be comin' right about now." Sonja implements a few instructions of this sort; "Get the potion and set it off" and "Hit it with a knife when it goes light" are examples.

There are large linguistic and computational literatures on temporal expressions; see, for example, [11, 44, 56, 82, 187, 209, 292, 297]. These literatures are concerned with mapping linguistic temporal expressions to internal temporal representations, typically in an interval algebra.

Sonja implements something quite different: its use of temporal expressions is *in* time as well as *about* time. Sonja's understanding of temporal expressions is constituted by its ability to manifest activity with the same temporal structure the expressions describe. For example, Sonja's use of "Get the potion and set it off" involves two activities, getting the potion and setting it off, which have the temporal relationship (succession) described by the instruction. I know of only one related project, Stucky's Pidgin (personal communication), an artificial language designed for situated communication between people and machines, which is similarly intended to be interpreted *in* time.

Spatial expressions Earlier in this chapter I have reviewed literature on the spatial grounding of language. Although this phenomenon is ubiquitous in Sonja's instruction use, it is particularly clear in the case of expressions involving prepositions; Sonja can use several instructions such as "Go in and get the amulet" and "Go around the top". Sonja's ability to use these instructions is grounded in its visual routines for parsing the world in terms of spatially extended objects such as rooms and obstacles and for figuring out spatial relationships between objects.

In my video corpus there are several instances of one player warning another that a particularly obnoxious monster has just appeared on the screen with an expression such as "Look out behind you!" These expressions fall into two classes: ones such as "Look out behind you!" that refer to directions relative to the heading of the player icon (the amazon in the case of the game Amazon), and others such as "Look out below!" which refer relative to the coordinate system of the screen. These classes correspond to the *intrinsic* and *extrinsic* uses of prepositions [225].[5] Sonja uses such warnings to switch attention to the indicated monster.

Indirect speech acts The instruction "Head left" in context usually does not mean simply to go left, but to go left in order to achieve a particular goal which requires going left, and to continue by actually achieving the goal. "Head left" is, thus, an indirect speech act [164, 212, 247], referring to some activity other than that it directly describes. Sonja uses the context to figure out what proposal "Head left" actually supports, and remembers this information so it can carry it out.

Similarly, I may say something declaratively from which I expect you to draw the inference that I am recommending a particular activity. Some examples from my video corpus are "Dynamite's on the ground!" "Here they come!" "There's two guys in front of you," and "We've got both barrels over here." These "instructions" result in visual activities that lead you to reregister the situation and consequently to act differently. The inference involved in understanding these indirect speech acts seems to be a matter of perception and action, not theorem-proving or symbol-manipulating. Having seen that "we've got both barrels over here," which you might not have noticed before it was pointed out to you, it may be obvious that the right thing to do is to pick them up and

---

[5]Retz-Schmidt [225] actually contrasts three uses, deictic, intrinsic, and extrinsic. Deictic uses are relative to the point of view of the speaker. Since all participants in video game discourse always face the screen, deictic and extrinsic usages are indistinguishable.

throw them at the enemies. The sole example in Sonja of a declarative instruction is "Scroll's ready."

Repairs Human language use is never perfectly communicative; people regularly misunderstand each other. Misunderstandings often result from differences in the set of entities the conversational participants are attending to, for instance. Typically people rapidly recover from miscommunication using any of several linguistic repair mechanisms [41, 134, 227, 244]. Repair is common in some discourse tasks, particularly those in which the interlocutors do not share perceptual access to the topic of discourse, for example when one gives instructions to another over a telephone line. Repair is rare in video game instruction, however. This is probably partly because there isn't time for it and partly because shared perceptual access to the situation means that misunderstandings are uncommon in the first place. (Two of the three examples of repair in my corpus occur in a short segment when an expert is instructing a complete novice who hasn't yet figured out what the icons on the screen mean.) It is also common, both in video game and other discourse, for minor misunderstandings to go undetected without significant consequence [134].

Sonja implements one repair, "No, the other one," which can be given as an instruction when Sonja has misidentified an ambiguous reference. In section 5.2.3, I explained that the interpretation of "No, the other one" depends on the linguistic context; which entity Sonja reregisters depends on what instruction has been given. For example, if Sonja is carrying out "Head down those stairs," "No the other ones" causes it to look for a new stairwell, whereas if Sonja is carrying out "Get the demon," "No the other one" causes it to look for a new demon. It is not clear what Sonja should do if it is carrying out more than one instruction when told "No, the other one." I think that a good theory of this would require serious analysis of turn taking and the temporal structure of discourse and other complex phenomena. Accordingly I have made an arbitrary implementation decision: Sonja reregisters *all* the entities that have been referred to by pending instructions when it is told "No, the other one."

A related approach to repair is taken in Goodman's FWIM system [99]. FWIM, like Sonja, is motivated by the observation that a hearer has limited resources for determining reference and that repair processes are consequently often required. Like Sonja, FWIM actively searches for referents; it differs in that this search is over a space of internal representations, rather than over external objects, and in its mechanism, which is relaxation. FWIM, like Sonja, uses spatial information in resolving references, but unlike Sonja its model of spatial computation is *ad hoc*. Also unlike Sonja, FWIM does not take purposes into account in choosing referents; it has a fixed task-independent preference ordering on possibilities.

5.4.5 Generating replies

Sonja has a simple linguistic output mechanism for generating replies to instructions. All of these replies are complaints, generated when Sonja can't make sense of an instruction. Examples are "I haven't *got* a key," "*What* demon?", "Go in *where*?", and "Use a knife for *what*?"; a complete list appears in figure 8.3 on page 164. There are many more situations in which Sonja might usefully generate complaints or other replies. For instance, Sonja doesn't complain when given a completely ambiguous reference, but chooses a referent arbitrarily.

Sonja only complains when an instruction can't make any sense: specifically, when it determines that one of the entities it refers to does not exist. Accordingly, Sonja clears the instruction buffer it complains, thereby rejecting the instruction. Since Sonja complains only when instructions could not possibly make sense, it does not allow the instruction-giver to reply to complaints. You can't tell Sonja which knife when it complains "*What* knife." This is acceptable because no reply (other, perhaps, than "Oops, sorry") could make sense. Sonja's existing instruction-taking mechanisms are sufficient to make sense of clarifying replies if Sonja were to complain of ambiguities. For Sonja to engage in more extended negotiation of reference [41] would in many cases require mechanisms for storing and using more of the linguistic context.

5.4.6 Some issues I'm ignoring

This book concentrates on understanding certain aspects of instruction use, and necessarily ignores many more. There are innumerable phenomena even in my video tapes that Sonja does not model. This section will discuss some of them; the list is not intended to be exhaustive.

Sonja makes less use of the timing of instructions as a resource for determining reference than it might. In my video corpus, the temporal course of an instruction or stream of instructions often tracks the activities it recommends. For example: " 'Kay, now go ba—keep going—take—left! left! Now go left again, now go down that, that alleyway... Turn—straight!—the way you are going now. Now take a right—take the first right." I don't see any way to model these phenomena without real time speech input; in Sonja, the game stops while instructions are typed. Davis's Back Seat Driver [54] (described further in section 5.5.2) carefully times the instructions it gives (such as "Bear left here") so they will end at the moment they are needed.

Sonja does not model many phenomena that arise from the interactive nature of situated instruction use. Several large literatures, such as discourse analysis [109, 135, 215], interaction structure theory [63], and conversation analysis [120, 164] study phenomena such as anaphora, rhetorical structure, gaze direction, gesture [178], turn taking, adjacency pairs, and prosodics [123, 214]. Sonja addresses none of these issues.

Sonja does not model many phenomena that arise from the embedding of discourse in a social as well as a physical situation. Issues of politeness, deference, formality, the maintenance of shared social as well as physical reality, and management of the participants' emotions are ignored. (Fillmore [82] provides a catalog of such phenomena under the rubric of *social deixis*; see also Grosz [105].)

5.5   Related work

5.5.1   Instruction taking

I'll review AI research first on instruction taking in general and then on natural language instruction taking in particular. I'll also describe some work on instruction giving, but not provide a full review, since Sonja does not address that issue.

AI's major model for instruction use is in the planning literature. (For reviews and analysis of the planning literature see for instance Agre and Chapman [7], Chapman [33], Georgeff [94], and McDermott [176].) A planner, given a goal and an initial situation, constructs a plan which is used by an executive. Executives are programming language interpreters, possibly with minor extensions; they execute a sequence of instructions blindly and mechanically. Several models of instruction use in the literature take instructions to be plans or plan fragments to be used by an executive; others take instructions to be goals given to a planner. (I'll discuss examples of each in this section.) I find neither model satisfactory, as I don't believe the planning model of activity; this work is motivated in part by a desire to replace this notion of plan use with a more flexible and hence more useful and realistic one. For further discussion, see Agre and Chapman [7] and Chapman [36].

More sophisticated ways of thinking about instruction use begin with McCarthy's proposed Advice Taker [175]. McCarthy described his motivation thus: "A machine is instructed mainly in the form of a sequence of imperative sentences [like a plan or program], while a human is instructed mainly in declarative sentences describing the situation in which action is required together with a few imperatives that say what is wanted." The Advice Taker was to be instructed as a human is. The Advice Taker was never implemented, but a program inspired by it, Mostow's "operationalizer" FOO [189], gets at some of the relevant intuitions. In these models of advice taking, as in Sonja, advice is not executable, but must be made useful. They differ in many other ways, however. The Advice Taker and FOO are given "high-level" descriptions of a domain, where the advice given to Sonja is quite concrete and specific to the immediate situation. Sonja takes advice at "run time," where FOO and the Advice Taker are given it at "compile time." FOO and the Advice Taker transform advice into an "operational" procedure that can be mechanically executed later, where Sonja uses advice only to manage an already-ongoing activity. FOO and the Advice Taker use theorem proving or related exponentially inefficient reasoning techniques to effect this transformation, where the machinery of Sonja is simple and seems more likely to scale.

Laird *et al.*'s Robo-Soar [159] takes advice in a real, incompletely-modeled robot arm domain. Robo-Soar, like Sonja, is not based on the planning model of activity, and accordingly its operation has some of the same flavor. As in Sonja, the advice given to Robo-Soar applies directly to the current situation, and is not construed either as plans or goals. Unlike Sonja, Robo-Soar learns from advice, reusing it in situations similar to those in which it was originally given. The advice given to Robo-Soar is of two sorts. First, when the system is unable to decide between alternative actions, the advisor can specify one. This is analogous to Sonja's use of advice to manage autonomous competences, except that that this advice must be couched in terms of Robo-Soar's internal processes, rather than in terms of the domain [98]. The advisor can therefore give direct advice about what may be rather abstract internal control decisions; this makes Robo-Soar a less natural fit to human advice-taking. Putting advice in terms of the system's structure rather than in terms of the domain also bypasses some of the problems of learning. Much of the difficulty of learning from the advice given to Sonja would be in figuring out which aspects of the situation make the advice valid and so which situations the advice should be applied to in the future; Robo-Soar does not face this problem. Robo-Soar can also be given a sort of advice that is used in recovering from an incorrect domain theory. This advice explicitly identifies to Robo-Soar the features of the domain relevant to the success or failure of particular strategies. This advice must be exhaustive, unlike the sorts of advice people typically give each other.

There's little work in the AI literature on the use of natural language instruction use. Winograd's SHRDLU [295] translated English instructions into procedures (plans) and executed them. The system did nothing except when instructed. The instructions were immediate, like Sonja's, not high-level like the Advice Taker's. My principal disagreement with this work is with the plan-based theory of activity that underlies it.

Vere and Bickmore's "basic agent" Homer [285] translates natural language commands into goals and passes them to a planner and executive. Homer operates in a simulated marine world and can take a broad variety of types of commands. Homer and Sonja are outwardly similar in their use of instructions, though Homer's sophistication and breadth is the more impressive. The two systems, furthermore, share a deeper motivation than exploring instruction use: the designers of both wished to go beyond AI research into particular areas such as planning, learning, or parsing, to construct a unified intelligence. Our approaches, however, are quite different, and this is reflected in the underlying architectures. Vere and Bickmore write that "The underlying thesis of this work is that AI component research and computer hardware have in fact progressed to the point where it is now possible, by a resolute effort, to construct a complete integrated agent." I disagree, for two reasons. First, I believe that existing AI theories of particular cognitive modules (components) are in fact inadequate. Planning is a clear example [7]; Vere and Bickmore do not address the problem of search control for planners, even though they report as a difficulty with Homer that, in its tiny simulated world, plan generation takes up to several minutes. Second, I think that existing AI theories reflect deeper misunderstandings. For example, I think that the particular modularity that most AI work assumes is incorrect, and that as a consequence theories of activity and of natural language that are not connected with perception from the outset probably never can be. Vere and Bickmore dismiss this concern by describing their agent as operating "at a cognitive level." Homer's simulated perceptual component is unrealistic, and I doubt that an autonomous cognitive level can exist.

Grosz has initiated a line of research on *task-oriented dialogues*: that is, conversations that naturally occur as a part of concrete activity. Her first empirical studies [104] were of experts directing apprentices in a mechanical assembly task. Her analysis emphasizes the importance of discourse context, including the configuration of the task equipment and the state of completion of the task [107], and accordingly the importance of shared visual access to the task equipment [104] and the resulting shared understanding of the activity [105]. These concerns are reflected in this book. Grosz further argues that the attentional state of the conversational participants is central to the structure of the discourse [104, 106]; she has developed this point in a recent paper with Sidner [110]. In Grosz's model attention focuses on parts of a semantic network representation. She argues for a hierarchical structure for discourse paralleling a hierarchical structure for activity; this hierarchical structure is supported by an attentional focus stack that is pushed and popped as subtasks are initiated and completed [103, 104, 106, 107, 110]. Sonja too makes attention a central structuring device for discourse. The attention mechanism I've implemented is narrower in scope than that of Grosz (as mine encompasses only visual attention). Sonja does not privilege hierarchical organizations of activity; I view hierarchical organization as an emergent phenomenon rather than as a correlate of particular machinery [4, 7]. Accordingly Sonja has no focus stack. However, it also does not address a hard problem the focus stack helps solve, namely resolving anaphora by consulting the linguistic context. Grosz's task-oriented dialog studies have been followed up by many other researchers; Grosz *et al.* [109] provide a survey.

Suchman's ethnomethodological study of an instruction-giving system based on the instructions-as-plans model [264] was one of the principal sources of the concrete-situated view of activity presented in chapter 2. It was also an inspiration for the design of Sonja. Her analysis emphasizes the importance of the indexicality of instructions. She points out that much of the work in using instructions is in resolving references (both to objects and to activities), so that instructions are not simply executed, but must be made relevant to the concrete situation. She found that in practice the instruction-giving system's plan-execution model of activity led to communicative breakdown. Users of the system would run into trouble in the use of instructions and then understood themselves as initiating repairs of various sorts, which the system had no understanding of. Consequently the system and its users would understand instructions differently, leading to further confusions. Sonja is intended to model aspects of the "situated inquiry" theory of instruction use Suchman proposes as an alternative. In particular, Sonja models the process of making-relevant; the process of linguistic repair, which is central in Suchman's analysis, Sonja models only sketchily. Another aspect of instructions Suchman discusses is their retrospective use to explain what has been done. Sonja does not model this at all.

5.5.2   Reference

There has been much work in both linguistics and AI on specification [14, 15, 16, 17, 108, 109, 155, 207, 256, 257]. I won't review that work here because Sonja isn't concerned with the subject. Some of these studies have explicitly mentioned the problem of external reference and have proposed grounding it in vision, but none have given an account of how to do so. Cohen's empirical study of the pragmatics of referring [42, 43] comes closest, as he is explicitly concerned only with perceptually grounded reference, but he grounds out in a generic PERCEPTUALLY-ACCESSIBLE predicate.

All systems I know of that provide external reference do so causally. Many AI systems have given causal grounding to their representations; the vast majority are vision systems (which represent what they see) and robotics systems (which represent what they manipulate or navigate about in). However, a few previous AI systems have given causal grounding to natural language representations.

Winograd's SHRDLU [295] pointed in the right direction. It allowed an interlocutor to refer to imaginary blocks in a simulated world. Reference was a product of the system's ability to perform simulated actions on the simulated blocks. This sort of reference is arguably causal and arguably even external, though the intimacy of the connection between SHRDLU and its blocks world makes the causal grounding a bit too easy. (The same perhaps could be said about Sonja, but interposing a realistic model of vision between language and Amazon is intended to deflect this criticism.) Similarly, Davey's tic-tac-toe player [51, 52] generated accounts of games it had actually played. His system deliberately exploited indexicality of reference to generate expressions like "the middle of the edge".

The TDUS system of Grosz and her colleagues [104, 229, 287] engaged in a dialog with a human user who was assembling an air compressor. TDUS could refer to objects with expressions such as "the aftercooler elbow"; this expression was causally connected with the actual aftercooler elbow by virtue of the human's ability to recognize it. This provides unarguably external reference, but offloads the work of achieving it onto the interlocutor.

Davis's Back Seat Driver [54] gives route instructions to a human driver. Like TDUS, it achieves external reference causally in virtue of its human user's perceptual abilities. It uses an annotated map in its model of the driver's visual abilities. For example, based on map locations, it generates instructions like "Look for Merit Gas on the left side." The system has no detailed model of the driver's visual processes, and its judgments of whether or not the driver will be able to see things is limited by the imprecision of the map.

Most systems that attempt causal grounding do so through machine vision. So far as I have been able to determine, none of these has quite made a full causal connection; in each some part of the process relating camera data to linguistic input or output is simulated.

The earliest such system I've found is Badler's [18], which anticipates the form of all the others. His intention was to build a system which would produce natural language descriptions from sequences of images of moving objects. His principal contribution was a general-purpose representation for motion and spatial relationships. This representation combined features of semantic networks and metrical representations from graphics algorithms. He presented unimplemented algorithms that would translate from image sequences to these representations and from the representations to natural language descriptions. The vision algorithms, we can say confidently with fifteen years of hindsight, wouldn't work. More seriously, there is reason to believe that the sort of metrical representations he wanted to extract from images cannot be had (see section 3.3.1), and that the sort of semantic network representations he proposed to give to a text generator are incompatible with essential connectionism. Nonetheless, his account of the aggregation of primitive motions and relationships into more abstract, meaningful ones is valuable.

The ALVEN system of Tsotsos *et al.* [280] built on Badler's work and incorporated more realistic vision algorithms with provision for noise and occlusion. Its final output was to be a frame representation suitable for text generation; the authors did not actually connect it to a text generator. Whether the implementation ever actually ran is unclear from the paper.

Four groups, working independently in the late Seventies, used representations similar to Badler's, though not all seem to have known of his work. Waltz and Boggess [288, 289, 290] considered the problem of constructing from a natural language description a spatial model to use in spatial reasoning. The system ran in some simple cases. Abe *et al.* [1] and Okada [204] describe implemented systems which constructed representations from stories with accompanying cartoon images. The visual and natural language processing in these systems seem in retrospect *ad hoc* and unlikely to generalize. A similar, unimplemented proposal was made by Marburger *et al.* [170].

This last work has been followed up by a series of projects in Germany which have continued through this decade [199, 225, 226, 245], particularly in the VITRA (visual translator) project. These systems produce natural language descriptions from sequences of images of moving objects. They are particularly concerned with the use of prepositions and motion verbs, and draw on a linguistic literature on the grounding of prepositions in spatial primitives; see, for example, Adorni *et al.* [2] and Herskovits [121]. The systems are all fairly similar for our purposes; I'll describe CITYTOUR [225, 245], which is best documented. CITYTOUR's visual system segments moving objects from the images, yielding a database of (object, location) pairs. A geometrical analysis system produces qualitative descriptions of the motions of the objects in the same ontology used by the natural language system. This ontology includes notions such as passing, being close to, following a path, and stopping. Finally a generation system produces text from this description.

CITYTOUR is the best implemented connection between language and vision to date. However, it has several weaknesses; most important is that the model of vision is crude and *ad hoc*. It requires a prior geometric model of the stationary background of the motion sequences and identifies only the bounding boxes of moving objects. In order to actually connect it to the language system, the types and orientations of the objects have to be entered by hand. It is not general purpose or motivated by a broader conception of vision. These deficiencies can probably be rectified. Were this done, the resulting system would differ from Sonja principally in that it would be a passive observer describing events, rather than an involved participant; and consequently it would provide more limited opportunities for linguistic interaction.

6 The peripheral systems

This chapter explains Sonja's peripheral systems, exclusive of the linguistic input system, which I've already described in chapter 5. Almost all of the chapter is concerned with vision, as the other peripheral systems are trivial. In particular it is concerned with the visual routines processor, as I have not implemented other visual systems.

Unlike some machine vision systems which seek engineering solutions by whatever means, Sonja's visual system is intended to model specifically *biological* vision. Sonja's VRP is, further, a model for *intermediate* vision. Unfortunately, relatively little is known about intermediate visual processing. There is little relevant neurophysiological evidence, for example. Progress at this point seems to require the construction of plausible models which can suggest questions for neuroscientific, psychological, and computational experiments. Such a model must respect the evidence that is available, even if it is scanty; the model this book proposes is informed by psychophysics, neurophysiology, and engineering considerations.

Intermediate vision, since it produces *compact* values from retinotopic images, must compute *non-local* properties of images: that is, it must perform computations which depend on large parts of the image. Furthermore, while it is logically possible that intermediate vision would also be uniform (so that all parts of the image would contribute equally to all intermediate computations), it seems clear that much of vision requires analyzing specific subparts of the image which correspond to distinct objects in the world. Thus it's also the job of intermediate vision to extract *spatially-specific* information from chosen parts of the image. This means that there must be operators which are capable of *finding* interesting subsets of the image (discussed in sections 6.1 and 6.2), and others which are capable of *manipulating* them (discussed in the rest of the chapter).

As I mentioned in section 3.3.3, Sonja's vision model is based largely on Ullman's visual routines theory. Ullman's proposal, however, is sketchy in many respects. Although other researchers have worked in the visual routines framework (for instance Mahoney [169] and Romanycia [231]), no one has produced an implementation that uses visual routines in a natural task domain. Thus I have had to extend the proposal and fill in many details. I've specified in greater detail the interfaces to the operators Ullman suggests, I've extended the set of operators, I've specified much more concretely the interface between the VRP and the central system, and I've worked out ways to compose operators into routines, which he addressed only briefly.

Section 6.1 describes visual attention, the ability to access subsets of the early retinotopic representations. Neurophysiological and psychophysical evidence suggest that visual attention is implemented with a mechanism that routes information from dynamically selected locations to the central system; this device is a key locus of the reduction of retinotopic representations to compact encodings. Sonja incorporates such a device.

Section 6.2 describes visual search, the ability to find locations in an image that have specified properties. Visual search has been shown psychophysically to depend on visual attention; in many cases it proceeds by serially enumerating and testing locations. Sonja is the first implemented system that models the psychophysically demonstrated properties of human visual search.

Section 6.3 describes intermediate objects, which are the state variables maintained by visual operators and used in communication between the central system and the visual routines processor. There are four sorts of intermediate objects, called markers, lines, rays, and activation planes.

Section 6.4 describes criteria for choosing visual operators. I describe local criteria on individual operators and global criteria on a set of operators. (Section 9.5.4 evaluates the set of visual operators I chose according to these criteria.)

Section 6.5 describes the specific visual operators used in Sonja. Figure 6.8 in that section gives a complete table of them with pointers to the subsections of 6.5 in which they are described.

Section 6.6 describes various human visual systems, other than the VRP, that are not modeled in Sonja. Modeling them might eliminate some weaknesses in Sonja. The systems I describe are shape matching, foveation, and spatial memory.

Section 6.7 describes Sonja's non-visual peripheral systems, particularly the motor systems.

For a minimal reading, you will want to read the first parts of sections 6.1 and 6.2 on visual attention and search, skipping the end bits where they get technical, and only the introduction of section 6.3 on intermediate objects. You'll want to look at figure 6.8 and flip through section 6.5 on the specific visual operators, because they are made extensive use of in chapter 8. The rest of this chapter is dispensable.

6.1 Visual attention

Visual attention is the ability to differentially apply visual processing to a subset of a scene. It is taken as consisting of two components: *overt* visual attention, or gaze direction, which can be studied with an eye tracker; and *covert* visual attention, which is neurally mediated and can only be studied indirectly. Following standard usage, I will use "visual attention" to mean covert visual attention when this will not result in confusion.

Visual attention is a central intermediate visual process, and one that is important in Sonja's operation. There are large psychophysical and neuroscientific literatures on the subject; I will review some of this literature in this section. While the data are uncertain and sometimes contradictory, there is broad agreement about some general facts.

The primary evidence for covert visual attention comes from psychophysical studies, for instance those of Posner *et al.* [218]. In a typical experiment, subjects are required to react to the onset of an event such as a light coming on somewhere in the visual field. The results of such experiments are that

- Reaction times are lower when the subjects are told where in the field the event will occur, suggesting that visual resources can more effectively be brought to the detection task when the location of the event is known.
- Covert visual attention is independent of (overt) gaze direction: it operates even when the subjects do not foveate the indicated location [195, 218], and brain lesions that eliminate voluntary eye movements do not affect covert attention [219].[1]
- Visual attention is at least partly cognitively penetrable and under voluntary control; the event location can be indicated by non-natural cues [218].
- The bulk of the evidence suggests that attention can be directed only to a single contiguous subset of the image [70, 218].[2]

---

[1]There may be weak interactions between covert and overt attention. Kröse, for instance, presents evidence that the detectability of a "T" in a background of "L"s is a function of retinal eccentricity [157]. Other researchers (such as Nakayama and Mackeben [195, p. 1639]) have failed to find such effects.

[2]Earlier studies by Shaw and Shaw [249, 250] suggesting that attention can be

- The diameter of the attended subset can be varied voluntarily [70, 136, 275, 277]. The possible shapes it can assume and the distinctness of its margin are uncertain [275].[3]

These observations are summarized as the *spotlight* model of attention, in which attention "illuminates" a chosen subset of the image. The nature of these subsets is unclear, so I will refer to them neutrally as "locations"; I'll have more to say about them in section 6.2.5.

Koch and Ullman [152] have proposed an *addressing pyramid* as the hardware supporting the attentional spotlight. (This proposal was inspired by neuroanatomical speculations of Crick [47]; similar proposals have been made by Anderson and Van Essen [13], Treisman and Gormican [278], Tsotsos [281], and others.) The addressing pyramid is similar in function to the addressing hardware of a conventional serial computer: it routes information from a selected part of a peripheral array to a central location. In the case of a conventional computer, this information is the contents of a memory location; in the case of the attentional hardware, it is the contents of the early representations in the attended location in the retinotopic array. The pyramid gets its name from its two-dimensional hierarchical tree organization. It consists of a series of exponentially smaller stacked layers that route information upwards to a central node (figure 6.1). Each level is composed of an array of nodes, each of which selects one of the nodes beneath it to route to its superior. Thus the system as a whole acts as a recursive *winner-take-all network* [80], eventually routing the contents of just one leaf node up to the root. These leaf nodes actually each contain the values of the early representations at one retinotopic location. I will describe how pyramid nodes choose among their subnodes in section 6.2.

A spotlight of variable diameter can be implemented by having some of the nodes send up a combination of the values of their inferiors, rather than choosing a single one. This has been suggested by Treisman and Gormican [278], who propose that interior nodes in the pyramid can, selectively, pass up the average of the early values of their inferiors,

---

split over arbitrary subsets of the image have not been confirmed by more recent work; but see Driver and Baylis [62].

[3]Eriksen and St. James [70] present evidence for an indistinct margin, with processing efficiency decreasing gradually from the center. Farah's results [73] suggest that attention can be directed to oddly-shaped regions, but this may instead be the result of an unrelated activation operation (see section 6.5.5).

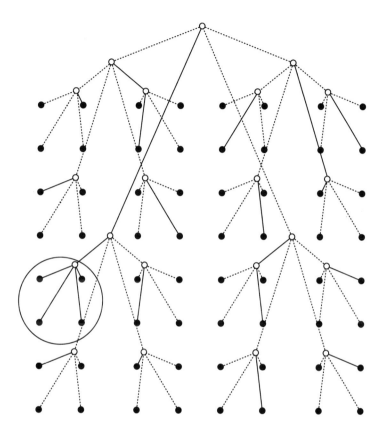

Figure 6.1
The addressing pyramid. Leaf nodes (solid circles) contain buses compactly
encoding early properties. Interior nodes (open circles) pass information from their
inferiors up to their superior. Selected communication paths are drawn as solid
lines, deselected paths as dashed ones. Here the encircled region (containing four
leaf nodes) is addressed. The interior node immediately above this region passes up
the average of the four leaf values, rather than selecting one. The other interior
nodes select just one of their inferiors to pass up early properties from.

rather than passing up the exact value of a single chosen inferior.

This addressing pyramid, then, is a key locus of the "collapse" of retinotopic representations into compact encodings that is criterial of intermediate vision. In effect it implements pointers into the image. In section 3.1.2 I argued against the use of pointers; the resolution involves three factors. Pointers into the image are not *general* pointers, from anywhere to anywhere, but range only over early representations. Moreover, they can only be accessed through a single root node, so the hardware cost is only linear, not quadratic, in the size of the retinotopic representations. Finally, addressing the visual image is probably so evolutionarily important that it would be worth devoting a substantial chunk of brain mass to the task. (An intriguing possibility is that this addressing machinery is reused for other purposes for which pointers would otherwise be necessary. Visual imagery might work by allowing the central system to "paint" on retinotopic representations using the addressing pyramid. Much of human thinking (of the sort often modeled with pointer computations in AI) might proceed by painting and accessing images through the addressing pyramid.)

Koch and Ullman propose implementing the pyramid in terms of a circuit of neuron-like elements; Sonja follows this proposal closely. I will describe the implementation further in section 6.2.

6.2   Visual search

Many of Sonja's visual operators are devoted to finding parts of the image which have specified properties. These operators are inspired by psychophysical research on *visual search*. (For surveys, see Julesz [136] and Treisman and Gelade [276].) In most psychophysical experiments, the sorts of properties searched for are very simple: "is red," for example, rather than "is a chair of some sort." Restricting attention to such simple properties has made it possible to isolate the mechanisms that probably underlie more complicated sorts of search. Fortunately, in Amazon, these simple properties are sufficient to locate the objects that are relevant to any task. Thus it was possible to implement the psychophysically demonstrated mechanisms without much speculative extention.

In Sonja visual search is a means to an end, as well as an object of study in itself. Psychophysicists have principally studied visual search in isolation and under artificial conditions. This has begged questions about the interface between these mechanisms and other visual and non-visual processes. For example, questions about the interaction between visual search and segmentation that must be answered to fully specify an implementation have gone unasked. (I'll take this point up in section 6.2.5.) More seriously, the role of visual search in broader activity has not been addressed. Sonja integrates the visual search mechanisms discovered psychophysically with other visual processes, and, further, integrates visual processes with action to achieve concrete ends.

This section first explains the psychophysical properties of visual search and the brain architecture they suggest, then explains Sonja's implementation of that architecture and compares it with related computational implementations.

6.2.1   Psychophysics of visual search

The central result of the visual search literature, due to Treisman and her colleagues [276, 278], concerns the distinction between *parallel* and *serial self-terminating* search. The experimental paradigm motivating this distinction examines the time required to determine whether or not an object with specified properties exists somewhere in an artificial scene. The results depend on the nature of the property and also on what objects are found in the scene (figure 6.2). Tasks varying on these dimensions segregate strongly into two classes. In the first class, the

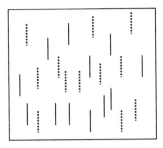 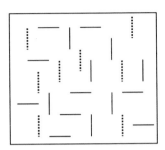

Figure 6.2
Psychophysical displays requiring, respectively, parallel and serial search.
Determining whether or not there is a horizontal line or whether or not there is a
dashed line in a display such as the first one takes time independent of the number
of objects. Determining whether there is a horizontal dashed line among vertical
dashed and horizontal solid lines (as in the second display) requires serial search
and takes time linear in the number of objects.

time required is independent of what is in the scene. In the second
class, time is a linear function of the number of "distractor" objects in
the scene, and on average is twice as long in cases in which the object to
be found is not present than when it is present. Treisman interprets the
first class as indicating that certain properties are computed in parallel
and in constant time over the entire visual field. In cases in which
the desired property is one of those computed this way, determining
whether or not any object with the property is present can be computed
in constant time as a global OR over the resulting retinotopic map. The
object, if present, is said to "pop out" of the display, and such properties
are called *pop out* properties. Treisman interprets the second class as
indicating that, in cases where properties are not computed in parallel,
visual attention must be applied sequentially to each location in the field
to determine whether or not it has the desired property. In these cases if
a single object of the desired type *is* present, on average half the objects
in the field will be examined before it is found; if one is *not* present,
every object in the field must be examined. This "serial self-terminating
search" accounts neatly for the reaction time data.

Given this paradigm, we can ask what features pop out. Treisman and
Gormican [278] report that colors, grey level, line curvature, line orientation, line length, line ends, directions of motion, stereoscopic depth

differences, and the proximity and numerosity of clusters of lines are pop out properties. These results are particularly interesting because there is convergent neurophysiological evidence for early retinotopic representations of many of these properties [172, 174]. On the other hand, intersection, line juncture, angle, connectedness, containment, and aspect ratio are not pop out properties. Neither are conjunctions of pop out properties.

Treisman's results have been replicated by many other researchers. Recently, some conflicting data and alternative explanations have been put forth [194, 279, 298]. I have adopted Treisman's model as it is the most generally accepted; new empirical results may force modifications. [4]

6.2.2 An architecture for visual search

These psychophysical results suggest an architecture like that of figure 6.3. Early modalities compute retinotopic maps bottom up. [5] Let us say that an early property consists of a *dimension* (which is a particular early modality) and a *value* on that dimension. Thus color is a dimension and red is a value. Each retinotopic map is retinotopically connected to an *activation map*. An activation map acts as a value filter; it has binary elements which are "on" at points where corresponding elements in the early map have the desired value. [6] A network extending globally over the activation map distributes the desired value to all the activation elements. (An alternative implementation would use a separate activation map for each early value. This would correspond to *value unit encoding*, which seems to be the rule for cortical neurons [19].) Another global network computes the global OR (figure 6.4). [7]

This much machinery is sufficient for tasks that require deciding whether or not there is a location in a scene which has a particular early

---

[4]For example, the results of Wolfe *et al.* [298] suggest that the activation maps described in the next section should be continuously graded, rather than binary.

[5]This is an abstraction from neuroscientific results, which show that retinotopic maps are actually computed in a cascade of stages [174]. The work of Moran and Desimone [188] suggests further that these stages are probably interwoven with the attentional pyramid: they found increasing effects of visual attention on the receptive fields of neurons in successively later areas of the visual cortex.

[6]Activation maps are not part of Treisman's original model, but seem necessary to avoid searching blank areas. Similar mechanisms have been proposed previously [152, 298].

[7]Alternatively, as Treisman and Gormican [278] have suggested, the global OR could be computed using the addressing pyramid by adjusting the diameter of the attended area to span the entire visual field.

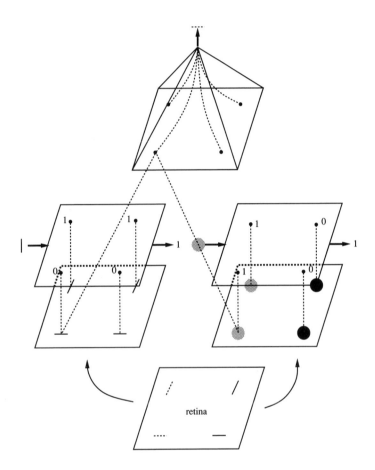

Figure 6.3
An architecture for visual search. In this example the retina is presented with lines
varying in orientation (horizontal, vertical) and color (symbolized by solid and
dashed). Two early maps compute these properties. Activation maps compute
whether a desired value (vertical or dashed, input from the left) is present in the
corresponding early maps at each point. A global OR (output on the right)
supports parallel search. The addressing pyramid supports serial search, routing to
the root (and thereby combining) all the early properties corresponding to a
particular addressed location (the lower left in this case). I have omitted most lines
connecting to pyramid leaf nodes to reduce visual clutter.

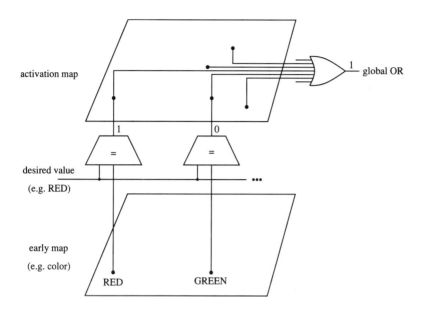

Figure 6.4
Structure of the activation maps. At each point the early value is compared with
the desired value to give a boolean activation value. A global OR of activation
values is computed over the entire map.

property, and therefore accounts for parallel visual search. What about combinations of early properties? A straightforward solution would be to provide activation maps for all possible combinations. There's a good engineering reason not to do this: there are too many combinations. Assuming that there are a dozen early maps, there would be $2^{12} = 4096$ combination maps. (Value unit encoding of the individual activation maps would increase the exponent substantially.) Since retinotopic maps each take up a significant chunk of cortex [174], this is infeasible. An alternative to this proliferation of maps is serial application of visual attention, as proposed by Treisman and others.

Serial visual search requires enumerating candidates and testing to see if they have the desired property. Various enumeration schemes are possible; I will propose a simple one which matches psychophysical results. To enumerate candidates, you pick one of the early dimensions involved in the compound desired property and enumerate all the locations that have the desired value on that dimension. For instance, if you are looking for a vertical blue edge, you can enumerate all the vertical locations and check if they are blue or enumerate all the blue locations and check if they are vertical. Enumeration involves repeated application of two primitives, *content addressing* and *return inhibition*, which affect the way nodes in the addressing pyramid select among their subnodes. In the remainder of this section I will describe content addressing, candidate testing, and return inhibition, and show how they can be combined into an algorithm for visual search.

In content addressing, the central system specifies an early dimension and value, and the addressing pyramid routes the early properties of an arbitrary location with that value on that dimension to the root. This is accomplished via the activation maps: the central system supplies the desired value to the relevant activation map and specifies that activation map as the relevant one for content addressing. Pyramid leaf nodes *disqualify* themselves from the selection process if the corresponding activation map value is zero. Disqualification propagates upwards; an internal node is disqualified if all its subnodes are disqualified. This system guarantees that the early values routed to the root node correspond to a location in the image whose activation value is one, and thus which has the desired early value on the specified early dimension. If there is no activated element in the specified activation map, the root node itself is disqualified; this corresponds to search failure.

For purposes of visual search, the root of the addressing pyramid is connected to circuits which determine whether the early properties presented there are the desired ones. In the worst case, this would entail circuits to compute the few thousand possible combinations of features. These circuits, operating on compact encodings rather than retinotopic representations, would easily fit into a small chunk of the brain. Having just one copy of these circuits, rather than a copy at each retinotopic location, is a tremendous hardware savings. We'll see in chapter 8 that Sonja actually only computes those combinations of features that are useful for its purposes; it does this in the registrars of the central system.

Suppose the currently attended-to location does not have the desired properties; we must reject it and find another. *Return inhibition*, when applied, prevents the currently addressed location from being considered a candidate in future content addressing. This allows candidates to be enumerated uniquely. Return inhibition requires that each leaf node in the pyramid keep a state bit which says whether or not it has been inhibited; inhibited nodes disqualify themselves. Klein [151] and Posner *et al.* [219] present psychophysical evidence for the reality of return inhibition.

In summary, an algorithm for serial self-terminating search in the proposed architecture goes as follows.[8]

1. Pick one of the conjoined early properties. Set the activation map for this property's dimension to filter for this value.
2. Use content addressing to find an activated location in the image. If there is none, return, signalling failure. Otherwise, the addressing pyramid will map the early properties of the found location to the root.
3. Check whether the addressed location has the desired combination of early features. If so, return, signalling success.
4. Otherwise, inhibit return to the currently addressed location. This means that future content addressings will find different locations. Go to step 2.

Sonja makes extensive use of this algorithm.

Treisman and Gelade [276] report that human subjects require about 60 milliseconds per iteration of the address, test, inhibit cycle. This

---

[8]Tsotsos presents a similar algorithm [281]. His is more complicated because it involves shape matching. I'll discuss shape matching further in section 6.6.

corresponds to examining seventeen locations per second. Sonja's cycle time varies because it was implemented on a serial machine, but on average it examines about as many locations per second.

6.2.3   Extensions

This section presents two extensions to the basic visual search paradigm which proved useful in Sonja but which are only weakly supported by psychophysical evidence. The first extension allows control of the order in which locations are enumerated; the second allows attention to be directed to locations based on their positions in the image, rather than on their early properties.

Controlling enumeration order   In many cases it is useful to control the order in which visual search enumerates locations. For example, domain knowledge often can tell you roughly where the sought location is likely to be.

Koch and Ullman [152], based on the psychophysical studies of Engel [68, 69], proposed a *proximity preference* mechanism for their model of the attentional pyramid. Proximity preference makes the location selected by the next content addressing as close as possible to the currently selected location.

Sonja provides a related form of proximity preference. It allows the central system to choose an arbitrary point of interest and causes content addressing to proceed in increasing order of distance from this point. This mechanism could be implemented using a damped spreading activation starting from the chosen point and enhancing winner-take-all units in proportion to the proximity to that point. The implementation actually uses explicit distance-comparison circuits. The chosen point is specified using a visual marker mechanism, explained in section 6.3. Sonja also includes a mechanism that constrains visual search to a specified region of the image or to locations lying along a specified line. In the latter case, locations may be enumerated in order along the line.

These enumeration order extensions to visual search are based solely on efficiency considerations. The only relevant psychophysical evidence I know of is due to Kröse and Julesz [158], who show that proximity preference does not *always* apply; this does not rule out its selective application under central control. It would be easy to do experiments to discover whether the human visual system has similar mechanisms. If not, people must do exhaustive searches in situations in which Sonja does not; this would result in somewhat different attentional performance.

Pointer addressing   In addition to content addressing, Sonja's visual system supports *pointer addressing*. In pointer mode, the central system can direct the pyramid to address an arbitrary (x, y) retinotopic location. This requires passing addresses *downward* through the pyramid and inhibiting the nodes that are not addressed. The pyramid can also pass addresses *upward*, providing the central system with the image coordinates of a location addressed by content.

There is little psychophysical evidence bearing directly on the question of whether the human visual attention apparatus supports pointer addressing; the question has not been asked explicitly before. The most relevant studies ask whether or not people can direct attention to points defined indirectly, for example as "two inches to the left of the big X". Some experiments have been done along these lines, but the results are inconclusive. Kröse and Julesz [158] present evidence that argues against such addressing; Posner *et al.* [218] and Nakayama and Mackeben [195, experiment 2] present evidence that argues for it. Pylyshyn [223] argues against it on *a priori* grounds.

Whether or not an attentional mechanism supports pointers affects possible implementation strategies for other sorts of visual machinery. For example, consider the problem of determining whether one location in an image is to the left of another. An architecture that supports pointers can subtract x coordinates to answer this question; an architecture without pointers must do something more complicated.

6.2.4   Related computational work

So far as I know, Sonja is the first implemented system to model the phenomena described in the psychophysical visual search literature I have discussed.

Several other researchers have presented implementations of visual attention. These implementations vary in their motivations, in the faithfulness with which they model psychophysical results, and in various engineering parameters. Among the last are the type of routing network used (retinotopic, hierarchical, or all-points), selective enhancement of signals from attended locations versus selective inhibition of signals from non-attended locations, and whether or not regions of variable diameter can be addressed.

Feldman and Ballard [80] provided the first suggestion I have found for a computational implementation of covert attention. They intended both to model Treisman and Gelade's [276] psychophysical studies and to solve the connectionist crosstalk problem. They suggested using a winner-take-all network; their discussion is abstract and apparently the suggestion was not implemented. Koch and Ullman [152] similarly did not implement their proposed pyramid.

The earliest implementation I have found is due to Fukushima [91]. He used a hierarchical winner-take-all network of connectionist units. His implementation seems to have been motivated principally by engineering concerns; it does not try to model psychophysical results accurately. For example, the attended subset of the image does not need to be contiguous.

Strong and Whitehead [262] present an implemented model of *overt* visual attention inspired by Feldman and Ballard's work and similarly intended to solve the crosstalk problem.

Mozer's [191, 192] implementation of covert attention models psychophysical results better than Fukushima's; it can attend only to a single contiguous region. His winner-take-all network is not implemented hierarchically (as a pyramid) but rather retinotopically. Koch and Ullman argue that a hierarchical organization results in faster convergence of the winner-take-all computation than would a locally connected network such as Mozer's. Mozer implemented addressing of continuously variable diameter regions; Sonja doesn't. Mozer's network operates by selective enhancement of signals from the attended region, rather than by selective inhibition of signals elsewhere (as does Fukushima's implementation and Sonja). Neurophysiological results suggest that the primate attentional system operates by selective inhibition.[9]

Ahmad and Omohundro [8] describe an implementation with a contiguous, variable diameter spotlight and boolean inhibition. This implementation is able to gate signals from the attended location to a central node in constant time by connecting the central unit to every unit in

---

[9]Moran and Desimone [188] found that neurons in area V4 of the visual cortex whose receptive fields (RFs) include the attended location respond strongly to stimuli at this location and weakly elsewhere in the RF, but neurons whose RFs did not include the attended location responded strongly to stimuli anywhere in the RF. Tsotsos [281] argues that selective inhibition should make the winner-take-all network converge more quickly.

a retinotopic array. This seems biologically implausible; Sonja uses a $log(n)$ depth fan-in tree instead.

6.2.5 Open questions

Many empirical and engineering questions concerning this architecture, beyond those posed earlier in this paper, remain open.

Current psychophysical evidence does not answer many questions concerning return inhibition. For example, is it applied automatically and uniformly, or selectively under central control? I implemented the latter. How are locations uninhibited? My implementation provides a global inhibition reset line which uninhibits all locations, providing a clean slate for a new search. Perhaps individual locations can be uninhibited, or perhaps inhibition just decays over time. Is there a limit on how many locations can be inhibited? What is the spatial resolution for inhibition? It can not be the case that enormous numbers of locations can be inhibited with great precision, or it would be easy to count patterns of many dots in arbitrary order.

Just what *are* the "locations" which the attentional spotlight looks at, content addressing finds, and return inhibition applies to? A simple hypothesis is that locations are the regions of the image found by a general-purpose preattentive segmentation process that partitions the image into relatively homogeneous regions. There is much psychophysical evidence that at least a first-pass segmentation is performed bottom-up [255, 275]. Psychophysical studies on attention have usually controlled out segmentation by using as stimuli displays of small geometrical figures neatly separated by a featureless white background, so little is known about interactions between attention and segmentation. More study of this interaction would be valuable; recent studies by Driver and Baylis [62] and by Farah *et al.* [74] support the hypothesis that attended locations are preattentively segmented regions.

6.3 Intermediate objects

Visual operators can maintain internal state, used to keep track of intermediate results during visual routines. We have seen one example already: the activated region that is computed in the first step of the containment routine (figure 3.3). Lacking empirical constraint on the nature of these intermediate representations, I have adopted Ullman's proposals, which were based on computational intuition, and extended them based on my own computational intuition.[10] These proposals might be tested psychophysically.

Sonja's visual operators manipulate four types of *intermediate objects*: *markers, lines, rays*, and *activation planes*. These representations are shared across operators, rather than being private to particular ones. Visual markers designate locations in the image. Lines (actually directed line segments) run between two points; rays extend from a point to infinity. Activation planes represent regions in the image. In figure 6.5, some markers, lines, rays, and activation planes are displayed graphically on top of a running Amazon game. The reverse-video polygons represent markers, the drawn lines represent line and ray intermediate objects, and the shaded regions represent activation planes. (These graphical representations should not be confused with the intermediate objects themselves; they are for debugging purposes only and can be turned on and off.)

The interface between the central system and the VRP is in part in terms of the intermediate objects. The central system can name intermediate objects; that is, it can pass values on buses which say which marker, line, ray, or activation plane to use in an operation. Some typical visual operators determine whether the distance between one pair of markers is greater or less than the distance between another pair; determine whether two markers are coincident; determine whether the angle between three markers, given in order, is clockwise or counterclockwise; draw a line between two markers; move one marker to where another one is; move a marker a specified distance in a given direction; cause a marker to track a moving object; determine whether a marker is within an activated region or a line intersects one; move a marker to the centroid of an activated region; determine whether a region is convex; and many other similar operations. These operators are all described in section 6.5.

The remainder of this section describes in turn markers, lines and rays, and activation planes.

---

[10]The only previous implementation of visual routines, due to Romanycia [231], used only retinotopic representations.

Figure 6.5
Intermediate objects displayed graphically. There is a right-pointing triangle marker on the amazon, a hexagonal marker on the amulet, a square marker inside the obstacle, and a diamond marker on the obstacle. A line connects two of the markers and a ray extends up and left from one of them. One activation plane covers the obstacle; another plane is a subset of the first (covering roughly the top half).

Figure 6.6
To determine whether there are four colinear points, you have to keep track of
points to apply the colinearity test to.

Markers

Many visual operations involve storing locations. For example, if you
want to know if there are four colinear points in an image, you have
to keep track of points to apply the colinearity test to (figure 6.6). Visual markers are a simple mechanism for keeping track of locations;
section 6.6 describes some others. The simplest implementation of location stores would be registers holding image coordinates. Since stored
locations are typically found using visual search, this implementation requires that the addressing pyramid be able to pass addresses in at least
the upward direction. In Sonja visual markers are additionally used to
store the early properties of the locations they mark. (These stored
properties are, of course, updated only when attention is directed to the
marker.)

Lines and rays

Lines and rays in Sonja may not correspond to any "things" in the
human visual system. They were an easy interface for a number of
operators which seem plausible, but which may well have some other
interface. Their principal use is to specify spatial limits for a search:
Sonja has operators that find things lying along a straight line or a ray.
Whether such limits can actually be put on visual search is unknown but
could readily be determined experimentally. One way to implement such
searches would be to "draw" the line or ray on a retinotopic map that is
ANDed into a search activation map. Then only locations lying on the

line would be candidates for content addressing. Another implementation would scan attention serially along a line. These implementations might be distinguished psychophysically by reaction time data.

Activation planes

Activation planes are used to keep track of interesting regions of the image, as in Ullman's routine for computing containment. They can be naturally implemented as retinotopic bit arrays, one bit array per plane; bits are turned on at points that are within the region of interest. This representation actually makes all the proposed activation operators easy to implement efficiently on massively parallel hardware. Lacking a ready massively parallel machine, I implemented activation planes in Sonja using edge lists and serial algorithms from computational geometry.

Psychophysical evidence could support or disconfirm the existence of activation plane hardware. I know of only one relevant study, due to Farah [73], who found that imaging a complex bounded form increased the detectability of events within the bounded region. This effect was found to be similar to attending to a colored form of the same shape. An activation plane would be a natural mechanism underlying this effect. Kosslyn has suggested an experiment (described by Ullman [283] but apparently never performed) that would give a more direct test. In it facilitation of later inside/outside judgements by a first judgement would suggest the existence of a representation of the extent of the bounded region.

How many activation planes are there? I know of no psychophysical studies of this question. The following informal observation may serve as the basis for an experiment. When staring at floors tiled with a regular pattern of identical tiles, I find that I can cause specific subsets to jump out: a hollow or filled square or hexagon (depending on the tiling pattern) or, more interestingly, disconnected sets like alternate tiles (resulting in a checkerboard appearance). This phenomenon is quite striking in that I can make quite elaborate patterns appear globally over a space of hundreds of tiles. The jumping-out tiles almost literally appear darker or colored. If this is the phenomenological correlate of activation, it suggests that there is only one activation plane available for this purpose, because despite much effort, I am completely unable to form even simple patterns that divide the surface into three sets rather than two. Simple psychophysical experiments might decide this question. In any case, Sonja uses three activation planes, but could probably get by with timesharing a single one.

6.4   Criteria on visual operators

There are two sorts of criteria that bear on choosing perceptual operators: local criteria on individual operators and global criteria on the set of them.

The local criteria I used were that an operator be plausibly implementable in essential connectionist hardware, general purpose, neurophysiologically and psychophysically plausible, and clean from an engineering standpoint.

• Each operator ought to be implementable in neurally plausible hardware (as specified in section 3.1). Ideally Sonja would implement each operator as an essential connectionist units. However, even the most powerful parallel computers available today would not have been up to the job of simulating the number of units required, and so I implemented most operators with conventional serial algorithms. However, I will sketch massively parallel, pointer-free implementations for each visual operator, thereby arguing that the constraints of biological plausibility do not rule them out *a priori*.

• The operators should be general purpose in two senses: they should not depend on the specific domain, and they should be useful for very different sorts of tasks. It's impossible to be sure without doing cross-domain and cross-task studies, but my intuition is that all Sonja's operators satisfy this criterion.

• Each operator's membership in the set ought to be supported by neurophysiological and psychophysical evidence. This is not true in Sonja. Most of the relevant experiments have not been done. Many of the operators in Sonja suggest tests for comparable human performance.

• Finally, I used straightforward engineering considerations to choose many of the operators. I used programmer's intuition to judge whether the postulated operators involved seemed clean. I admitted only a few kludgy operators, in cases in which "doing the right thing" seemed like it would be a lot of work and not particularly edifying. I am reasonably sure that none of these operators does anything that could not be done cleanly.

My global criteria on the set of operators were that the set span the space of visual analysis tasks, that it make programming visual routines easy, and that it make learning visual routines easy. I was less successful in satisfying these criteria; I will postpone analyzing the set according to these criteria until section 9.5.4.

- We want a "spanning" set: that is, a set of operators that together are sufficient for any task. Here "any task" may mean "any psychologically plausible task" or, for engineers, "any task in the class of domains of interest." Thus the set of visual operators, when combined into routines, are to form a finite means for the realization of an infinite collection of possible visual processes.
- A set of operators should not only make it possible to implement any visual task, it ought to make it *easy*. From an engineering standpoint, the VRP should present a nice programming system.
- A set of operators should also make it easy to *learn* new visual routines.

6.5   The specific operators

This section describes the specific visual operators Sonja uses. This set substantially extends the set proposed by Ullman [283]. I've implemented many other operators, some interesting in their own right, that didn't get used in the final version of the system; I omit discussion of them for brevity.

Visual operators are to be thought of as bits of hardware each dedicated to performing a specific visual operation. Primitive operations and operators correspond one-to-one: although it is logically possible that individual pieces of visual hardware could compute several distinct operations, the proposed primitive operations are sufficiently dissimilar that it seems more likely that functions are allocated statically. Because visual operators support intermediate vision, their purpose is to give compact answers to compact questions about non-compact representations such as image regions and activation planes.

In the most general case, illustrated in figure 6.7, a visual operator takes its input in the form of one or more of the retinotopic maps and in

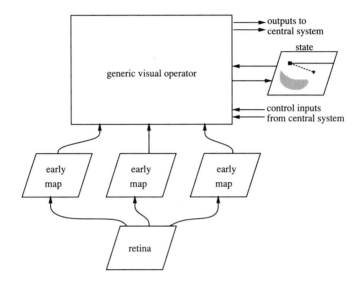

Figure 6.7
A generic visual operator. The visual operator, on the basis of control inputs from
the central system, produces compact outputs from the retinotopic maps. It may
maintain some state, which can be shared with other visual operators.

addition one or more control signals from the central system; maintains state, which typically is shared with other operators; and produces as output to the central system one or more compact encodings. Operators can be degenerate in all the corresponding possible ways: an operator may not depend on retinotopic maps, or may not take control inputs from the central system (in which case it operates *bottom-up*), or may not depend on state, or may not side-effect the state it does use, or may not produce any values for the central system, but rather operate by side-effect only.

The subsections of this section correspond to a somewhat arbitrary categorization of operators into six groups. The first group is concerned with visual attention and search; the corresponding subsection, 6.5.1, fills in some details left vague in sections 6.1 and 6.2. Subsection 6.5.2 describes an operator for tracking moving objects. 6.5.3 describes operators concerned with geometry: distances, directions, and angles. Subsection 6.5.4 describes operators for direct manipulation of intermediate objects and 6.5.5 describes operators involving activation planes; together these can be used to determine topological properties such as containment and connectedness. Subsection 6.5.6 describes operators for finding edges and gaps in them. Subsection 6.5.7, finally, describes a housekeeping operation called "blanking." Figure 6.8 presents a table of Sonja's visual operators and the subsections that document them.

By convention, the names of operators that change the state of intermediate objects end in an exclamation mark (`content-address!`), and those that implement boolean tests end in a question mark (`distance-within?`). Operators with side-effects have an enabling boolean `doit?` control input; the operator is a no-op unless this input is high.

Sonja's VRP includes multiple copies of some visual operators. The reasons for this are explained in section 7.2.7. Since a visual operator is a fixed piece of hardware, only as many operations of a given type can be performed simultaneously as there are chunks of hardware (operators) that implement that operation.

6.5.1   Visual attention and search

I have explained the implementation of visual search in section 6.2; this section explains the details of the interface between it and the central system. This interface is in terms of visual operators which encapsulate the addressing pyramid, thereby integrating it into the architecture of

Class of operators	Operator name	Subsection
Visual search	`content-address!`	6.5.1
	`content-address-activated!`	
	`scan-along-line!`	
	`scan-along-ray!`	
	`inhibit-return!`	
	`uninhibit-return!`	
Tracking	`track!`	6.5.2
	marker-`disappeared?`	
Geometry	`greater-distance?`	6.5.3
	`distance-within?`	
	`marker-to-activated-region-distance-within?`	
	`markers-coincident?`	
	`marker-to-marker-direction`	
	`aligned?`	
	`angle-ccw?`	
	`marker-line-angle-ccw?`	
	`marker-ray-angle-ccw?`	
	`random-direction`	
	`touching?`	
	`corner-free?`	
Direct manipulation	`warp-marker!`	6.5.4
	`walk-marker!`	
	`draw-line!`	
	`draw-ray!`	
Activation	`activate-connected-region-of-type!`	6.5.5
	`activate-connected-region-not-type!`	
	`activate-connected-region-not-type-from-gap!`	
	intermediate-object-`activated?`	
	`activation-touches-edge?`	
	`mark-centroid!`	
	`convex?`	
	`expand-to-convex-hull!`	
	`transect-activated-region!`	
Edges and gaps	`find-edges!`	6.5.6
	`enumerate-gaps!`	
	`gap-orientation`	
Blanking	*intermediate-object*-`blanked?`	6.5.7
	`blank-`*intermediate-object*`!`	

Figure 6.8
Sonja's visual operators and the sections that document them.

figure 3.5.

Attention supplies early properties to the central system. I gave the VRP as plausible an interface with the central system as I could, but made no attempt to make the connection between early and intermediate vision realistic. Sonja does no pixel-wise early processing. Instead, the visual operators have direct access to the data structures representing video game objects that Amazon maintains for its own purposes. I will talk about the implications of bypassing early vision in section 9.5.1.

Thus, to implement content addressing, I needed a simulated implementation of early processing. This implementation is in terms of seven early dimensions. I chose these dimensions and the values Amazon objects have on these dimensions somewhat arbitrarily; my main concern was to ensure that some objects would pop out and that others would require slow serial searches. Some of the dimensions are found in human early processing: grey level, speed and direction of motion, line orientation, and perhaps overall size. Orientation is defined principally in terms of the presence or absence of diagonal elements; the horizontal vs. vertical orientation of doors and the orientations of scroll characters are also accessible. Two other simulated dimensions are arbitrary and probably not biologically accurate: I called them "fiddliness," corresponding roughly to the amount of detail in the icon, and "boxiness," corresponding to whether or not the icon is roughly rectangular. Figure 6.9 presents a table of all the icon types in Amazon and the early properties Sonja's visual system assigns them. Early properties are *not* computed at run time, but are fixed properties of icons. The implementation does not model the internal structure of the icons; they are treated as homogeneous blobs.

The operator `content-address!` implements content addressing. It takes as inputs an enabling `doit?` signal and an early (dimension, value) pair to find. Because one typically wants to keep track of the addressed location, the operator takes a marker as an additional input; the marker is moved to the center of the addressed location. Optionally `content-address!` can take as input another marker representing the locus of proximity preference (section 6.2.3).

Three operators put spatial limits on content addressing. `content-address-activated!` requires that the found location be within an activated region. `scan-along-line!` and `scan-along-ray!` address the first location with a given early property found along a line or ray.

Object type	boxy?	size	fiddly?	diagonal?	darkness	speed
free space	0	*undefined*	0	0	zero	zero
wall	1	large	1	0	medium	zero
door	0	large	0	0	medium	zero
stair	0	large	1	0	large	zero
bread	1	large	0	0	medium	zero
scroll	1	large	1	1	medium	zero
amulet	0	medium	0	1	medium	zero
potion	0	large	0	1	medium	zero
key	0	medium	1	0	medium	zero
sitting knife	0	small	1	1	medium	zero
flying knife	0	small	1	1	medium	fast
fireball	0	small	0	0	medium	fast
shuriken	0	small	1	1	medium	fast
amazon	0	medium	1	1	medium	slow
demon	0	large	1	1	medium	slow
ghost	0	large	0	1	medium	slow
pile of bones	0	large	1	1	*variable*	zero
hut	1	large	0	1	large	zero

Figure 6.9
The fixed early properties of object types in Sonja. These early properties are not
realistic, but were assigned arbitrarily in order to explore visual search. Some other
properties (e. g. direction of motion) vary according to the situation.

The operators `inhibit-return!` and `uninhibit-return!` perform the operations they are named for and take only the enabling `doit?` signal as input. Sonja takes icons to be the "locations" to which return inhibition applies; see section 6.2.5.

Sonja's visual system can operate in two modes, with and without a detailed simulation of the attentional pyramid. The actual circuit implementation of attentional pyramid is prohibitively slow on a serial machine because it involves tens of thousands of circuit elements even at the 16×16 resolution I implemented. This implementation can be switched out in favor of a fast implementation that accesses Amazon data structures directly.

6.5.2   Tracking

An ability to *track* several moving objects simultaneously is very useful in playing video games. My informal observations of human players suggest to me that people can to track up to four or five moving things simultaneously; Pylyshyn and Storm [223, 224] present psychophysical evidence for about the same numerical limit on tracking. [11]

Sonja tracks moving objects with visual markers. The operator `track!` causes a marker, passed as an input, to track the motion of the thing it marks. As many copies of `track!` are required as things can be tracked simultaneously; Sonja uses three. The VRP also provides `disappeared?` operators which tell whether a tracked thing has been lost. In the implementation, things are lost only when they disappear: when a monster or pile of bones is killed, a goody is picked up, or when something passes off the screen. Presumably more realistic visual systems could not do so well; preattentive tracking would have to use unstable early clues to segment the tracked object from the background. Horswill [129, 130] describes some dynamics that ameliorate the effects of losing track of objects.

In the human visual system, tracking presumably works by segmenting the optical flow field. How this works in detail is unclear (see Thompson and Pong [271] for an explanation of the issues and some computational

---

[11] Pylyshyn argues that this ability contradicts the finding that people can attend to only one location at a time. No such contradiction is necessary, however, if attention is required only to support full access to *all* early properties. Full access is not necessary for tracking, which needs access only to motion computations. The tracking hardware probably has a separate, dedicated addressing scheme for a motion map.

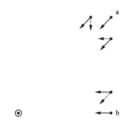

Figure 6.10
Major and minor components of directions to the circled point. The major
component is drawn as a solid arrow and the minor component as a dashed one. In
two cases (*a* and *b*) the two components coincide.

approaches) but there is no doubt that the human visual hardware supports tracking [239].

6.5.3 Distances, directions, and angles

Sonja's VRP provides a series of operators which compute geometrical
relationships between intermediate objects. These operators manipulate distances, directions, and angles. All of these operators are implemented as numerical computations in terms of the pixel coordinates of
intermediate objects. Directions are coded in terms of the eight possible
movement directions in Amazon. Directions passed to the VRP are just
coded as one of the eight. Directions passed back from the VRP are
coded as ordered pairs of values out of the eight, a *major* and *minor*
component representing the nearest and next nearest of the eight directions to the actual direction. (See figure 6.10.) This encoding provides
sufficient resolution for the purposes to which the system is put.

The operator `distance-within?` is a predicate on two markers and
a distance; it tells you whether the distance between the two markers is greater or less than that given. `marker-to-activated-region-
distance-within?` is the analogous predicate on a marker and an acti-
vation plane. `greater-distance?` takes two pairs of markers and tells
whether the distance between the first pair is more or less than the
distance between the second. `markers-coincident?` tells whether the
distance between two markers is zero.

`marker-to-marker-direction` tells the direction from one marker to another. `aligned?` tells whether or not two markers are aligned in one of the eight directions.

Three operators, `angle-ccw?`, `marker-line-angle-ccw?`, `marker-ray-angle-ccw?` determine whether or not an angle is counterclockwise; they respectively take three markers, a marker and a line, and a marker and a ray as arguments.

`random-direction` returns a random direction each tick. Presumably there is more than enough noise in the brain to make such an operator feasible. This operator is used to implement random wandering in Sonja's navigation routines (section 8.7.6).

Two operators determine whether locations (interpreted as Amazon icons) are adjacent to each other. `touching?` takes as arguments a marker and a direction; it tells whether or not the Amazon object under the marker is touching something else on the specified side, or whether there is free space in that direction. `corner-free?` similarly determines whether there is free space adjacent to a given corner of an object. These operators probably ought to be decomposed into routines over more primitive operators that would shift attention to the indicated edge of the icon and check for free space.

6.5.4 Marker, line, and ray manipulation

Two operators provide direct manipulation of marker positions. `warp-marker!` moves one marker to be coincident with another. `walk-marker!` moves a marker a specified distance in a specified direction. These are implemented by side-effects to the coordinate information markers maintain. Similarly, `draw-line!` takes two markers and a line and causes the line to extend from one marker to the other, and `draw-ray!` extends a given ray from a given marker in a given direction.

6.5.5 Activation

The primary use of activation planes is to fill (activate) a bounded region. Ullman [283] suggests that what counts as a boundary may be task-specific (and thus presumably supplied as a parameter by the central system). Lacking evidence about the nature of this information in the human visual system, I had the operator take a disjunction of icon types that are allowed in the activated region. Ullman suggests further that short gaps in surrounding edges may optionally count as boundary segments for the activated region, and Sonja provides an optional gap filling facility.[12]

I implemented three different activation operators; they could be merged without too much difficulty. `activate-connected-region-of-type!` takes a marker which will be inside the final activated region, an activation plane to mark the region with, and type information about what sorts of things should be included in the activated region. `activate-connected-region-not-type!` is the same except that the type information is negated. The two are implemented somewhat differently, because free space is not represented explicitly in the game code, and `activate-connected-region-not-type!` but not `activate-connected-region-of-type!` can activate free space. Finally, `activate-connected-region-not-type-from-gap!` works similarly, except that the marker argument will not be in the activated region, but rather marks a gap in the boundary which should be counted as if boundary elements were there. `activate-connected-region-not-type-from-gap!` takes an extra argument to specify which side of the boundary should be activated, which would otherwise be ambiguous. All three operators take a boolean argument which specifies whether or not the edge of the screen should count as boundary for activation. All three operators return a single boolean value, which tells whether or not activation succeeded. Activation succeeds unless the edge of the screen does *not* count as a boundary and the activated region runs off the screen (corresponding to the "point at infinity" test). (Bypassing early vision made it unclear how to model the edge of the Amazon screen. These and a number of other visual operators treat the edge of the screen in *ad hoc* ways.)

I implemented the activation operations in terms of an inner loop which traces the perimeter of the activated region. This loop turned out to be the hardest two pages of code I've ever written; I'd guess I spent twenty percent of the total implementation time debugging it. Though conceptually simple, the various special cases made it very complex.

Ullman proposes a better way to implement activation, in terms of a locally-connected retinotopic array of processors. Each processor maintains a bit which tells whether or not it is activated and a bit which

---

[12]Psychophysical study of gap filling in edge tracing, postulated as a related operator, is reported by Jolicoeur *et al.* [133]. Ullman [282] suggests that gap filling is a ubiquitous operation in early vision and proposes neural networks for the operation.

tells whether or not it is a boundary point. You turn the `activated?` bit on in the processor corresponding to the marked point from which activation begins, and then you repeatedly propagate activation: each activated processor tells all its neighbors that it is activated; if they are boundary points they do nothing; otherwise, they set themselves activated. Repeat until no new processor is activated. I didn't implement this because I was using a serial machine. Mahoney [169] and Shafrir [248] describe still faster divide-and-conquer activation algorithms.

Three operators, `marker-activated?`, `line-activated?`, and `ray-activated?` determine whether other intermediate objects intersect activated regions. Operations like these could be implemented by connecting corresponding elements in the retinotopic arrays representing the various sorts of intermediate objects. For instance, in section 6.3 I suggested implementing lines by "drawing" them on a retinotopic array of computational elements; `line-activated?` could be implemented by having these elements communicate with corresponding elements in the activation array to determine if they represent a point that is both activated and on the line; computing a global logical OR over the array will yield the desired result. A fourth operator, `activation-touches-edge?`, determines whether an activated region runs up against the edge of the screen.

Sonja's VRP provides several other operators that manipulate activation planes. `mark-centroid!` puts a marker on the centroid of an activated region. Actually my implementation does not compute an accurate centroid, and Sonja's use of the operator doesn't depend on such accuracy. A biologically plausible implementation might use a spreading activation computation [87]. `convex?` tells whether an activated region is convex, and `expand-to-convex-hull!` takes two activation planes and makes one be the convex hull of the other. Computing convex hulls is probably not psychologically realistic, but for the purpose I put it to, a realistic and equally useful operation would be to compute a Gaussian blurring of a region; such blurring operations are have been demonstrated neurophysiologically in human early vision [172].

`transect-activated-region!` takes two activation planes, a line, and a direction. It sets one of the activation planes to be the subset of the other plane that is on the side of the line indicated by the direction. (See figure 6.11.) One way to implement transection would be in terms of the activation propagation algorithm I've already described; it

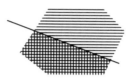

Figure 6.11
Transecting an activated region with a line. The horizontally hatched region is
transected by the line; the vertically hatched region is the subset below the line.
The overlapping of the hatches yields a plaid pattern.

would require setting the `boundary?` bits in elements corresponding to
locations along the line.

6.5.6   Gaps and edges

Open doorways are important features in Amazon. Sonja's VRP provides an operator which finds *gaps*, which are candidate doorways. Gaps
are places where a wall ends, there is some free space, and then there is
another wall. These can be defined in terms of edges found in a coarse
scale space. The human visual system does compute edges at coarse
scales, and as I mentioned earlier line ends terminators are computed
early. My implementation treats gaps as though they were also detected
early, which may not be psychophysically accurate. People certainly can
find gaps with serial search of line ends [278], and Sonja's operation does
not depend on its ability to enumerate gaps in unit time.

`enumerate-gaps!` takes three arguments: a marker to move to the
next gap found, a boolean that says whether to actually move the
marker, and a boolean which says whether to initialize return inhibition
for gaps. The operator `gap-orientation` determines the orientation of
a gap.

Gap finding depends on edge finding. The human visual system computes edges constantly. This was too expensive for Sonja, and not really
necessary. Sonja's visual system finds edges only on command, using
the `find-edges!` operator. This operator is passed an early property
that defines the edge.

6.5.7   Blanking

Blanking is a sort of housekeeping operation. A blanked intermediate object is unused and has no spatial information associated with it. Each intermediate object has an operator which tells whether or not it is blanked. There are also operators which blank objects. There is no explicit way to unblank an object; operators which side-effect objects unblank them when they move them. In implementation, blankedness is just a bit associated with each intermediate object.

6.6   Other visual systems

Several visual systems coexist with the postulated visual routines processor I have described. I haven't modeled these other visual systems in Sonja; adding them might solve some problems I ran into. I'll discuss shape matching, foveation, and spatial memory. (Spatial memory is not a strictly visual phenomenon, but is closely linked with vision.)

Shape matching

Much work in machine vision has concentrated on *shape matching*: given a geometrical model of an object and a part of an image, determine whether a projection of that object could give rise to that image fragment. This problem originally seemed very difficult, but recent progress [64, 65, 101, 102, 127, 128, 167] suggests that it may be quite simple and computationally inexpensive—particularly after a heuristic bottom-up segmentation has been performed.

Shape matching is *not* object recognition. It is in general neither necessary nor sufficient for object recognition. For example, in many video games, objects can be identified by single early properties; shape matching is not necessary if types and colors correspond one-to-one. Similarly, we are able to recognize an unfamiliar object as a chair in spite of its failing to geometrically match any chair we've seen before; shape matching is not sufficient. Matching is useful nevertheless. The members of many classes of objects are rigid and all have the same shape. Shape matching is probably the right way to recognize paperclips, for instance.

Ullman proposed in [283] that visual routines are a preprocessing stage for shape recognition. More recent work suggests that the two are parallel channels each connecting the early maps with the central system. It is tempting, in fact, to identify shape matching and the visual routines processor with the *temporal* and *parietal* visual processing streams described by Ungerleider and Mishkin [174, 284]. In this model, supported by physiological, anatomical, and clinical evidence, two streams of visual transformations diverge early and lead respectively to the temporal and to the parietal cortex; the former is concerned with object recognition and the latter with assessment of spatial relationships. In clinical studies, damage to the parietal cortex affects perception of position and movement and leaves object recognition unimpaired. Temporal lobe lesions, on the other hand, affect "object recognition" but not the discrimination of spatial relationships. It would be interesting to know whether object recognition in this case extends to the sorts of recognition tasks that seem to require visual routines, or whether only shape matching is affected.

Foveation

The human retina has a region of maximal acuity called the *fovea*. Typically people *foveate* objects of greatest interest, moving their eyes so that the corresponding image falls on the fovea. There are five separate systems controlling foveation in human vision (for reviews, see [20, 100]). There has been little research on foveation in the machine vision literature. (Ballard [20, 21] provides reviews of some.) I conjecture that this is because foveation is the most clearly cognitively penetrable visual operation, and machine vision has until now made almost no contact with AI studies of activity.

Sonja has no account of foveation. Many of the operations for which Sonja uses markers may involve foveating eye movements in human vision. Though I have not tried to incorporate a theory of foveation into Sonja's model of vision, I see no obstacles to doing so; indeed Sonja's architecture seems better suited to incorporating such a theory than most, because it models task-specific central control of visual processing.

People typically make several large eye movements per second; yet the world does not seem to jump in the opposite direction several times per second. This phenomenological stability shows that at some stage of processing the visual system translates retinotopic coordinates into some other coordinate frame. It is still unclear at what level of processing this translation occurs; for discussion, see Feldman's "Four Frames Suffice" paper [77] and the peer commentary on it. This raises the question of whether intermediate objects are preserved across eye movements, or whether they must be recomputed. I have, thus far, spoken of the early maps as retinotopically organized, but if they were instead organized in head-centered coordinates, for instance, the intermediate objects would be preserved automatically. Alternatively, they might be explicitly updated by signals from the oculomotor systems. Because Sonja does not model eye motion, I have not had to take a stand on these issues.

Sudnow [265] presents a phenomenological account of the central role of foveation in human activity: learning to play video games, in particular. This account suggests that an understanding of foveation is a prerequisite to a theory of visual skill acquisition (for which see section B.3.4). For a psychophysical and computational studies of the role of foveation in object recognition, see [261] and [20] respectively.

Spatial memory

Sonja's intermediate objects provide mechanisms for remembering the locations of external objects. Additional mechanisms would be required to model people's ability to remember locations. The intermediate objects can only represent visible objects, but people can remember the locations of objects that are no longer visible.

Psychological evidence has led several researchers [77, 220] to propose that there are several spatial memory mechanisms. It seems, for instance, that one is head- or body-relative and might be good for remembering the positions of nearby cars when driving on the freeway [21, 223], and that another represents the structure of large-scale space and might be good for remembering while at work where in the lot you parked your car [301]. The latter mechanism has been identified with the hippocampus on neuroscientific grounds [66].

These spatial memories differ from the intermediate objects in that they can not be used directly as arguments to visual operators, provide less precise spatial localization, and allow storage of many more locations. This tradeoff is similar to memory hierarchy in serial computers, and probably is due to a similar engineering trade-off: intermediate objects require a lot of hardware, so you can't afford many of them, while the spatial memories are probably cheaper per item stored. Presumably as in conventional computers items can be moved between intermediate objects and spatial memory: you can choose to remember the location of the object currently indexed by a visual marker, for instance. Later you could "retrieve" the object and put a visual marker back on it. Because spatial memory is imprecise, and because eye and perhaps body movements may have occurred in the meantime, retrieval might entail eye motion and visual search, but these would be informed by the rough knowledge of where the object is. Pylyshyn [223] presents a model similar to this; Waddell and Rogoff [286] demonstrate that spatial memory is not automatic but enabled by visual tasks.

Spatial memory would be a useful extension to Sonja because it would allow the system to keep track of things that are currently offscreen. It could, for instance, make a cognitive map of the dungeon, which would improve its navigational skills. More importantly, it would provide a new form of grounding for deictic representations. Currently Sonja grounds all deictic representations in perception, but the theory of deictic representations admits several other possible groundings, memory among them. Memory grounding for deictic representations would enable routines such as registering that *the-room-with-the-potion-is-locked*, realizing that *I-don't-have-a-key*, remembering where *the-nearest-key* is even though it is offscreen, getting it, and returning to open *the-room-with-the-potion*.

6.7   Sonja's other peripheral systems

A complete agent has many peripheral systems. The only one I've modeled seriously in Sonja is the visual routines processor. Section 5.3 has already described Sonja's linguistic input system (consisting of the instruction buffers).

Four of Sonja's motor operators correspond to the interface the videogame provides. go! corresponds to the joystick; the direction given it on each tick is the one in which the amazon icon moves. shoot!, turn-key!, and use-potion! correspond to buttons on the videogame console. shoot! takes a boolean input which says whether to shoot a shuriken or a knife.

say! models speech output; it takes a string argument and writes it on the linguistic interaction window with a prepended greater-than sign (figure 5.1).

have-knife? and have-key? are boolean "sensory" modalities. I don't know how people keep track of whether or not they have such tools; I know I'm not very good at it. I've thought about implementing circuitry in Sonja to keep counts of knives and keys but haven't gotten to it.

7 The central system architecture

This chapter describes the implementation technology of Sonja's central system. It is all quite technical and will interesting primarily to those engaged in building similar systems.

Since the central system is a circuit, I wrote it using a circuit description language, MACNET. (I also used MACNET to build the attentional pyramids described in section 6.1.) Section 7.1 describes MACNET.

Aspect registrars are written in MACNET directly; proposers and arbiters are written in a *macrology* (a system of related macros implementing a Lisp-embedded language), described in section 7.2, which compiles into MACNET. The arbitration macrology has a primitive for describing proposers and various constructs for specifying arbitration.

Section 7.3 describes the debugging facilities I used in constructing Sonja.

Section 7.4 describes related work: other languages people have used for describing the circuitry of situated agents.

7.1 MACNET

MACNET is a small, Lisp-embedded language. It allows you to construct circuits by connecting together *primitive machines*. A primitive machine has a set of inputs, which are the outputs of other machines, and a single output. You can think of the inputs and outputs as narrow buses. Since only types that could be passed via compact encodings are allowed, each primitive machine can only correspond to a simple digital circuit. In fact, in Pengi and until late in the implementation of Sonja, only boolean values were allowed, the only primitives were gates, and other types had to be implemented explicitly with buses of boolean wires.

For each primitive, there is a constructor function. For example, a call on `andg` builds an AND gate; `org`, `invert`, and `latch` build OR gates, inverters, and latches. The return value of one of these constructor functions is an object representing the output wire of the gate; the arguments are the input wires. `eqm` generates a machine whose boolean output tells whether its two inputs wires have the same value on them. `ifm` generates primitive machines with a boolean control input and which selectively switches one of the other two inputs to the output. `condm` is a special form with `cond` syntax which expands into calls on `ifm`. The special form `constant` returns a wire which always has a constant value on it. A special form `defm` allows you to define your own primitives.

That is pretty much all there is to MACNET; the rest is Lisp. The usual Lisp control structures suffice to build complex circuits. For example, we can define nonprimitive gate types by function composition:

```
(defun xorg (a b)
  (org (andg a (invert b)) (andg (invert a) b)))
```

Since MACNET wires are Lisp data objects, we can use Lisp compound data structures to represent complex circuits. For example, we can use a list of wires to represent a bus:

```
;;; Binary to unary decoder.
(defun decode (bus)
  (let ((n (length bus))
        (negated (mapcar #'invert bus)))
    (loop for i from 0 to (1- (expt 2 n))
          collect
            (apply #'andg
                   (decoder-line-inputs i n
                                        bus
                                        negated)))))
(defun decoder-line-inputs (i n bus negated)
  (loop for j from 0 to n
        for jth in bus
        for jth-bar in negated
        collect (if (logbitp j i) jth jth-bar)))
```

MACNET is designed to build networks in a "forward" direction: you construct the inputs to a gate before you construct the gate itself. Most of the time this works fine. Occasionally, though, you want to be able to refer to a gate before constructing its inputs. MACNET provides for this by letting you construct an *interface node*, which you can think of as an identity gate: it has one input which is connected directly to the output. You can make an interface node without specifying its inputs and use it in place of the gate you haven't built yet; when you do build the gate, a call on the function `set-input!` will connect it to the interface node.

This is a pretty ugly kludge, and it can easily lead to bugs. If you rearrange your code without thinking carefully, so that the `set-input!`

occurs before the interface node is constructed, you will get the old version of the interface node from the last time the circuit construction program was run as part of your circuit. This results in bizarre, hard-to-debug errors.

What you'd really like is to be able to write order-independent code, with transparent forward references to bits of circuitry that haven't been constructed yet. It's conceptually easy to do this: you want the variables that refer to gates to be logical variables, not program variables. In section 7.4, I describe REX, a language similar to MACNET which has such a facility.

MACNET goes to some, but not great, effort to optimize circuits, mostly by constant folding.

MACNET doesn't operate at run time; a MACNET procedure is run just once to build a circuit before the system runs. Sonja's circuit simulator uses the circuit descriptions MACNET builds to engender action at run time. There's nothing interesting about this simulator.

Human neural "circuitry" is certainly asynchronous. Sonja's circuitry is clocked. This simplified the implementation, and I couldn't see any relevant hard issues it evaded.

7.2   The arbitration macrology

I *could* have written Sonja entirely in MACNET, but it would have been hard. Consider the specification of a typical effector wire leaving the central system. The MACNET expression for this wire would be an enormous tree rooted in sensory inputs. Writing this expression directly would be awkward. Thus I developed an *arbitration macrology* to provide modularity to make it easier to design central circuitry. This macrology compiles down into MACNET circuitry.

Lacking any psychological or neuroscientific theory of how arbitration actually works, I designed what amounts to a programming language. It supports the three-phase central system architecture of registrars, proposers, and arbiters that I proposed in section 3.2.2. The kinds of arbitration it provides were rich enough to support the kinds of tasks Sonja engages in. In particular, it is *not* a simple priority scheme; most of the complexity supports ways of taking environmental conditions into account in choosing between alternative courses of action. I make no

claims for the completeness, optimality, or psychological plausibility of
the macrology.

The arbitration macrology defines an ontology of proposers, operations, proposals, conditions, overridings, defaults, hierarchy, and discrimination. I'll explain these in turn.

7.2.1   Proposers

Proposers we have seen before: they are bits of circuitry that "have
an opinion" about something Sonja should do. An *operation* is a parameterized thing the system can do. Each peripheral operator is an
operation, parameterized by its inputs; there are other operations we'll
get to soon. A *proposal* is the set of actual parameters that a proposer
thinks the operation should be given at a particular time. Because the
formal parameters of operations are implemented as buses, a proposal
corresponds to a set of values on such buses.

The form (propose *proposer-name operation-name &rest alist*) defines a proposer. The *alist* is an alternating list of names of parameters
of the operation and values for them, given as MACNET buses. For
example,

```
(propose compute-obstacle-centroid mark-centroid!
  marker *obstacle-marker*
  plane *temp-plane*
  doit? (andg *expand-to-convex-hull!-done?*
              (invert *unregister-goal-obstacle?*)))
```

defines a proposer named compute-obstacle-centroid, which wants
to set the inputs of the peripheral operator mark-centroid!. It proposes that the marker and plane arguments of mark-centroid! should
be wires that are passed in the Lisp variables *obstacle-marker* and
temp-plane, which must be bound in the context in which this expression is evaluated. It builds an inverter with the call to invert, and
an AND gate with the call on andg. compute-obstacle-centroid proposes that the doit? input to mark-centroid! should be the output
wire of the AND gate.

7.2.2   Conditions and overridings

In general, there may be several proposers for any given operation with
alternative theories about what its inputs should be. The job of the ar-

bitration macrology is to construct circuits which choose one of the competing proposals and route it to the operation's inputs. There are several ways of specifying how arbitration is to occur; the simplest are conditions and overridings. A *condition* specifies when a proposer could possibly be valid. If a proposer's condition is not true, the proposer is not a candidate for setting its operation's inputs. The form (`condition` *proposer-name wire*) specifies a proposer's condition. A *proposer overriding* specifies that one proposer should always be preferred to another, so long as the first proposer's condition is true. The form (`overrides-proposer` *overriding-proposer &rest overridden-proposers*) specifies proposer overridings.

```
(propose align-with-the-goal heading
   direction *amazon-to-goal-minor*)
(condition align-with-the-goal
           (andg *goal-registered?*
                 ;; only align with bad guys
                 *goal-is-enemy?*
                 ;; don't get yerself wedged
                 (invert *amazon-stuck?*)))
(propose face-the-goal heading
   direction *amazon-to-goal-major*)
(condition face-the-goal (andg
                         ;; you have a goal to shoot at
                         *goal-registered?*
                         ;; there's nothing in the way
                         (invert *goal-obstacle?*)
                         ;; you're lined up with the goal
                         *aligned?-result*
                         ;; it's something to shoot at
                         *goal-is-enemy?*))
(overrides-proposer face-the-goal align-with-the-goal)
```

This code fragment defines two proposers for the operation **heading** and arbitrates between them. Each proposer has a condition, which is a small boolean circuit. The starred Lisp variables are bound to wires; most are the output of other circuits, and some come from sensory operators. **face-the-goal** overrides **align-with-the-goal** if the conditions of both are true.

Proposer overridings invalidate particular proposers. It may also be useful to invalidate a particular *proposal*. Thus, for example, under certain conditions you may want to specify that any proposer who suggests heading left is invalid. The (**overrides-proposal** *proposer operation &rest alternating-parameters-and-values*) form allows this. It says that when *proposer* is valid, any proposer who proposes that *operation* be given *alternating-parameters-and-values* as parameters should be invalidated. The values in *alternating-parameters-and-values* are specified by buses and are computed at run time.

As it happened, I ended up never using **overrides-proposal**. I also never used a recursive overriding feature I implemented based on the model of Agre's running argument architecture [4]. I think both might be useful in the design of other systems similar to Sonja.

7.2.3   Defaults

The arbitration macrology provides a facility for *default proposers*, which are proposers which are implicitly overridden by all regular proposers. Thus a default proposer's proposal is taken only if all the regular proposers's conditions are invalid. **propose-default** constructs a default proposer; a typical example is

```
(propose-default opportunistic-search content-address!
  moved-marker *opportunistic-marker*
  proximity-marker *amazon-marker*
  early-dimension (constant 'darkness)
  early-value (constant :non-zero)
  doit? *t*)
```

which specifies the default inputs to the operation **content-address!**. One can imagine more than one level of default, priority schemes, and so on; I didn't find them necessary.

7.2.4   Hierarchical arbitration

The arbitration macrology is *hierarchical* in two dimensions: it provides for abstract proposers and abstract operations.

An *abstract proposer* makes proposals which are too complex to be simply specified by a single concrete proposer. Consider, for example, wandering around in the maze. This is conceptually a single sort of action which it is useful to be able to talk about, but it is actually implemented in terms of several concrete proposers. For example, wander-randomly proposes going in a random direction; keep-wandering-in-same-direction proposes continuing to wander in whichever direction we're currently headed; and wander-per-advice proposes to wander in whichever direction the advisor suggests. A great many other proposers have theories about which direction to go in; it would be a lot of work, and bad modularity, for them all to have to know about the three different ways that wandering is implemented. So there is a single abstract proposer **wander** which *subsumes* these three. **wander** makes a single coherent proposal based on arbitration among **wander-randomly**, **keep-wandering-in-the-same-direction**, and **wander-per-advice**. **wander** can then be conditionalized and overridden as a unit. (**abstract-proposer** *proposer-name operation-name*) constructs an abstract proposer, and (**subsumes** *abstract-proposer proposer*) specifies a subsumption relationship. Here is part of the code for wandering in Sonja, simplified somewhat for clarity:

```
(abstract-proposer wander heading)
(subsumes wander keep-wandering-in-same-direction)
(propose keep-wandering-in-same-direction heading
   direction *sensed-amazon-motion-direction*)
(condition keep-wandering-in-same-direction
            *amazon-moving?*)
(subsumes wander wander-randomly)
(propose wander-randomly heading
   direction *random-direction*)
(overrides-proposer keep-wandering-in-same-direction
                    wander-randomly)
(subsumes wander wander-per-advice)
(propose wander-per-advice heading
   direction ...)
(condition wander-per-advice ...)
(overrides-proposer wander-per-advice wander-randomly)
```

(I've omitted the details of **wander-per-advice** because it depends on the discrimination constructs of section 7.2.5.)

An *abstract operation* consists of a set of named buses called *ports*. Proposers can make proposals about what the values on these buses

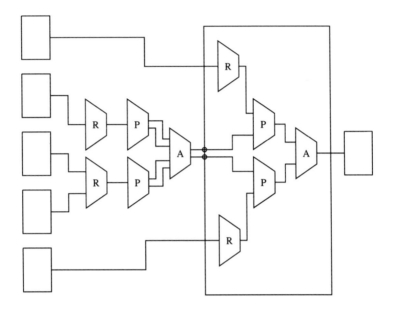

Figure 7.1
An abstract operation. The small rectangles represent peripheral operators and the
trapezoids represent bits of circuitry in the central system. The abstract operation
per se consists only of two buses (ports), appearing with circles around them in the
middle of the figure. The values on these buses are arbitrated by the arbiter (labeled
A) in the center. Two proposers have theories about what values the ports should
take on. The ports are used as inputs to other proposers for another operation.
This organization allows the designer to view all the circuitry inside the large
rectangle as a black box parameterized by the values on the ports. The rectangle,
however, is only a way of thinking, and does not correspond to any machinery.

should be; the proposals are arbitrated using the same arbitration
macrology I have described. This in effect allows you to parameter-
ize chunks of circuitry: all the circuitry that takes the operation's buses
as inputs can be thought of as a parameterized black box from point of
view of the circuitry that sets the buses (figure 7.1). Abstract operators
allow a conceptual layering of the central system: operations at higher
levels are implemented by patterns of activity at the next lower level.

(**abstract-operation** *operation-name &rest ports*) specifies an abstract operation. (**port** *abstract-operation-name port-name*) returns the
bus that is the port named *port-name* of the abstract operation named
abstract-operation-name.

Here is an example, taken from Sonja's navigation code.

```
(abstract-operation navigate
  destination-marker)
(propose-default goal-is-destination head-for-goal
  goal-marker (port navigate destination-marker))
...
(propose navigate-to-monster navigate
  to-marker *monster-marker*)
(condition navigate-to-monster
          (invert *monster-marker-blanked?*))
...
```

navigate is the abstract operation which implements Sonja's ability to move the amazon about on the screen. It has one port, a marker which designates the location the amazon should head for. navigate is implemented in terms of another abstract operation, head-for-goal; in the simplest case, navigate simply passes along the destination and lets head-for-goal do the work of moving the amazon. The default proposer goal-is-destination implements this case. The other cases are complex, and I've omitted them. Various proposers for navigate have opinions about where the amazon should head. For instance, navigate-to-monster proposes heading for the monster by supplying a marker that tracks monsters as the destination-marker of navigate. There are many other such proposers with complex arbitration between them.

7.2.5 Discrimination

As explained in section 5.4.2, instructions to Sonja serve to manage existing competences, largely by affecting arbitration decisions which Sonja is not competent to make on its own. There are many cases in which Sonja is capable of undertaking either of two fairly complex tasks, both of which are plausible in a given situation. An advisor with a better understanding of the game may be able to choose between them when Sonja can't. This I term *discrimination*.

Arbitration among a set of proposals for an operator that are all valid on the basis of conditions and overriding can be swayed by wires that *support* or *object to* some of these proposers. If, among such a group

of proposers there is one that is supported, it wins. Similarly, if one
is objected to, it loses. (Being objected to is not the same as being
overruled; a proposer that is objected to may still win if it is the only
one that is valid on the basis of conditions and overriding.) Typically
instruction buffers support or object to various proposals.

What happens in a group of proposers, all valid on the basis of conditions and overriding, when support or objection does *not* discriminate
among them (as when no advice is given)? The natural thing is to
choose one arbitrarily. I found that this made debugging tricky; if I
wrote the arbitration a bit wrong, unpredictable things would happen.
Accordingly, I introduced a run-time arbitration error checking facility
(described in section 7.2.6) that would signal an error if more than one
proposer was valid. I also provided a form `indifferent` which declares
that it is OK for more than one proposer to be valid; `indifferent`
is useful in cases where discrimination is used. (`indifferent` *&rest
proposers*) specifies that error checking should not be applied to unar-
bitable conflicts between the *proposers*, and that one should be chosen
arbitrarily.

```
(indifferent navigate-to-bones
             navigate-to-goody
             navigate-to-stairwell
             navigate-to-monster)
(propose navigate-to-monster navigate
  marker *monster-marker*)
(condition navigate-to-monster
           (invert *monster-marker-blanked?*))
(supports (told-to kill-the-monster) navigate-to-monster)
(objects-to (told-to dont-kill-the-monster)
            navigate-to-monster)
...
```

We saw earlier that various proposers such as `navigate-to-monster`
have opinions about where Sonja should go. In general it is very difficult to make this decision; it can depend on complex features of the
situation. Sonja is able to take some of the these features into account;
these are expressed in terms of conditions and overridings. For instance,
it knows that it doesn't make any sense to chase a monster if you aren't
registering one. That is what the condition on `navigate-to-monster`

is for; `*monster-marker-blanked?*` is high when no monster is registered. However, Sonja can't always make the best decision itself. In the worst case, all four of the `indifferent` proposers might be valid simultaneously. Sonja can use advice to help when several alternatives seem equally plausible. The instruction buffer `kill-the-monster` is set when the advisor suggests "Get the monster;" `dont-kill-the-monster` is set when the advisor instructs Sonja "Don't bother with that guy." The calls on `supports` and `objects-to` make these instruction buffers to support and object to the proposer `navigate-to-monster`. `told-to` is a special form that returns the valid line of an instruction buffer (section 5.3).

Just as it is possible to override a proposal regardless of who made it, it is possible to support or object to a proposal regardless of its proposer. For instance, one may say "Head left!" and thereby support whichever proposer is arguing for that move. The form (`supports-proposal` *wire operation-name &rest alternating-parameters-and-values*) says that *wire* supports any proposer that wants to set the parameters of *operation* to the given *values*. `objects-to-proposal` works similarly. The circuits these forms generate include latches to keep track of which proposer they support. This is because when the advisor says "Head left!" he intends you to head left for a specific reason; it's not just generally a good idea to go left. There may be some other reason for going left a few seconds later, but the advisor does not intend his advice to support that. This mechanism is part of the way Sonja implements indirect speech acts (section 5.4.4).

7.2.6 Arbitration compilation

The various special forms I have described are implemented in terms of MACNET primitives; they compile proposers and arbitration down into gates. This process is painfully complicated in practice, and writing and debugging the arbitration compiler took me a couple of months.

The arbitration compiler, as well as constructing the circuitry that sets the inputs to the various effector operators, builds circuitry which detects runtime arbitration errors. An arbitration error occurs when there is more than one proposer for an operation that is valid after all arbitration (including discrimination) is taken into account, or when no proposer is valid. This runtime error checking was a significant aid in debugging Sonja's central network.

7.2.7 Arbitration in practice

Sequencing One way to achieve sequential action is with a program counter or other control state. Sometimes this is the only way to achieve it. I've deliberately added features to Amazon to force such situations and implemented some routines in Sonja that depend on control state. (See particularly section 8.5.) This is atypical, however.

In the typical case, each action has perceptible consequences. These consequences can be registered and used to condition the next action in the sequence. Most action sequencing in Sonja arises this way. This sort of dynamic action sequencing adds flexibility to the system's operation under conditions of uncertainty. If an action does not have the desired effect, the "next action in the sequence" will not occur; some other action appropriate for the new situation will occur instead. Similarly, if serendipitous events bring Sonja closer to achieving a goal than would normally be expected, the system will not continue to carry out unnecessary actions, but rather will proceed from the new situation. Sonja performs actions because they make sense in concrete situations, not because they are the next step in a program.

Operator duplication Earlier I said that arbitration addresses the problem of different proposers wanting a peripheral operator to do different things. Why would this happen? Consider that the visual operators are intended to be domain-independent. Many different visual routines with entirely different purposes might want to know whether two markers are coincident, for example; and if the two markers are parameters to this operator, the chunks of circuitry subserving these two routines are liable to want to check for coincidence of *different* pairs of markers. Now, this can be more or less of a problem. In the typical case, these two routines will only apply under quite different circumstances, and it will be easy to compute based on registered aspects which should have access to the operator at any given time. This case is the one the arbitration macrology was designed for.

If the two routines need to occur under the same circumstances, this won't work. This might happen, for instance, if you need to monitor two similar conditions using routines which require the same operator. In a first version of Pengi, I timeshared the contended-for operator among the routines. This required the use of a ring counter to arbitrate access to the operator. It also required circuitry depending on the output of a shared sensory operator to check the phase of the counter to determine the meaning of the output; it would mean unrelated things according to the value of the counter. This seemed like a kludge and made writing central circuitry painful. Agre suggested simply duplicating the operator in these cases, and that is the approach I have taken in Sonja.[1]

I believe this duplication is a reasonable solution. The total number of operators of any given type that are required is only as many as the total number that are actually required *at any given time.* There's reason to think that this number should never get very high. Video games are made interesting by being difficult: by pushing some part of human computational machinery close to its limit. Different games press different parts, but most are difficult because they require that you keep track of several moving things and the relationships among them at once. Thus, video games probably require more simultaneous visual computation than just about any other activity. It seems to be possible to play Pengo and Amazon with only a few-fold duplication at worst.

Another mitigating factor is that what counts as a single operator depends on how heavily parameterized it is. One operator can be split into several by substituting constants for the parameters. For example, is there a single operator that tells you whether a marker (supplied as an argument) is blanked, or is there one operator for each marker? If all the parameters of an operator are eliminated this way, it becomes bottom-up, and no arbitration is necessary because there can be no argument about the operator's parameter values. Lacking any theory of how heavily parameterized operators should be, I have made arbitrary decisions.

Proposer splitting There's another use for the arbitration macrology. The parameters an operator should be given within the course of a particular routine may depend on various conditions. In such a case, the values the associated circuitry propose could be computed by gating either one or the other into the proposer according to the condition:

```
(propose some-proposer some-operation
   parameter1 (ifm some-condition one-value another-value))
```

---

[1]One cannot, of course, duplicate motor operators, because the physical effectors they connect to cannot be duplicated.

Indeed such code appears frequently in Sonja. However, it's sometimes more convenient to write the same thing another way:

```
(propose propose-one-value some-operation
   parameter1 one-value)
(condition propose-one-value some-condition)
(propose propose-another-value some-operation
   parameter1 another-value)
(overrides propose-another-value propose-one-value)
```

This style is more convenient when `one-value` and `another-value` are computed in lexically distant places. I didn't plan for this use of the arbitration macrology, but it turns out to be handy.

Arbitrating access to intermediate objects All of what I've said about arbitration so far has concerned the arbitration of the parameters given to operators. In writing the central system it is necessary to ensure not only that two proposers don't get access to the same operator, it is necessary to ensure that two operators don't try to side effect the same intermediate object. A marker can only be moved to one place at a time; and it doesn't make sense to simultaneously move it and blank it. The arbitration macrology does not provide any special support for avoiding such collisions; it's the central system writer's responsibility. Multiple side-effects on an intermediate object *are* trapped as run time errors, however.

7.3   Debugging facilities

MACNET has a feature I haven't talked about so far, which allows you to give names to machines. For example, you can write (**named-andg** *name &rest inputs*), which creates an AND gate named *name*. MACNET maintains a hashtable mapping names to machines. In the Sonja code, I named any machine I expected to have to refer to in debugging.

The first debugging technique I developed for Pengi was **why**, a function which, given a machine or machine name, printed out a derivation of its value, using indentation to represent the logic tree:

```
(why 'under-attack?)
#<OR-GATE UNDER-ATTACK?: NIL> which is the OR of
 #<AND-GATE 94473485: NIL> which is the AND of
  #<OR-GATE 94472418: T> which is the OR of
   #<DELAY, output NIL, state NIL> which is the delay of
    #<I-NODE SHOOTING?: NIL>
   #<OR-GATE HEADING-TOWARD-MONSTER?: T>
  #<I-NODE DISTANCE-WITHIN?1-RESULT: NIL>
 #<I-NODE DEMON?-RESULT: NIL>
```

Gates are printed as #<*type name: truth-value*>. Gates without a name are numbered. The top level OR gate has two inputs, an AND gate and an interface node (which, recall, can be thought of as a buffer or just a wire.) Recursion stops whenever it hits a named gate.

Simultaneously with why, I implemented a logic analyzer: you could give it a list of named gates and it would display their values as the system ran. This turned out, oddly enough, not to be very useful. I'm not sure quite why not; perhaps because the set of gates I wanted to look at in the course of debugging was constantly changing.

What I actually used to debug Pengi was a combination of why with single stepping and breakpoints. Single stepping pauses the combined Sonja-Amazon system just after the central system runs on each tick. Then you can apply why to various machines and try and figure out what happened. You give the breakpoint facility the names of machines to break on, and then it pauses the system whenever those machine change state. More generally, you can give it the description of a new machine which it will construct and connect into the existing central network; this allows you to add test hardware and break on complex conditions.

Debugging this way worked pretty well for Pengi. That Pengi had no state in the central system and constantly displayed all the state in its peripheral system on the screen made it easy to figure out what was wrong when it did something silly: I could read the problem right off the gates. Sonja's a little trickier to debug since it does have state, but it has little compared with most programs, and it's usually pretty obvious what's going on. The exceptions to both these claims were various sorts of timing errors, which I spent enormous amounts of time on. These were due to bugs in the logic simulator and in the way in which Amazon and Sonja interfaced and in the way the central network hooked up to the peripheral system. Eventually I got it right and didn't have to think about it any more.

Sonja's circuitry is an order of magnitude more complex than Pengi's. why was not sufficient for understanding the deeply nested circuitry, much of it built automatically by the arbitration compiler. I needed a higher-level tool.

show-operator-frame, like why, shows the state of the central network, but it does so symbolically, in terms of the arbitration macrology.

```
(show-operator-frame 'go!)
Operation GO!, with inputs from WANDER-RANDOMLY:
  DIRECTION: :LEFT
No outputs.
Direct proposers:
* WANDER: valid
    Overridings:
      FACE-THE-GOAL, which fails
      PASS-OBSTACLE, which fails
      ALIGN-WITH-THE-GOAL, which fails
      CHASE-THE-GOAL, which fails
* WANDER-RANDOMLY: valid
    Overridings:
      WANDER-PER-ADVICE, which fails
      KEEP-WANDERING-IN-SAME-DIRECTION, which fails
    Subsumers: (WANDER)
  WANDER-PER-ADVICE: invalid
    Condition false
    Indifferent with KEEP-WANDERING-IN-SAME-DIRECTION
    Subsumers: (WANDER)
  KEEP-WANDERING-IN-SAME-DIRECTION: invalid
    Condition false
    Indifferent with WANDER-PER-ADVICE
    Subsumers: (WANDER)
  FACE-THE-GOAL: invalid
    Condition false
  PASS-OBSTACLE: invalid
    Condition false
  ALIGN-WITH-THE-GOAL: invalid
    Condition false
    Overridings:
      FACE-THE-GOAL, which fails
      PASS-OBSTACLE, which fails
  CHASE-THE-GOAL: invalid
    Condition false
    Overridings:
      FACE-THE-GOAL, which fails
      PASS-OBSTACLE, which fails
      ALIGN-WITH-THE-GOAL, which fails
No default proposers.
```

show-operator-frame takes the name of an operation (go!) as its argument. It tells you what proposer for that operation is currently setting
the proposer's inputs (wander-randomly). It lists the inputs and out-

puts of the operation and displays the values on these buses symbolically. go!, the effector operator which actually moves the amazon icon on the screen, has no outputs. go! has many proposers, most of which are not listed here. Only those relevant to determining the inputs to the operation are listed: many others are subsumed by an abstract proposer which is overruled, for example. Valid proposers are starred; it's possible for several to be valid, as in this case, because they form a subsumption chain. Each proposer is listed with the associated arbitration machinery: its conditions, overrides, discrimination, and so forth.

show-instructions similarly shows the state of the instruction buffers symbolically. Here's what its output looks like when the instruction "Get the potion and set it off" is given:

```
(show-instructions)
  GO-AROUND
    DIRECTION: :LEFT
  NO-THE-OTHER-ONE
  SCROLL-IS-READY
  GO-FOR-DOOR
    END: :LEFT
  HIT-IT-WITH-A-KNIFE-WHEN-IT-GOES-LIGHT
  USE-A-KNIFE
· USE-A-POTION
  LOOK-OUT-ABSOLUTE
    DIRECTION: :LEFT
  LOOK-OUT-RELATIVE
    ROTATION: :LEFT
  GO-OUT
  GO-IN
  SUGGESTED-NOT-GO
    DIRECTION: :LEFT
  SUGGESTED-GO
    DIRECTION: :LEFT
  IN-THE-ROOM
* REGISTER-THE-POTION
  REGISTER-THE-KNIFE
  REGISTER-THE-BREAD
  REGISTER-THE-AMULET
  REGISTER-THE-KEY
  DONT-PICK-UP-THE-GOODY
* PICK-UP-THE-GOODY
  DONT-GO-DOWN-THE-STAIRWELL
  GO-DOWN-THE-STAIRWELL
  DONT-KILL-THE-BONES
  KILL-THE-BONES
  DONT-KILL-THE-MONSTER
  KILL-THE-MONSTER
    TYPE: AMAZON
```

The starred instruction buffers are valid; that with a dot in front of it
(USE-A-POTION) is pending. The fields of instruction buffers that have

them are printed indented. The values of the fields of invalid buffers are meaningless.

These two tools made debugging the central system straightforward.

7.4 Related work

In this section I will compare MACNET and my arbitration macrology with specification languages developed by other groups designing situated agents. Although there are many differences, they don't seem to matter much. I think that this is because arbitration is actually an easy problem; any reasonably programmable scheme will work just fine. I'll talk more about this in section 9.3.

MACNET is based on NODNET, a language originally designed by Terman as the input language for a much more sophisticated circuit simulator [270].

Other researchers building situated agents have also used what amount to circuit description languages.

REX [138, 142], the circuit description language used by the Situated Automata group (principally Rosenschein and Kaelbling) to build computational machinery embedded in robots [233, 235], is very similar to MACNET. There are probably at least four reasons for this. First, that group shares most of my intuitions about how embedded computations should be designed. Second, we share in particular the idea that digital circuits are the right way of describing embedded computations. Third, the problem of digital circuit description is so simple that similar results were inevitable. Fourth, I participated in the development of REX.

The principal difference between REX and MACNET is that REX provides logical variables, thereby solving more cleanly than MACNET the problem of forward references.

Just as I found that raw MACNET was too low-level to write complex systems in, the Situated Automata group found REX too low-level and wrote two languages on top of it which correspond roughly with my arbitration macrology. Kaelbling's GAPPS [139, 141] is a language for specifying an action selection network; its function is roughly parallel with that of my arbitration macrology. Rosenschein's Ruler [234] is a language for specifying perceptual systems which also compiles into REX. It doesn't correspond to anything in Sonja, whose perceptual systems are written in unconstrained Lisp.

The MIT mobile robot group has developed a series of circuit specification languages descending from Brooks's *subsumption language* [25, 28]. The primitive units of the circuits these languages generate are finite state machines. These run asynchronously, in contrast with the synchronous circuits generated by MACNET and REX. The languages provide *inhibition* and *suppression* mechanisms roughly parallel to my conditions and overrides. In the original formulation, these mechanisms made inhibition and suppression discrete actions whose effects persisted for variable periods depending on numerical time constants. Although not enforced by the language, the original formulation of the subsumption architecture mandated *layered* construction, in which the finite state machines are organized into equivalence classes which are totally ordered, with suppression and inhibition constrained to respect the layer hierarchy. Abstract operations in Sonja support a similar organization. The most recent subsumption language also provides for defaults and a form of modularity similar to abstract operations [29].

The most complex application of the subsumption architecture is in Connell's thesis [46] which describes a coke-can collecting robot. Connell's experience with the original subsumption architecture led him to abandon the principle of strict layering. He also eliminated the original architecture's time constants in inhibition and suppression, resulting in purely combinational arbitration. These changes have been adopted by Brooks. Connell further required that all internal state be *ephemeral*: no state element could go for more than a few ticks without being updated. This ensures that the robot's activity stays closely linked to perception, and that it cannot get confused by out-of-date information. Connell made extensive use of external memory. These changes make the subsumption architecture and my arbitration architecture more similar. My arbitration architecture has no time constants. It is combinational except for the latching of proposal discrimination, which is required in order to remember the relevance of given instructions, and this and the instruction buffers are the principal form of persistent (non-ephemeral) state.

Agre's running arguments system [3, 4] was the immediate model for my arbitration macrology. This system incrementally compiles a running rule language into a dependency network. The dependency network can be viewed as digital circuit, and is thus analogous to Sonja's central system. Sonja central network differs in allowing state and in being hand written. The rule language supports a model of argumentation (descended from that of Doyle's SEAN [57]) involving proposals, support, and objections. The semantics of these operations are different in Sonja but the intuition is similar.

8 Sonja

This chapter explains how Sonja works as a whole system to play Amazon and to use instructions. This entails explaining the wiring of the central network and its interactions with the peripheral systems, with Amazon, and with an advisor.

I begin, in section 8.1, by repeating the scenario presented in chapter 1, explaining how Sonja did what it did. These explanations are imprecise and intended to give a sense of how Sonja operates without going into technical details.

Section 8.2 then discusses various implementation issues which are manifested in many parts of the central network, for example real time performance, the allocation of intermediate objects, and projection.

Sections 8.3–8.7 describe the specific routines Sonja engages in and the central circuitry that enables them. Sonja does three sorts of things: it collects goodies, it clobbers monsters and piles of bones, and it navigates around the maze. These are in increasing order of complexity.

Section 8.3 documents the central circuitry that implements the registration of the amazon and its aspects. This section also explains in detail the code that generates this circuitry. The rest of the code is similar, so I don't present any other examples.

Collecting goodies requires that they be registered. Section 8.4 describes the registration of goodies, stairwells, and piles of bones. Section 8.5 describes the special registration of scrolls. After goodies are registered, collecting them just entails getting to them, because to pick up a goody in Amazon all you have to do is to run into it. Thus collection largely reduces to navigation.

Section 8.6 explains how Sonja kills monsters and bone piles. Combat requires registering monsters. In general there can be a great many monsters on the screen, so you have to register the relevant ones, which are ones you can kill and ones that can kill you. You can kill things which you are aligned with in any one of the eight directions (because shots in Amazon always move along one of those directions) and which you have a clear shot at. If you aren't aligned with anything that you have an unobstructed shot at, you can choose an enemy to kill and try to get aligned with it. (This is a somewhat different sort of navigation than that needed for collecting goodies, which gets you all the way to a location.)

Finally, section 8.7 describes navigation. Because Sonja has the same top-down view of the Amazon maze that a human player has, this is not navigation in the normal sense, but rather involves guiding the amazon from place to place on the screen. The navigation routines involve the most complex and interesting visual processing. In spite of this, Sonja's navigation ability is quite crude because the problem turned out to be harder than I expected and because it had little to do with the points I wanted to make in this book. I implemented two major navigation routines: one for *passing around* an obstacle which neither you nor your goal are in the convex hull of; and one for *entering* or *exiting* a room when either you or your goal but not both are within it. Sonja gets confused in situations that do not fit either of these descriptions. Accordingly, as discussed in section 4.3, I revised the maze to contain only obstacles of sorts that Sonja could navigate around or through.

For reference, figure 8.1 presents a table of some of the deictic representations Sonja registers, along with the sections of this chapter that explain how they are registered and how they affect arbitration. Figure 8.2 presents a similar table of routines Sonja engages in. (I've omitted purely visual routines from this table.) Recall that deictic representations and routines exist only in a theorist's description of an agent's interactions; they are not objective features of its construction, nor do they necessarily correspond with specific bits of machinery. Thus, there can be no definite lists of them; these figures just display some of the deictic representations and routines that I analyzed Sonja in terms of as I was constructing it. Figure 8.4 repeats figure 5.2, the table of instructions and their buffers, for reference. Figure 8.3 lists all the replies Sonja generates.

Deictic representation	Section described in
I've-been-cold-booted	8.3
the-amazon-is-stuck	8.3
the-amazon-is-under-attack	8.6
the-amazon-is-in-a-room	8.7.3
the-amazon's-heading	8.3
the-bones-are-dark	8.4
the-bones-have-just-gone-light	8.6
the-goody	8.4
the-scroll-is-ready	8.5
the-stairwell	8.4
the-ghost	8.6
the-demon	8.6
the-monster-is-dangerous	8.6
the-fireball	8.6
the-demon-that-breathed-the-fireball	8.6
the-target-is-an-enemy	8.6
the-destination	8.7
the-destination-is-in-a-room	8.7.3
the-goal	8.7.3
the-direction-to-the-goal	8.7.3
the-obstacle	8.7.3
the-direction-to-pass-the-obstacle	8.7.3
the-room	8.7.4
the-doorway-of-the-room	8.7.4
the-gap-in-the-wall	8.7.4
the-door	8.7.4

Figure 8.1
Some of Sonja's deictic representations and the sections they are described in.

Routine	Section described in
Shoot-the-enemy	8.6
Throw-a-knife-at-the-enemy	8.6
Pick-up-the-goody	8.7.1
Navigate-to-destination	8.7
Navigate-to-goal	8.7.3
Align-with-the-enemy	8.7.3
Pass-the-obstacle	8.7.3
Deglitch	8.7.3
Enter-the-room	8.7.4
Open-the-door	8.7.4
Exit-the-room	8.7.4
Head-in-the-recommended-direction	8.7.5
Wander	8.7.6

Figure 8.2
Some of Sonja's routines and the sections they are described in.

```
Hey, I can't find the amazon!
WHAT ghost/demon/monster/bones/key/amulet/
        potion/knife/bread?
What?  I can't see any ready scroll!
But I'm not IN a room!
Go in WHERE?
Use a knife on WHAT?
I haven't GOT a knife!
I'm severely confused -- I shouldn't be saying this!
```

Figure 8.3
The linguistic outputs generated by Sonja. (Cf. section 5.4.5.)

Instruction	Instruction buffer(s) set	Field
Get the monster/ghost/demon	`kill-the-monster`	`type`
Don't bother with that guy	`dont-kill-the-monster`	
Head down those stairs	`go-down-the-stairwell`	
Don't go down yet	`dont-go-down-the-stairwell`	
Get the bones	`kill-the-bones`	
Ignore the bones for now	`dont-kill-the-bones`	
Get the *goody*	`pick-up-the-goody`	
	`register-the-`*goody*	
Don't pick up the *goody*	`dont-pick-up-the-goody`	
	`register-the-`*goody*	
Head *direction*	`suggested-go`	`direction`
Don't go *direction*	`suggested-not-go`	`direction`
Go around to the left/right	`go-around`	`direction`
Go around the top/bottom	`go-around`	`direction`
Go on in	`go-in`	
OK, head out now	`go-out`	
Go on in and down the stairs	`in-the-room`	
	`go-down-the-stairwell`	
Go on in and get the bones	`in-the-room`	
	`kill-the-bones`	
Go in and get the *goody*	`register-the-`*goody*	
	`in-the-room`	
	`pick-up-the-goody`	
Get the potion and set it off	`register-the-potion`	
	`pick-up-the-goody`	
	`use-a-potion` (chained)	
Scroll's ready	`scroll-is-ready`	
On your left! *and similar*	`look-out-relative`	`rotation`
On the left! *and similar*	`look-out-absolute`	`direction`
Use a knife	`use-a-knife`	
Hit it with a knife		
when it goes light	`hit-it-with-a-knife-when-it-goes-light`	
Use a potion	`use-a-potion`	
No, the other one	`no-the-other-one`	

Figure 8.4
Sonja's instruction buffers and the instructions that set them. Some instructions
have variant forms. `pick-up-the-goody` and `use-a-potion` are chained together
when the instruction "Get the potion and set it off" is given.

8.1   Scenario

When the scenario of section 1.1 begins, Sonja finds that it is not registering the amazon, and accordingly uses a visual search to find it. Having found it, Sonja tracks it with a marker (figure 8.5).

The instruction "Go in and get the amulet" tells Sonja that it should be looking for an amulet in a room. Sonja starts a new visual search for an appropriate amulet. The first amulet it finds is the one on the right (figure 8.6). Sonja applies the containment visual routine of section 3.3.3 to determine whether this amulet is in a room; it is not. Thus the visual search continues to the next amulet, the bottom left one; the containment routine determines that this amulet is in fact in the room (figure 8.7). Sonja then finds the doorway of the room by enumerating gaps (figure 8.8) and heads for it.

Meanwhile, Sonja has registered the nearest monster, using a visual search with proximity preference. This monster is a ghost and it is relatively far away, so it is not a threat and Sonja ignores it. Eventually, however, the ghost gets to be close enough to be dangerous, and Sonja kills it (figure 8.9). Sonja then registers the demon. At this point the advisor says "Use a knife." In general, Sonja may have to do visual work to determine what the knife is to be used for. In this case, Sonja is already engaged in combat with the demon, and so does not consider the possibility of using the knife to open a door. Rather it immediately uses the knife to kill the demon.

Having clobbered the monsters, Sonja heads into the room by passing first one and then the other doorway marker (figure 8.10). When Sonja turns down to get the registered amulet, the advisor says "No, the other one!" This instruction restarts Sonja's visual search for an amulet in a room. Sonja finds and retrieves the top amulet.

Figure 8.5
Sonja finds and marks the amazon using visual search.

Figure 8.6
Sonja finds an amulet with visual search. However, this amulet is not in a room as
required.

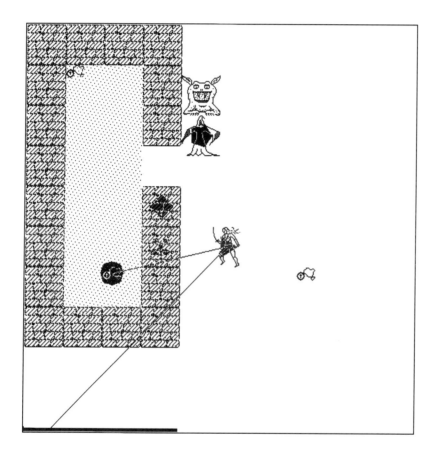

Figure 8.7
Sonja finds an amulet in a room. The interior of the room is activated with a
speckle pattern. Sonja activates the obstacle to getting to the amulet with a hatch
pattern.

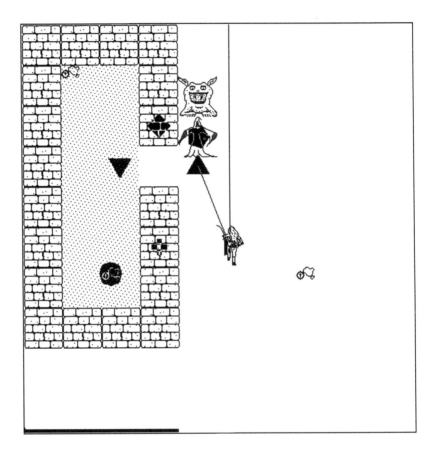

Figure 8.8
Sonja finds the doorway to the room by enumerating gaps and heads for the outer
end of it.

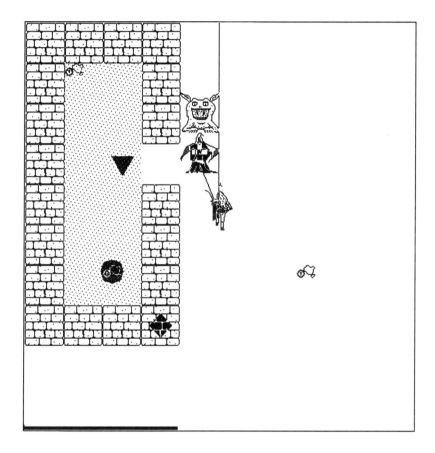

Figure 8.9
Sonja kills the ghost when it gets close enough to be a threat. A shuriken is visible
immediately above the amazon.

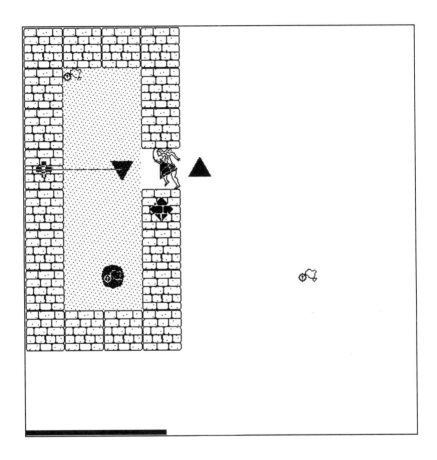

Figure 8.10
Sonja enters the room by passing the doorway markers in turn.

8.2   Global implementation issues

Real time and clocking

Sonja runs in sync with Amazon. Thus, the outer loop of the combined Sonja-Amazon system is

Run one step of the Amazon game. Update the screen.

Run the sensory systems; present inputs to the central system.

Use the logic simulator to run the central system, propagating boolean values through the network.

Clock the central system state elements.

Run the effector systems.

A central claim about Sonja is that if it were implemented in essential connectionist hardware it would run in real time. This means that the system would have a small constant cycle time (well under a second) and that it would provide a vector of actions to Amazon on every tick. Sonja is actually implemented in simulation on a serial machine, so it is not in fact real time. I have tried to make the system run as nearly as possible in real time given hardware limitations.

There are several reasons Sonja can not run in real time on available hardware. First, Amazon itself is so computationally intensive that it uses up all the cycles of my computer when a human is playing it. (It runs at about twenty ticks per second, fast enough that motion looks smooth and flicker-free.) Since Amazon and Sonja run on the same machine, Sonja *couldn't* keep up with the game unless it did no computation at all. Since Sonja and Amazon run in sync, Sonja does provide a vector of actions on every tick, but its cycle time varies. There are several reasons for this variability. One is that I have used iterative algorithms to implement operations which would be constant time on a parallel machine. For example, the circuit simulator is event-driven, and the time it takes to update the central network is proportional to the number of machines whose output changes in response to a new vector of sensory inputs. Usually this number is small, and the update takes less than a tenth of a second. Occasionally it can take up to about half a second. Similarly, I argued in section 6.5 that there are fast, bounded-time parallel implementations for all the visual operators, but my serial simulations often take time quadratic in the complexity of the scene. This occasionally delays the system for up to about a second. A final reason is that the system doesn't quite fit into main memory and takes unpredictable page faults. Overall, Sonja plays Amazon at about half real time, with occasional pauses of up to a couple seconds.

Because Sonja's visual and central systems run synchronously on a unit-time clock, the VRP supports the fiction that all the visual operators run in unit time. This is not only neurophysiologically implausible (the brain is not clocked), it is specifically contradicted by psychophysical evidence that the time required to discriminate values on a single early dimension increases continuously with their similarity [278]. I don't think that this unrealism has any great consequence.

Allocating intermediate objects

I used a static intermediate object allocation strategy. That is, the same intermediate object is always used for any given purpose. On the other hand, each intermediate object may be put to more than one purpose. In a static allocation strategy, it is possible to use a intermediate object for two purposes only when you can be sure these two purposes will not overlap in time. Thus, for instance, a particular activation plane is used both to represent the convex hull of obstacles and to determine whether an obstacle runs off the screen. These two tasks never overlap in time. In a more complex domain, a dynamic allocation strategy with a freelist might be preferable.

Sonja uses eleven markers, one line, two rays, and three activation planes (figure 8.11).

Projection

Projection is the registration of likely outcomes of events. We saw in section 2.7 that projection in Sonja is accomplished by visualization; that is, by running visual routines. A visual routine can be used to register what would happen in alternative possible future circumstances.

It is difficult to say just which of Sonja's routines constitute projections. The problem is that (like any physically implemented agent) Sonja can collect information only about the current situation; this informa-

Display	Entity	Global variable
Markers:		
right triangle	*the-amazon*	*amazon-marker*
cross	*the-target*	*target-marker*
pentagon	*the-monster*	*monster-marker*
hexagon	*the-pile-of-bones*	*bones-marker*
septagon	*the-stairwell*	*stairwell-marker*
octagon	*the-goody*	*goody-marker*
nonagon	*the-fireball*	*fireball-marker*
square	*the-obstacle*	*obstacle-marker*
up triangle	*outside-the-doorway*	*doorway-outer-marker*
down triangle	*inside-the-doorway*	*doorway-inner-marker*
diamond	*something*	*opportunistic-marker*
Line:		
	amazon-to-goal	*goal-line*
Rays:		
	heading-direction	*heading-ray*
	demon-direction	*demon-ray*
Activation planes:		
increasing hatch pattern	*the-obstacle*	*obstacle-plane*
decreasing hatch pattern	general purpose	*temp-plane*
grey wash	*the-room*	*room-plane*

Figure 8.11
Sonja's intermediate objects, with their statically-allocated uses, graphical displays, and global variables.

tion can be used to project futures, but the registered aspect can be expressed either as a statement about the future or the present. For example, the same aspect could be described as *this-monster-is-dangerous* or *this-monster-will-hurt-me-if-I-don't-do-something-about-it*; the same entity can be described as *the-thing-I'm-facing* or *the-thing-I'd-hit-if-I-threw-a-shuriken-now*. As with all other aspects, we see that projections are postulated by an outside observer and not an objective feature of an agent's operation. I will, however, point out several visual routines which are probably best thought of as projections.

Instruction buffer clearing

In most cases, it's obvious when a buffer should be cleared; so obvious that in what follows I won't bother to describe the buffer clearing logic. For example, the instruction buffer for "Get the ghost" should be cleared when the ghost is killed or when visual search for a ghost fails. In a few other cases, it's not obvious when to clear the buffer, and I haven't gotten to implement logic to do so; these instructions currently have unlimited temporal extent.

Defined machine types

MACNET primitively supplies boolean gates and `ifm` switches on arbitrary types. It also provides a way to define new machine types. The only nonprimitive machines Sonja's central system needed compute with directions. For example, one computes the opposite direction from a given one, and another tells whether or not a direction is diagonal. I also used arithmetical machines in the addressing pyramids to implement proximity preference.

8.3   Registering the amazon and its aspects

When Sonja is cold-booted, all the intermediate objects are blanked. It is cold booted when a new Amazon game begins, when the amazon goes down a stairwell to a new level of the dungeon (so that the entire configuration on the screen changes), or on command (for debugging). It's easy to register this condition: a particular marker, `*amazon-marker*`, displayed as a right-pointing triangle, is dedicated to tracking the amazon icon at all times; if the `*amazon-marker*` is blanked, Sonja knows it's been cold booted.

The first order of business when cold-booted is to register the amazon using the visual search algorithm of section 6.2.2. Specifically, Sonja enumerates things whose value for the early dimension `size` is `medium`. It checks each thing to see if it has the conjunction of early features that are criterial for amazonhood, namely being `fiddly` and `diagonal` in addition to having size `medium`. Sonja tracks the amazon when it finds it. If the search fails, the system complains "Hey, I can't find the amazon!".

Sonja registers *the-amazon-is-stuck* in terms of two operators, one of which determines whether the amazon is moving and another of which determines whether it is touching something in the direction it is facing. If the amazon is not moving and it is touching something, it is stuck. (The amazon briefly ceases moving, without being stuck, after shooting.) Sonja also draws a ray from the amazon in the direction it is heading. We'll see that this ray is used in various places to determine where the amazon or its projectiles will end up.

The remainder of this section documents the code which engenders the amazon registration process I've just described.

```
(defun register-the-amazon ()
  (set-input! *found-amazon?*
              (andg (invert *amazon-marker-blanked?*)
                    *amazon-fiddly?*
                    *amazon-diagonal?*
                    (eqm *amazon-size*
                         (constant :medium))))
  (propose uninhibit-amazon uninhibit-return!
    doit? *t*)
  (condition uninhibit-amazon (invert *found-amazon?*))
  (propose find-the-amazon content-address!
    marker *amazon-marker*
    proximity-marker *nil*
    early-dimension (constant 'size)
    early-value (constant :medium)
    doit? *t*)
  (condition find-the-amazon (invert *found-amazon?*))
  (overrides-proposer find-the-amazon
    find-the-monster register-simply
    find-a-door opportunistic-search)
  (propose barf-no-amazon say!
    utterance (constant "Hey, I can't find the amazon!")
    doit? *t*)
  (condition barf-no-amazon
             (andg (invert *found-amazon?*)
                   *content-address!-failed?*))
  (propose track-amazon track!1
    marker *amazon-marker*
    doit? *found-amazon?*)
  (propose check-touching touching?
    marker *amazon-marker*
    direction (port heading direction))
  (setq *amazon-stuck?* (andg (invert *amazon-moving?*)
                              *touching?-result*))
  (propose draw-heading-ray draw-ray!1
    ray *heading-ray*
    origin *amazon-marker*
    direction (port heading direction)
    doit? *found-amazon?*))
```

This bit of code defines a Lisp function, **register-the-amazon**, which when called (with no arguments) creates the chunks of central network responsible for registering the amazon and its aspects. This function does *not* run while Sonja is playing Amazon. It is called just once

during the central-network creation process by a Lisp function called
wire-sonja which creates the whole central network. The body of
register-the-amazon consists mainly of a series of calls on the special
forms of the arbitration macrology. It is just a Lisp function, though, so
there can be other arbitrary bits of Lisp in there, such as calls on setq.
There are also calls on MACNET primitives such as andg and invert.

The first form in the body of register-the-amazon is a call on
set-input!, which sets the input of interface nodes (section 7.1).
found-amazon? holds an interface node, used in several places, whose
output is supposed to say whether or not Sonja is registering the amazon. The input of *found-amazon?* is set to be the conjunction of
four conditions which together determine that the amazon marker is in
fact over an amazon. The global variable *amazon-marker-blanked?*
contains the sensory input wire from the operator which checks to see
whether or not the amazon marker is blanked. *amazon-fiddly?*,
amazon-diagonal?, and *amazon-size* store the early properties
of the location the amazon marker marks. These stored properties are
updated at each step of the visual search.

The next form in register-the-amazon creates a proposer named
uninhibit-amazon. uninhibit-amazon is a proposer for the operator
uninhibit-return!, the operator which clears all the return inhibition
bits in the leaf nodes of the addressing pyramid. The operator takes
one input, the boolean enable line doit?. The condition on uninhibit-
amazon clears return inhibition whenever the amazon marker is found
to be blank, which is to say whenever the system is cold booted and a
new search needs to begin.

The proposer find-the-amazon enables the operator content-address!. The proposer selects the size activation map and supplies
:medium as the desired value. The condition on find-the-amazon ensures content addressing until the amazon is found. Because registering
the amazon is more important than anything else, find-the-amazon
overrides all the other content addressing proposers. Not shown here is
the operation of inhibit-return!, which inhibits rejected items during
a search. This operator is turned on by default in a different part of the
code. Together find-the-amazon and this default implement the visual
search for the amazon.

The proposer barf-no-amazon causes Sonja to complain "Hey, I can't
find the amazon!" when the search fails. It is a proposer for say!,

the operator implementing Sonja's "linguistic" output system. Because there are many other proposers for `say!`, `barf-no-amazon` has a validity condition: it makes a proposal only when the amazon has not been found and search has failed. `*content-address!-failed?*` is an output of the `content-address!` operator; it is high when the `doit?` input was high on the last tick (that is, when content addressing was requested) and all locations with the desired early value have been inhibited.

The proposer `track-amazon` causes one of the tracking operators to track the amazon. The operator is enabled as soon as the amazon is found.

The proposer `check-touching` sets the inputs of the `touching?` operator; it tells `touching?` to see if there's something touching the object under the `*amazon-marker*` in the direction (`port heading direction`). `heading` is an abstract operation whose `direction` port contains the direction given to the motor operator that determines which direction the amazon will go on the next tick. Thus, `check-touching` tells the VRP to check whether the amazon is touching something in the direction it is heading at the time the check is performed. `*touching?-result*` is the boolean output wire of the `touching?` operator. `*amazon-moving?*` is set elsewhere; it contains the output wire of an operator that determines whether or not the thing under the amazon marker is moving on the screen.

The proposer `draw-heading-ray` makes the `*heading-ray*` emanate from the amazon in the direction the amazon is heading. More exactly, it tells the VRP to draw the ray in the same direction Sonja tells the motor system to make the amazon head in. An alternative would be to draw the ray in the perceived direction the amazon is heading; this would make changes in the ray heading lag behind those of the amazon heading by one tick. `draw-ray!1` is one of two ray-drawing operators; we'll see the other, `draw-ray!2`, used in section 8.6. This is an example of the duplication of peripheral operators (see section 6.5).

8.4   Simple registrations

Sonja uses visual searches similar to that for the amazon to register stairwells, piles of bones, and goodies (keys, amulets, potions, knives, and food).

As described in section 5.4.1, instructions that refer to objects typically support visual searches for their referents. Instructions such as "Get the bones," "Head down those stairs," and "Get the *goody*" (where *goody* is one of "key," "amulet," "potion," "knife," or "bread") set buffers that condition visual search proposers. For instance "Head down those stairs" sets the instruction buffer `go-down-the-stairwell` whose validity bit conditions the proposer `register-the-stairwell` which proposes searching for a stairwell. This search is quite efficient, because stairwells have a rare early property, namely `darkness large`; typically there are at most two or three such dark things visible. The termination test for the search is that the stairwell marker be on a stairwell. This means that if the marker is *already* on a stairwell when the instruction is given, no actual search is performed. If search fails, Sonja complains "WHAT amulet" or "WHAT pile of bones" or whatever.

When there's nothing specific that Sonja needs to register, a default proposer for `content-address!` performs *opportunistic registration*. This proposer, `register-opportunistically`, specifies the `*opportunistic-marker*`, the early dimension `darkness` and the desired value `:non-zero`, and thereby enumerates all objects. Sonja checks each object to see if it is interesting: for example if it is a dangerous monster or useful goody. There's no way to avoid enumerating everything if you want to be able to find interesting things of arbitrary types, because there is no single early property that interesting things share that is not also shared by the walls. Accordingly, these default searches can take many ticks, thereby in some instances significantly degrading Sonja's play. This mirrors human performance, and provides useful opportunities for instructions to specify what to look for. When an interesting object is found, the marker for that sort of object is moved with `warp-marker!` to the location of the opportunistic marker.

The instruction "No, the other one" is Sonja's example of a *repair*. It causes Sonja to *reregister* entities. If you say "Get the bones" and Sonja starts heading for the wrong set of bones, you can say "No, the other ones," and Sonja will find another set to head for. When the instruction buffer `no-the-other-one` is valid, visual search is enabled even if the marker is over what would otherwise be a search-terminating object. Thus reregistration simply restarts whatever search process has already occurred.

8.5   Registering scrolls

Scrolls must be registered specially, as it matters whether or not they are ready. (Recall that a scroll is ready when all the characters on it point inward.) I deliberately made registering the readiness of a scroll an expensive operation for Sonja; it must serially check the orientation of each of the four characters in turn, thus tying up attention for a substantial fraction of a second. (This does not, I think, model human registration of scroll readiness, which I suspect depends on unit-time shape-matching; see section 6.6.) Sonja uses `walk-marker!` to move the scroll marker from one character to the next (figure 8.12); the required distances and displacements are specified by constant bits of circuitry. Sonja uses state to keep track of which character it is looking at. This is the only state in Sonja that is reminiscent of a program counter; it is in fact a length-four ring counter. This counter could readily be removed; for example if Sonja used two markers, one of which stayed at the center of the scroll, it could register which character the other marker was on with `marker-to-marker-direction`. However, I specifically invented scrolls to experiment with visual routines involving control state.

Sonja needs to use a bit of state to remember the outcome of the scroll readiness registration routine. This is unfortunate, because the scroll can stop being ready and Sonja won't notice. Again, however, this deliberately mirrors human performance in analogous cases: if, because of capacity limitations, you fail to notice a change, you may do things that wouldn't make sense if you had noticed it. When Sonja finally gets to the scroll, if it runs into it and the scroll does not vanish, that indicates that it has actually stopped being ready, and Sonja then unregisters it and gives up.

Because checking the readiness of scrolls is expensive, Sonja does it spontaneously only when `register-opportunistically` happens to land the opportunistic marker on a scroll. This means that it is useful for a kibbitzer to say "Scroll's ready," lest that event be missed. When that advice is given, Sonja performs a visual search specifically for scrolls (enumerating `diagonal?` things) and uses the readiness-registering routine to check each visible scroll in turn. If it can't find a ready scroll then, it complains "I can't see any ready scroll!". If Sonja is told "Scroll's ready" and has found one and then told "No, the other one," it will look for another.

Figure 8.12
Registering the readiness of a scroll. The scroll marker is over the lower left-hand
character of the nearest scroll.

8.6 Combat

Registration of the enemy is prerequisite to combat. Sonja registers
only one monster at a time, though human players clearly often register
several monsters. There are situations in which Sonja will fare ill as a
result, particularly ones in which a group of monsters too large to fight
off at once threatens to surround the amazon but in which a retreat
is possible. Sonja never retreats because it registers only one monster
at a time and so can not assess the magnitude of a threat. However,
in most cases, the best defense is a good offense, and registering only
the-monster-to-attack is quite adequate. Additional markers could be
used to register more than one monster; a variable diameter attentional
spotlight (section 6.1) might be a good way to implement the registration
of clusters of monsters.

In the simplest case, Sonja simply registers the monster *nearest* the
amazon as *the-monster-to-attack*, using a visual search with proximity
preference. The search enumerates slow-moving things; the only such
objects are monsters and amazons. By default, the search terminates
when either a ghost or demon is found; an instruction to "Get the ghost"
or "Get the demon" specializes the search. Because monsters move, they
have to be tracked, using `track!2`.

Typically the nearest monster will be a ghost, in which case Sonja can
dispatch it quite quickly. Demons are more of a challenge, and because
they can cause damage from afar it is important to kill them as quickly
as possible. Thus, once a demon is spotted, search is inhibited, and
Sonja "locks onto" the demon. (Sonja does not lock onto demons when
it has been explicitly told to "Get the ghost." Another exception is when
Sonja has been told "Get the monster" or "Get the demon" and then
is told "No, the other one." In the latter case, return to the demon is
inhibited, and search is repeated.) Sonja complains if these instructions
are given and no monster of the appropriate sort can be found.

It is important to register demons as soon as possible. Often a human
player will first notice a demon by noticing a fireball near the amazon;
Sonja does likewise, using opportunistic registration to find fireballs.
When a fireball (and its direction of motion) is registered, Sonja uses
`draw-ray!` to extend a ray from the fireball in the opposite direction:
towards its source, a demon. Then Sonja uses `scan-along-ray!` to find
the demon (figure 8.13).

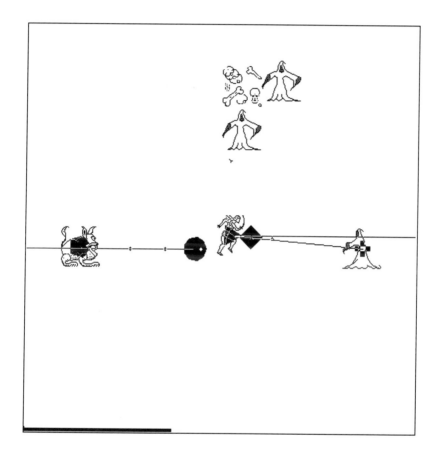

Figure 8.13
Registering a demon from its fireballs. Sonja has noticed the rightmost fireball and tracked it with the nonagonal marker. It has extended a ray from this marker in the direction opposite the fireball's motion and used that to find the demon. Having found the demon and tracked it with the pentagonal marker, Sonja will head for it in order to kill it.

Sonja uses warnings such as "Look out behind you!" to find demons. When such a warning is given, Sonja extends a ray from the amazon icon in the specified direction and uses `scan-along-ray!` to find a demon (figure 8.14). In the case of an intrinsic prepositional use (section 5.4.4), the specified direction is relative to the Amazon; and since the amazon's heading can change rapidly, the direction is latched at the moment the warning is given. This ray search technique often does find the appropriate demon, though sometimes it fails because the demon is not aligned with the amazon well enough for the ray to actually pass through it. A better model of this phenomenon would involve a visual search whose spatial scope was controlled more broadly on the basis of the specified direction. The ray used for finding a demon based on a warning is the same as that used for finding a demon based on a fireball's trajectory, so the two registration routines can not operate simultaneously.

Having registered the monster, Sonja registers whether the amazon is under attack: whether the monster is dangerous. If the monster is dangerous, Sonja needs to dispatch it immediately; otherwise it can be ignored for a while if necessary.

Demons are always dangerous. A ghost is dangerous if it is close by and if it could reach you. Since monsters move at constant speed, a fixed distance threshold is adequate to determine closeness; Sonja uses 100 pixels, as determined by `distance-within?`. A ghost can reach you if you are heading in its general direction; those behind you or on one side are usually no threat because you can run faster. (There are several sorts of exceptions to this rule which Sonja doesn't handle. Sonja's performance could be substantially improved by increasing the accuracy of this registration, but I haven't bothered.) A nearby ghost can also catch up with you if you have just shot at something else, and so are immobilized for a little while.

We'll see later that the navigation code tries to align the amazon with monsters and piles of bones; you have to be aligned with something in one of the eight directions in order to shoot it, because projectiles are sent in the direction the amazon is facing and travel in straight lines. Once the amazon is aligned with the target, it faces it and shoots.

Sonja also shoots *opportunistically*, based on projecting *the-thing-I'd-hit-if-I-shot-now*. Recall that a ray is extended at all times from the amazon in the direction it is headed. Sonja uses `scan-along-ray!` to find the first thing along this ray (dropping the *target* marker on it)

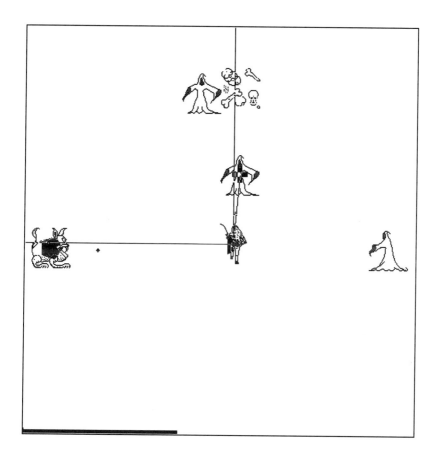

Figure 8.14
Registering a demon based on advice. The instruction "On your left!" has recently
been given. Sonja has extended a ray in the specified direction and used it to find
the demon. On this tick, Sonja has registered the demon; on the next tick it will
turn the Amazon to face and shoot it.

whose `speed` is not `:fast`. This target is what a shuriken would most likely hit if the amazon were to shoot. Since monsters always head toward the amazon, they rarely pass out of the path of a shuriken that has been fired at them. The not-`:fast` constraint allows Sonja to ignore projectiles (shuriken and fireballs) in computing the target.

Unless there are good reasons not to, Sonja shoots whenever it finds that the target marker is on a monster or pile of bones. This opportunism (figure 8.15) dramatically improves Sonja's performance. It seems to me introspectively that I do something much like this when playing; I'm constantly looking out in front of the amazon to see what I would hit. Sonja's performance probably rather *too* good, actually; it can find in unit time things arbitrarily far along the ray, which I'm not sure I can. This may account for Sonja's superhuman combat performance; see section 9.6.2.

The actual conditions under which Sonja shoots are quite complicated. You want to retrieve ready scrolls as quickly as possible, lest they stop being ready before you get to them, and accordingly Sonja does not take opportunistic shots when there is a scroll ready. Sonja does not take opportunistic shots at a pile of bones if it has been given an instruction to do something else, because killing a pile of bones takes many shots and therefore a long time. On the other hand, Sonja is willing to suspend advice in order to opportunistically kill monsters, which typically doesn't take more than a second or two. Sonja doesn't take opportunistic shots at one monster if it is under attack by another, but will rather reorient to face the attacker.

Sonja's motor system, when told both to change direction and to shoot, shoots in either the old or new direction arbitrarily. This could be fixed, but the central system compensates by inhibiting changes of heading when it wants to shoot.

Sonja sometimes throws a knife (rather than a shuriken) to kill a monster or pile of bones. Sonja doesn't have enough global understanding to judge whether an enemy is worth using a knife on, so it is conservative and uses knives this way only when instructed to. But the instruction "Use a knife" is ambiguous as to which way it is to be used; knives can also be used to open doors, and Sonja must decide which is intended. (This is Sonja's clearest example of indexical reference to an activity.) If the amazon is currently heading for a door, demon, or pile of bones, Sonja supposes that the instruction is referring to that target. (This

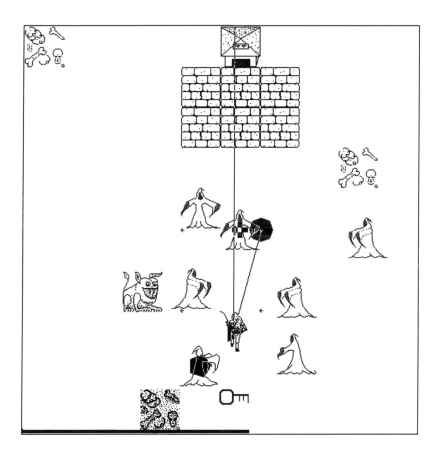

Figure 8.15
Opportunistic shooting. The nearest monster, the pentagon-marked ghost, is
nonthreatening. Sonja has just noticed the knife marked with the octagon and
turned toward it. The heading ray intersects another ghost, that marked with the
cross, indicating that Sonja can shoot it opportunistically.

exploits the fact that the instruction giver can see which direction the amazon is facing, and will reflexively take this into account in giving the instruction. Since instructions can determine focus of attention, the sequence of instructions "Get the monster," "Use a knife" given in rapid succession will unambiguously recommend using the knife on the monster.) Otherwise, if Sonja is currently registering one of these types of objects, it will take that to be the referent. Finally, Sonja will actively look for a door, demon, or pile of bones if it is not already registering one and this instruction is given. Once Sonja has figured out what it will use the knife on, it latches that, because in general it may have to do arbitrary amounts of other stuff before it gets around to actually using the knife; there may be many enemies and obstacles between the amazon and the thing the knife is to be used on.

Sonja complains "Use a knife on WHAT?" if it fails to register any suitable use. (The system does not provide a way for the advisor to answer this question.) Sonja also complains "I haven't GOT a knife!" if the instruction is given and it knows it hasn't got a knife. In this case Sonja ought to try to register a knife on the ground, collect it, and use it, but I haven't implemented that.

The *temporal expression* "Hit it with a knife when it goes light" also suggests using a knife, but is unambiguous about what it is to be used on: a shadowed pile of bones. Recall that such a pile is invulnerable. Sonja registers when a pile of bones goes light, using attentional access to the **darkness** early dimension of the pile. A pile of bones can be seen to have gone light when it is light now, when (using a delay) it was previously dark, and when the marker has not been moved (lest moving it from a dark object to a light pile of bones confuse the issue). When Sonja notices that a pile of bones has gone light, it latches this fact; the latch is cleared when the pile of bones is destroyed or a different pile of bones is registered (due to the operation of "No, the other one") or the pile goes dark again. When this latch is high and Sonja has a clear shot at the pile of bones, it actually throws the knife.

Potions kill all visible enemies, but are scarce. Deciding when it is sensible to use one requires taking into account how bad the current situation is, how bad likely future situations will be, and how many potions you are likely to find in the future. Sonja is not smart enough to estimate any of these factors, so it uses potions only when the instruction "Use a potion" is given it.

8.7   Navigation

I mean "navigation" metaphorically: getting from one point to another
in the dungeon. This problem is quite different from that faced by a
robot navigating in real space because Sonja, like a human player of
Amazon, has a bird's-eye view of the dungeon. I'll describe the relationship between Sonja's approach to navigation and those in the robotics
literature in section 9.6.5.

8.7.1   Uses of navigation

The navigation routines together implement an abstract operation navigate, which takes as its argument a marker which marks a *destination*
to get to.[1] The five proposers for navigate are navigate-to-goody,
navigate-to-monster, navigate-to-stairwell, navigate-to-door,
and navigate-to-bones, representing the five entities that Sonja might
want to navigate to. Arbitration among these five proposers is complex,
and depends on aspects of these entities that Sonja registers and on what
instructions have been given.

navigate-to-goody and navigate-to-stairwell are supported and
objected to by "Get the *goody*," "Head down those stairs," "Don't go for
the *goody*," and "Don't go down yet." These proposers are conditioned
by not being under attack from a monster; if you are under attack, you'd
better deal with it before going after a goody or stairwell. (There are
some exceptions to this, as when the stairwell is nearby and your health is
very low, so that it is a means of escape; Sonja doesn't know about these
cases.) navigate-to-goody is also supported by noticing a ready scroll:
it's important to get to those quickly, before they become unready again.
On the other hand, if the registered goody is a scroll and it is *not* ready,
a condition ensures Sonja will not head for it. navigate-to-monster
is supported by advice to "Get the monster" (or ghost, or demon) and
objected to by "Don't bother with that guy." navigate-to-bones is
supported by "Get those bones" and objected to by "Ignore those bones
for now."

---

[1] It also requires as arguments various properties of the marker, such as the direction from the amazon marker to it; this simplifies the circuitry somewhat, for
uninteresting reasons.

8.7.2   Approach to navigation

There are well-known algorithms for navigating in mazes seen from above; depth-first search is an obvious one, and probably one can't do much better in the general case of complex and deliberately confusing mazes. I have not adopted such a solution. Search algorithms (in the technical sense of "search") violate the constraints of essential connectionism. For instance, they require that you keep an unbounded stack of backtrack points. Moreover, Amazon's mazes are simple enough that it's visually *obvious* how to get about in them; search would be overkill.

It seems cognitively plausible to me that an Amazon player has visual routines whose job it is to determine how to get from one point to another. Navigation thus depends mainly on continuous visual analysis of the current situation; the process is guided by visual feedback and little state is involved. It seems, further, plausible that there are several of these routines, and that they are specific for different sorts of situations. For example, different routines might analyze the scene in terms of obstacles to go around, rooms to go into or out of, or passageways to go down.

A further advantage of this approach is that plausible navigation routines seem to neatly correspond to English prepositions in many cases, so the machinery needed to accept spatial instructions and the machinery needed to get about can overlap heavily. For example, a routine for registering rooms can subserve both the routine for entering them and that for making sense of instructions such as "Go *in* and get the amulet."

I have, in fact, only implemented a few such routines, and they are less general than I'd like; it turned out to be harder to write them than I expected. Half the central system code and well over half the time I spent implementing Sonja went into navigation. I'll talk about the reasons for and implications of this in section 9.6.5. As I explained in section 4.3, since navigation is not a central concern in this work I chose to restrict the sorts of dungeon mazes I'd run Sonja in rather to than implement more general navigation routines. In most situations not covered by the routines I implemented Sonja spins the amazon in place; in some others it heads off in a random direction.

The navigation routines I did implement are not particularly interesting for their own sake—being strictly domain dependent, and not

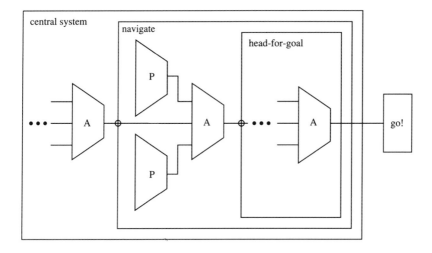

Figure 8.16
The internal structure of the navigation circuits. Various proposers have theories
about where the Amazon should go; these are arbitrated by the leftmost arbiter,
which sets the **destination** port of the **navigate** abstract operation. **navigate**
passes to **head-for-goal** either the destination or one or the other end of a channel
passing through the door to a room. (The room and doorway registrars are not
illustrated but would be at the left end of the **navigate** box.) **head-for-goal**
eventually figures out which direction the amazon should actually go and passes
that to the peripheral operator **go!**. (**head-for-goal** is actually implemented in
terms of yet another abstract operation, **heading**, not illustrated here.)

very successful in their one domain—but I think they are interesting as
examples of complex visuomotor activity.

I implemented routines for heading for a destination, for aligning with
an enemy to get a clear shot at it, for entering and for exiting rooms,
and for passing convex obstacles. Internally, **navigate** is implemented
in terms of another abstract operation, **head-for-goal** (figure 8.16).
navigate figures out whether or not the amazon will have to go through
a doorway to get to the destination. If so, the *goal* is the doorway;
otherwise it is the destination. **head-for-goal** is responsible for getting
the amazon to the goal; it knows how to pass around some kinds of
obstacles on the way.

8.7.3   Head-for-goal and obstacle passing

The abstract operation `head-for-goal` gets the amazon to the goal (which is either the destination or a doorway), passing around obstacles as necessary. `head-for-goal` takes a marker to head for as an argument.[2]

Whenever there is a goal, Sonja uses `draw-line!` to draw a line to it from the amazon. (We've seen this line in several previous figures.) Sonja uses `scan-along-line!` to determine whether this line intersects anything that would constitute an obstacle. Walls and hutches constitute obstacles, as do scrolls unless they are known to be ready.

So long as there is no obstacle, the amazon can head directly for the goal. (Keep in mind that the amazon moves continuously, or, more exactly, one pixel at a time.) This default method is implemented by the abstract proposer `chase-the-goal`, which subsumes `chase-the-goal-normal` and `chase-the-goal-deglitched`. `chase-the-goal-normal` simply sends the amazon in the major component of its direction to the goal. (The major and minor components of directions were explained in section 6.5.3; they are found using `marker-to-marker-direction`.) I'll discuss `chase-the-goal-deglitched` later.

If the goal is a monster, we want to be able to shoot at it, rather than to get to it. If there is no obstacle between the amazon and the monster, traveling in the minor component of the direction from the amazon to the monster will align the two; see figure 8.17. Once aligned with the monster, Sonja turns to face it in order to shoot.

If there *is* an obstacle to getting to the goal (as determined by `scan-along-line!`), a marker is dropped on it (figure 8.18). Typically, the obstacle is a largish object; simply putting a marker on it somewhere is not enough to know how to pass it. In order to discover its extent, Sonja uses `activate-connected-region-of-type!`, passing it the obstacle marker, a type specification for obstacles, and an activation plane. This activates the whole obstacle (figure 8.19). This is the foremost example of Sonja's doing visual work to individuate its own objects. The video game code does not individuate obstacles; it rather represents uniform fifty-pixel square "chunks" of wall at particular coordinates. This code does not represent adjacency relationships between chunks, much less connectedness.

---

[2]It actually also requires the minor and major components of the direction from the amazon to the goal to be passed as arguments.

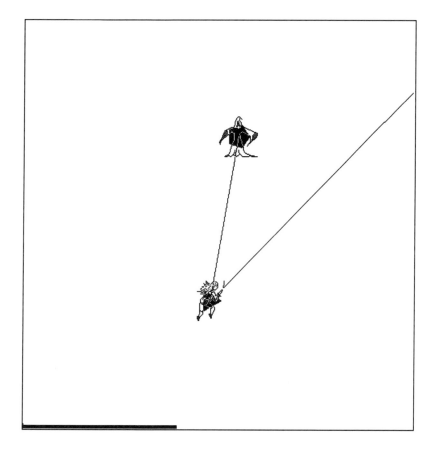

Figure 8.17
Aligning with the goal monster. The major component of the direction to the ghost
is upwards; the minor component is up and right. Heading up and right aligns the
amazon with the ghost so it can shoot at it.

Figure 8.18
Marking the obstacle by finding the first thing along the line between Sonja and the destination. The obstacle marker is the square one.

Figure 8.19
Activating the obstacle with the diagonal increasing hatch pattern plane.

Once we've found an obstacle, we need to discover whether or not it is really the responsibility of `head-for-goal` or of the room registration machinery. The room registration machinery will take over if and only if the obstacle is a room and the amazon is outside it and the destination inside it, or vice versa. (These two cases correspond to entering and exiting respectively.)

Sonja's visual routine for determining whether or not something is in a room is similar to the abstract containment routine proposed by Ullman and discussed in section 3.3.3. To determine whether or not something is in a room, Sonja grows an activated region outward from the thing until it runs into an obstacle boundary. This is the functionality provided by `activate-connected-region-not-type!`, to which Sonja passes the amazon or destination marker, the obstacle type, and an activation plane as arguments. (We've seen this in figure 8.7.) `activate-connected-region-not-type!` knows to skip over short gaps in obstacles, which constitute doorways (section 6.5.6). It also can be directed to fail if it runs into the edge of the screen; Sonja does so direct it. The edge of the screen corresponds to the "point at infinity" of section 3.3.3; if the activated region extends that far, the object is not bounded by a room, or at any rate not one that is currently wholly visible.

If Sonja is in a room and the goal is in the same room, or if neither is in a room, then the entering and exiting code is not applicable. Responsibility for getting to the destination rests in such cases with `head-for-goal`. `head-for-goal`, however, is designed only to *pass* obstacles with the property that neither the amazon nor the goal is in their convex hull. It often succeeds in other cases, and there is some extra circuitry that tries to encourage this, but it is only heuristic. This means that obstacles that are neither rooms nor passable may cause Sonja to do something nonsensical.

The passing code has one decision to make: which way around the obstacle to go. This decision is quite complicated in general. By default, the best way around is the shortest. However, if part of the obstacle is offscreen, the apparently shortest way around may not in fact be shortest. There is an unbounded set of further considerations which depend on where in relationship to the amazon, goal, and obstacle other relevant features may be. Sonja does not take these considerations into account, and so may act suboptimally. This is a good opportunity to give the system a suggestion; the advisor can say "Go over the top" or whatever.

In order to discover which is the shortest way around the obstacle, Sonja finds the centroid of its convex hull. First it uses `expand-to-convex-hull!` to activate the convex hull of the obstacle with the `*temp-plane*`. Then it uses `mark-centroid!` to move the obstacle marker to the centroid of the convex hull (figure 8.20). Sonja can then get an idea of which way around the obstacle is shorter by examining the angle between the goal, the amazon, and the centroid (using `angle-ccw?`). It is usually the case that the shortest way around has the same sign as this angle. In the figure, for instance, the shorter way around is counterclockwise.

Next Sonja needs to determine whether the obstacle extends off screen in the direction the amazon would pass it if we took the apparently shortest way around. If so, it would typically do better to go the other way, because the obstacle might extend arbitrarily far offscreen. Sonja determines whether the obstacle passes off screen by activating the portion it would pass around and determining whether that portion touches the edge of the screen. Specifically, Sonja uses `transect-activated-region!` to activate the portion of the obstacle that is on the appropriate side of the goal line (figure 8.21). Sonja then uses `activation-touches-edge?` to determine if the obstacle runs off the screen in the direction it hopes to pass.

As the amazon moves, the screen may move over the underlying world, and more of the obstacle may be revealed. The newly revealed part will not have been activated. For this reason, the output of `activation-touches-edge?` is latched. A timer is used to force reregistration of the obstacle every few seconds, so that newly revealed parts of it can be taken into account. This kludge would not be necessary if Sonja could afford to continuously update the registration of the obstacle, as would be possible in a parallel implementation.

Thus, finally, Sonja has a best guess as to which way to go around: the apparently shortest way unless that runs off the screen. (Sonja doesn't check to see if the longer way also runs off the screen. In such cases there isn't much to go on, and in any case it never comes up in the mazes I've used.) This guess is overridden by advice such as "Go around the top." Sonja does some simple geometry to determine whether such an instruction advises going clockwise or counterclockwise around the obstacle depending on its position relative to the amazon.

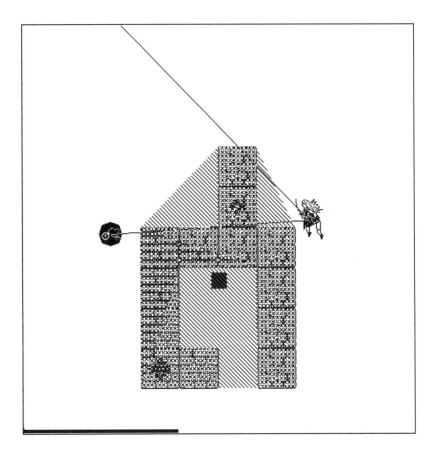

Figure 8.20
Marking the centroid of the convex hull of the obstacle to find the shorter way
around. The shorter way is given by the sign of the angle between the destination,
amazon, and obstacle markers: counterclockwise, in this case.

Figure 8.21
Activating the apparently shorter part of the obstacle on the decreasing hatch
pattern plane. The upper portion is in both activated regions, yielding a lozenge
pattern; overlaid on the bricks, this looks much like a random stipple.

Passing the registered obstacle is implemented by the abstract proposer `pass-obstacle`, which figures out which actual direction to go given knowledge about whether to pass clockwise or counterclockwise. This involves several cases, which are implemented by concrete proposers subsumed by `pass-obstacle`. I'll discuss them in turn.

`initialize-passing` sets the amazon's heading to the major component of the direction to the goal. This is guaranteed to cause the heading ray to pass through the obstacle, a condition Sonja senses with `ray-activated?`. Sonja then tries successively more indirect candidate directions: the proposer `search-for-heading` sets the amazon's heading to be 45 degrees from its current heading, rotated in the direction opposite to that in which the amazon will pass around the obstacle. (See figure 8.22.) `search-for-heading` is valid for as long as the heading ray is activated. The proposer `continue-passing` makes the amazon keep going in a valid direction once one is found.

Eventually Sonja will have gone far enough in the found direction that it can turn to head more directly towards the goal. The proposer `rotate-back-to-check-passing` periodically overrides `continue-passing` and forces Sonja's heading 45 degrees closer to the goal (the opposite rotation from that of `search-for-heading`). (A timer is used to condition `rotate-back-to-check-passing`; it goes off once every 17 ticks.) If the heading ray is still clear of the obstacle, `rotate-back-to-check-passing` applies again, so that it keeps rotating until it has gone too far and has run back into the obstacle (figure 8.23). Then `search-for-heading` will kick in and rotate out one increment so that the ray is in the clear again. In figure 8.24 we see Sonja having gone far enough that a new heading is valid.

This implementation of passing is a good example of Sonja's avoidance of program counters. It involves two "loops": searching for a valid heading and repeatedly rotating back. These loops are emergents resulting from the interaction of various bits of circuitry that "communicate" only via the position of the heading ray. No central system state is involved.

Sonja unregisters the obstacle by blanking the obstacle marker and activation plane. The unregistration routine occurs when the goal line no longer intersects the obstacle activation region, which indicates that the obstacle has been passed; when when the goal has changed, so there may be a different obstacle which should be registered instead; and when the obstacle should be reregistered on account of screen motion.

Figure 8.22
Searching for a heading. Sonja rotates the amazon, and the heading ray,
progressively clockwise, until the ray no longer intersects the obstacle. In this case
Sonja first tries heading left, finds that that intersects with the obstacle, and so
tries heading up and left, then finally straight up, which succeeds.

Figure 8.23
Rotating the heading ray back until it hits the obstacle.

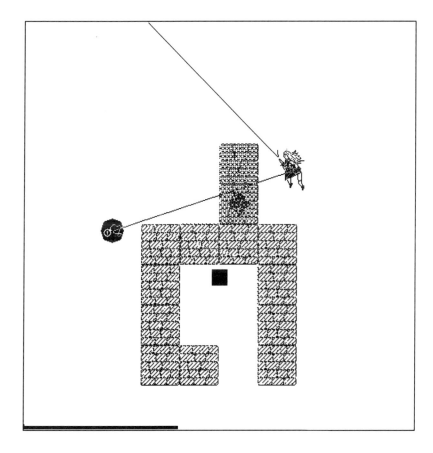

Figure 8.24
Sonja has gone far enough that a new heading will work.

Earlier I mentioned a proposer `chase-the-goal-deglitched`. Deglitching is an unfortunate ugly special case, best explained by reference to a diagram; see figure 8.25. The problem is that because the line runs only from the center of the amazon to the center of the destination, some actual obstacles may not be detected. Sonja can detect this situation: if it is stuck (not moving and touching something) and if no obstacle is registered by the goal line, deglitching is required. Glitching is possible only when Sonja is heading in a nondiagonal direction, because complaint motion guarantees the amazon will head around an obstacle if it is heading in a diagonal direction. Accordingly, Sonja deglitches by switching to one of the two diagonal directions closest to the desired nondiagonal direction. Sonja chooses this direction by using `corner-free?` to check the two corners of the amazon corresponding to the possible diagonal motions to see if they are up against something. For example, in figure 8.25, the two closest diagonal directions are up and to the left and down and to the left. The corresponding corners are the top left and the bottom left ones; of these the top left one is free, so Sonja heads the amazon up and to the left. I'll discuss an alternative to deglitching in section 9.6.5.

8.7.4 Rooms

Recall from section 8.7.3 that Sonja uses an activation operator to determine whether the amazon or the destination or both is in a room. If the amazon is in a room and the destination is not in the same room, the amazon must first exit; if the destination is in a room and the amazon is not, the amazon must enter. The entering and existing routines are also cued by instructions such as "Go on in."

The entering and exiting routines entail first registering the doorway through which to pass. There are three doorway registration routines corresponding to different reasons for passing though one: because you need to enter or exit to get to the destination, because you've been told to "Go in" to an unspecified room, and because you've been told to "Use a knife," perhaps to open a door.

The first doorway registration routine looks for a doorway into the room whose interior has been activated on the room activation plane. This is the room that Sonja must enter or exit. Doorways are defined in terms of gaps between connected edges composed of walls; the routine uses `find-edges!` to find these gaps. It uses `enumerate-gaps!`

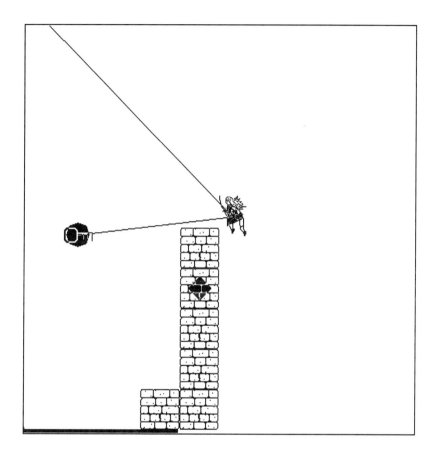

Figure 8.25
Deglitching. In this scene, Sonja would like to move the amazon directly left, as
that is the closest direction to the goal. However, there's a wall in the way. (It
doesn't look as though the amazon is colliding with the wall, but it is. Amazon
represents all objects in terms of the rectangular bounding boxes; the amazon
extends out to the left as far as the sword does.) Because the goal line does not
intersect the obstacle, the normal obstacle passing code does not apply.
Accordingly, Sonja must head in one of the diagonal directions closest to the desired
direction. These are up and to the left and down and to the left. Sonja checks the
corresponding corners of the amazon (the top left and bottom left corners) to
determine which is free; the top left one is. Accordingly, Sonja heads up and left.

to put the outer doorway marker on successive candidates. If a gap is found to be within 50 pixels of the activated region (using `marker-to-activated-region-distance`) it must be a doorway to the room. This routine is also used to register the room the amazon is in when the instruction "OK, head out now" is given. That instruction also causes Sonja to activate the interior of the room the amazon is in so it can find the right doorway. If the amazon is not found to be in a room, Sonja complains "But I'm not IN a room!"

The second doorway registration routine is used to find arbitrary doorways in response to the instruction "Go on in." It also uses `enumerate-gaps!`, but the search criterion is that the gap be a doorway to a room. To determine this, Sonja uses `activate-connected-region-not-type-from-gap!` to attempt to activate the interior of a room opening out from the gap. In general Sonja has to apply this operator twice, once on either side of the gap. Sonja restarts this search when told "No, the other one."

The third doorway registration routine finds an arbitrary door using visual search. This routine is triggered by the instruction "Use a knife." It too is restarted by "No, the other one." (This isn't a natural use of the English instruction; specialized repairs such as "No, use it on the other door" would be easy to add, but I haven't bothered.)

Sonja's strategy for entering through a doorway is first to go to a point just outside it and perfectly aligned with it and then to head for another point just inside it and also aligned with it. This strategy avoids a problem illustrated in figure 8.26: putting a single marker in the middle of the doorway would often make the goal line pass through the walls of the room. This bit of wall can not be treated like other obstacles, but belongs to the room being entered. There actually can be obstacles to getting to a doorway, and Sonja would have to differentiate the two cases. Doing so would be possible, and would allow Sonja to use compliant motion [173] to solve what is in effect a peg-in-hole problem. A compliant solution would be neater, but the one I have adopted does work.

Sonja uses two doorway markers, and outer and an inner one (figure 8.27). As soon as the right doorway is registered, using the outer marker, Sonja uses `warp-marker!` to move the inner marker to the same point, and then `walk-marker!` to move the two markers to their final positions. The right directions to walk the markers depend on the orientation of

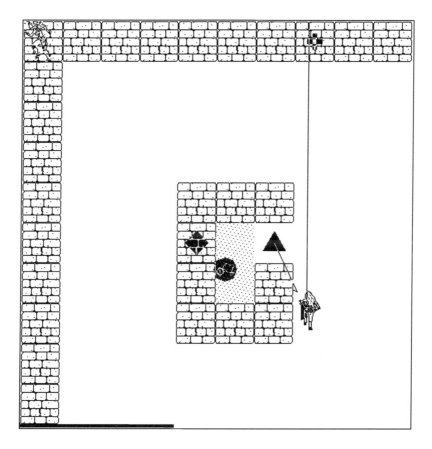

Figure 8.26
If Sonja used only one marker for doorways, it would have to figure out that the bit
of wall the goal line passes through is not an obstacle to be passed, entered, or
exited, but part of the room the doorway belongs to.

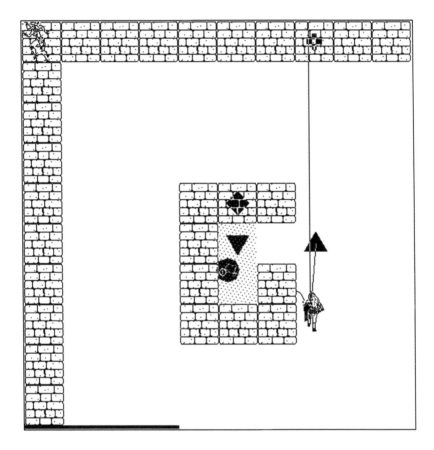

Figure 8.27
Entering a doorway. Two markers mark points just outside and just inside the
doorway. Sonja heads for these points in turn. Here Sonja is heading for the outer
doorway marker.

the doorway, computed by `gap-orientation`.

Two proposers for the abstract operation `head-for-goal` get the amazon to and through the doorway. `head-for-doorway-first-marker` makes the goal be the outer marker (if the amazon is to enter) or the inner one (if it is to exit). Sonja determines when the amazon has reached the first doorway marker using `markers-coincident?` and latches this fact. This latch is used to enable `head-for-doorway-second-marker`, which sends the amazon through the doorway. Sonja unregisters the doorway when it has passed through it, or when it changes its destination.

Recall that Sonja always has a destination as well as a goal. When Sonja is told to "Go in" or "head out," the destination is one of the doorway markers. This is implemented by the `navigate` proposer `navigate-to-doorway`.

When Sonja runs into a door in the course of passing through a doorway, it must open it with a key or knife. Sonja prefers to use keys, since knives can also be used to kill monsters. It will use a knife if it has no key or if it has explicitly been told to "Use a knife."

Instructions such as "Go in and get the amulet" depend on the entering routine: once an amulet in a room is found, the usual navigation routines take over and get the amazon in. Thus, unlike instructions such as "Get the potion and set it off," in which temporal sequencing depends on instruction buffer chaining, the sequencing of "Go in and get the amulet" falls out of the physical constraints of the domain automatically. There is no way to get the amulet without going into the room first.

The instruction buffer `in-the-room` is used to signal that an entity referred to in an instruction must be in a room. As we've seen Sonja has to check each new destination to see if it is in a room anyway, in case it has to enter. `in-the-room` operates by restarting referent searches if the found referent is discovered *not* to be in a room. This means that the entire "Go in and..." class of instructions actually involves only two lines of code in addition to that already required for room entering.

8.7.5 Suggested-go

The instruction buffers `suggested-go` and `suggested-not-go` correspond to instructions such as "Head left" and "Don't go up." They use proposal support and proposal objection to affect proposers for navigate and for wander (described in section 8.7.6). Because of the way proposal support and objection are latched (section 7.2.5), they continue to affect only the proposer they are relevant to at the time the instruction is given. Thus in effect Sonja latches the activity indexically referred to by the instruction.

suggested-go is cleared only when the amazon gets stuck against a wall trying to carry it out. This is indeed one way to see that the advice is no longer relevant, but there are many others I haven't implemented. suggested-not-go is one of the several instruction buffers that is never cleared (because the conditions under which that should be done are complicated, and I didn't get around to implementing it). (This doesn't mean that once you say "Don't go up" Sonja never will. It means it won't go up on the say-so of the proposer which was suggesting going up at the time you gave the instruction.)

8.7.6   Wandering

If Sonja is not registering any destination (which happens only when there is nothing on the screen except obstacles and the amazon) it has no way of knowing which way to go. (Remember that it has no memory for things off the screen.) It will, therefore, *wander* randomly unless advised otherwise.[3] Wandering is implemented by the abstract proposer wander. The subproposer wander-randomly picks a random direction to wander in. Once Sonja has started wandering, the proposer keep-wandering-in-same-direction keeps a steady heading. This proposer actually senses the current direction of motion, thus in effect using the world to keep track of three bits worth of state. When the amazon gets stuck (by wandering into an obstacle) wander-randomly kicks in again and chooses a new direction.

Eight additional proposers, one for each direction, are used to implement wandering per advice. These are supported by instructions such as "Head left" using proposal support.

---

[3]Wandering has been partially described in section 7.2.4.

9 Analysis

This chapter analyzes Sonja with an eye to evaluation. I have presented both some ideas and an implementation; the chapter tries to determine how they relate to each other. (Numerous local analyses and suggestions for future research appear elsewhere in the book.)

There much disagreement over how to evaluate AI research in general. Section 9.1 begins the chapter with a philosophical discussion of this problem. I argue that much AI research contributes approaches rather than specific technical results, and that this is legitimate. I also argue that the role of an implementation in an AI paper is as an illustration, and that the process of implementing an AI system is itself a valuable form of understanding.

Section 9.2 considers Sonja as an implementation of the concrete-situated approach to activity described in chapter 2. Sonja successfully demonstrates most but not all aspects of this approach.

Section 9.3 discusses Sonja's architecture. The principal conclusion is that the problem of action selection is easy and has been overemphasized.

Section 9.4 analyzes Sonja's instruction use, particularly issues in reference and reflexivity. Sonja illustrates most of the themes of chapter 5.

Section 9.5 analyzes Sonja's visual system. I discuss the problems of early vision, object recognition, and three-dimensional vision which Sonja passes over. I also analyze the VRP in terms of a set of global criteria posed in section 6.4.

Section 9.6 evaluates the system as a whole. I evaluate Sonja as a technology for concrete activity and for Amazon playing in particular. I discuss navigation particularly.

9.1 Evaluation

9.1.1 Results and approaches

There is no generally-agreed upon way to evaluate work in AI. This poses both practical and theoretical problems for the field: it makes it hard both to choose research directions and to justify the value of the field as a whole.

Many intellectual fields have generally accepted standards for research. These standards define what it means to be a *result* in the field. By a result I mean a piece of work reported in the accepted way. (Research may have many results, in the everyday sense of the term, which do not constitute results in this sense.) Different fields have different criteria of resulthood. These criteria are complex, and mastering them is a large part of becoming a skilled practitioner in the field. Speaking roughly, however:

- In mathematics, *theorems* are results.
- In science, *experiments* that test *theories* are results.
- In engineering, *demonstrably superior technologies* are results.
- In philosophy, *rigorous arguments* are results.[1]

AI has partly adopted each of these criteria of resulthood. Some AI papers contain theorems, experiments, technologies, arguments, or combinations of these. There is much argument within the field as to the relative importance of these criteria. There are, for instance, AI researchers who insist that unless a paper has a new theorem in it, it's not worth reading. That AI has no criteria for resulthood of its own, and must make do with those inherited from other fields, is part of what makes it hard to evaluate AI research, and part of the reason AI is fragmented into mutually incomprehending schools.

The problem runs deeper than this, however. Many of the most respected and influential papers in AI contain no results of any of these sorts. Three examples are Hayes's Naive Physics Manifestos [115, 116], McCarthy's Advice Taker paper [175], and Minsky's Frames paper [184]. These papers prove no theorems, report no experiments, offer no testable scientific theories, propose technologies only in the most abstract terms, and make no arguments that would satisfy a serious philosopher. Do these papers offer results of some other sort, a sort perhaps unique to AI? I think not.

What these papers offer, I think, is an *approach*. An approach is a way of doing research: a way of looking at phenomena, of choosing issues to explore, of stating and attacking problems. These papers have been influential because they show us powerful ways of thinking about the central issues in AI. They repay reading over and over: turning to the Frames paper when stuck will often yield fresh inspiration and new ideas.

---

[1]In Anglophone philosophy at any rate. Continental philosophy works differently.

I think that most researchers read papers AI papers with an implicit understanding that some of the best ones offer ways of thinking rather than results. I think that there are two reasons this understanding is sometimes resisted. First, criteria of resulthood inherited from other fields are justified partly by the authority of those fields. For instance, one can argue that theorems are important because mathematicians say so, and mathematics is safely established as the Queen of the sciences. AI is less well established and perhaps insufficiently secure to adopt its own criteria of resulthood. Second, approaches are inherently nebulous; it is harder to determine whether a paper contains a new approach than to determine whether it contains a new theorem. It is also difficult to evaluate approaches. However, it is difficult to evaluate results as well. Once one has determined that a paper contains a new theorem, one must ask whether the theorem matters. There are no guidelines for making this judgment. Thus, criteria of resulthood only postpone the real problem of evaluation.

AI has, thus far, produced no theorems important enough to be commonly known by name in the field, let alone any known in computer science or mathematics generally. With the exception of work in early vision, AI has produced few scientific theories that have withstood testing; and indeed few AI papers report experiments that would be recognized as rigorous by a biologist. AI has produced many technologies, but few have been demonstrated as superior to alternatives. It is common for mainstream computer scientists to say of AI that the few worthwhile programs it has produced could have equally well been implemented in C using standard software engineering techniques and that the bulk of work in the field has no obvious application. This is quite true, but misses the point: AI technologies are for the most part not interesting for their short-term applications but for their role in a broader view of what it takes to create intelligence. That is, their value derives from the approaches that gave rise to them. Finally, AI has produced few solid philosophical arguments; philosophers of mind, including those who propound computational theories of mind, routinely ignore work done by AI researchers.

This is not, I think, cause for shame. We should, rather, accept that AI is *largely about* approaches, and not feel that this makes the field "unscientific" or "immature."

Reading an AI paper is harder in some ways than reading papers in

the other fields I've mentioned. It requires a deeper engagement of the
critical faculties. One must ask not merely "does this paper have a
result in it?" but "is this paper saying something important?" There
is no formula for answering this question. This difficulty can make AI
frustrating, but also makes AI more interesting. We should celebrate it.

9.1.2 Implementations

Most AI papers report on an "implementation": that is, a program
which stands in some relationship to the text of the paper. What is that
relationship? Why do we do implementations?

There are two obvious answers, derived from scientific and engineering
practice respectively. On the first account, an implementation might be
an experiment testing a theory, or an apparatus with which to conduct
such an experiment. This story could account for only the small fraction of AI work which involves testable scientific theories. On the second
account, an implementation is an instance of a technology, and can be
subjected to empirical tests to demonstrate its superiority. This story
does not explain why most AI programs, including most of the famous
ones, are subjected to only cursory testing and are rarely systematically
compared with alternative technologies. Researchers who believe that
AI should be more like science or more like engineering argue that implementations should be required to test theories or that they should be
subjected to rigorous comparative efficacy testing. I believe that while
experiments with and tests on implementations can indeed be valuable
(just as I think theorems and arguments can be valuable) I think that
implementations are typically valuable for other reasons. I believe that
this is implicitly recognized by most AI researchers. Papers describing
systems that run only on a few carefully selected examples are regularly
accepted by journals and are in many cases regarded as seminal. I believe that this is, again, not something we should be ashamed of, but
something we should accept as an integral part of the nature of AI.

I believe that implementations in AI most often serve as *illustrations*
of approaches. Approaches are in large part inarticulable. They are
learned largely by apprenticeship: if you study with a connectionist or
a logicist, you will learn to think and talk and write like a connectionist or a logicist. Yet the individual nature of apprenticeship means it
can disseminate new approaches only slowly; papers transmit ideas more
broadly and so more quickly. If we can not fully articulate approaches,

they must be communicated largely by example. An approach is a way of doing research; an implementation provides an illustration of that way. Like a diagram, an implementation is a concrete artifact which communicates an abstraction. An implementation successfully communicates an approach when it engenders imitations. NOAH [238] is a good example: though Sacerdoti's thesis makes few if any theoretical claims and though he reports only a handful of trivial tests of the program, NOAH has spawned hundreds of variants. Approaches are learned in part from the practice of reimplementing illustrative programs.

Other sorts of illustrations are possible. For example, Hayes's Naive Physics Manifesto argues for a particular way of doing research involving logical axiomatizations of physical phenomena. By itself, the paper might have been too abstract to be influential. Accordingly, he illustrated it with the Ontology for Liquids paper [117], which provides an example of the sort of research he advocates. The importance of this paper is not that Hayes provided the right ontology for liquids (he probably didn't, and an ontology of liquids is in any case of limited inherent interest) but that it demonstrates that concrete work of the sort the Manifesto proposes is possible. These two papers have enabled researchers to productively analyze many other aspects of naive physics.

Why illustrate approaches with programs, specifically? An AI implementation is a designed artifact. Following Cross [50], I believe that *design is a way of knowing.* It is often thought that the value of design derives from the usefulness of the artifacts it produces, or from the explicit theoretical knowledge that results from the design process. Cross argues, in contrast, that design has *intrinsic* value apart from these derived forms of value. Designing is itself a way of making contact with and thereby understanding the world. This form of understanding can not be directly communicated; it must be experienced. This experience is facilitated by examination of designed artifacts. In other words, learning design requires illustrations.

Cross's paper explains the widespread but rarely articulated intuition that implementation is not merely theory testing but is the center of AI practice; that understanding flows principally from the design process. Cross suggests that design, as a way of knowing, is focused on synthesis, rather than analysis, and that it is solution-directed, rather than problem-directed. These aspects of AI implementation balance and complement the analytical and problem-centered focus of the result-oriented practices that derive from other fields.

9.1.3   How to evaluate this work

This book offers relatively few results; its value, if any, lies mainly in its approach and in the illustrative value of the implementation.

In terms of the criteria of resulthood I've discussed,

- The book has no theorems.
- The book describes no experiments. Many aspects of the visual architecture are sufficiently precise and detailed that they could be taken as theories about the human brain and subjected to psychophysical experiment. I would find such experiments interesting, but I am not particularly committed to any of these aspects of the architecture.
- I have presented some arguments, principally in chapter 3 (on architecture). I like the argument that skill acquisition implies a visual routines architecture, for instance, but it certainly would not hold up under rigorous logical scrutiny.
- The book could be construed as offering a technology for building situated agents. My earlier work with Agre on Pengi [5] has often been so construed, and Pengi is often cited as the first "reactive planning" system [7]. We have argued elsewhere [7] that the technologies in Pengi and Sonja are indeed superior to some alternatives, but I have not focused on such comparisons in this book. As I said in section 2.4, I don't think these technologies are especially interesting in their own right.

This book should be evaluated the same way other AI papers offering approaches should be evaluated. Did it suggest new ways of looking at your research problems? Did you get new ideas from reading it? Does the way I have incorporated neuroscientific and psychophysical evidence appeal to you? Are you inspired to build systems similar to Sonja? If so, the approach I have outlined is useful.

9.2   The concrete-situated approach

An approach, I've argued, is largely ineffable. Nevertheless, in chapter 2 I've tried to make explicit part of the concrete-situated approach I have taken to constructing Sonja. This section argues that Sonja successfully demonstrates most but not all aspects of this approach to activity.

Sonja is a model of *routine* activity. There is much that we still don't know about routine activity, but Sonja's success suggests that some of what we do know may be right. Sonja effectively exploits routineness; the implementation is able to cope with what would otherwise be a difficult domain by separating routine performance from novel problem solving. Sonja addresses only the former; an account of the latter will eventually be necessary. The concrete-situated approach holds that routine activity should be understood before novel activity; our eventual understanding of novel cases will rest on our understanding of the routine ones.

Sonja makes extensive and varied use of its concrete *situation* in choosing what to do at each moment. Most importantly, its activity is grounded in perception. It does not need to simulate or reason from first principles. Sonja can also exploit certain aspects of its social situation, specifically by making sensible use of externally supplied instructions. These instructions are similar to those actually given by human video game experts.

Sonja's activity is *interactive*. Sonja is constantly engaged in tight interaction with other processes (monsters) that are beyond its control. Sonja's activity is immediately responsive to opportunities and contingencies that arise in the course of activity. Accordingly, Sonja routinely engages in patterns of activity that more complex than its own structure considered in isolation predicts.

Sonja's activity is *improvised*. The system recomputes at each instant what it should do next. This gives its activity greater flexibility than systems based on control structure ideas can exhibit.

The improvised organization of Sonja's activity leads to a broad variety of emergent *dynamics*. For instance, the system can and regularly does interleave actions that are in pursuit of distinct goals, exhibit hierarchically organized activity, interrupt an activity to pursue an emergent possibility, attempt alternative means to an end, abort a course of activity when it becomes clear it will not succeed, and keep retrying a method until it finally succeeds, all without any machinery specifically dedicated to these effects.

Sonja's activity regularly falls into *routines* that are determined jointly by the structure of the system and the structure of its environment. These routines operate at various levels of abstraction. If you put Sonja into the same dungeon ten times, it will act much the same way each

time. It won't act *quite* the same way, because its activity is partly
random (specifically in wandering, section 8.7.6), and more importantly
because its environment is partly random. So Sonja has a routine for
getting itself out of the nasty situation it finds itself in when the game
begins, and a routine for getting into the room that's just off the left
of the screen when the game begins, and so on. None of these routines
are reflected in the code, which makes no assumptions about dungeon
layout. More abstractly, Sonja has a characteristic way of getting into
rooms (involving getting first to a point just outside the doorway) which
is also a routine, and one which does reflect specific machinery. Similarly, your routine for making coffee in the morning may or may not
involve machinery in your head that makes reference to your specific
coffee pot. Routines, we see, are a dynamic phenomenon which can not
be understood by reference to mental machinery alone.

Sonja's activity exploits *deictic representation*. Standard AI representation schemes would be a liability in playing Amazon; they represent
both too much (everything on the screen, regardless of relevance) and
too little (because they don't directly represent functionality). Sonja in
each Amazon-playing situation represents exactly and only the things it
needs to. The causal grounding of Sonja's deictic representations gives
it the access to the domain it needs for tight interaction. The representations don't get out of date and do provide the information needed for
effector control.

Sonja does *not* model two important aspects of the concrete-situated
approach, *development* and *embodiment*.

Because Sonja does not model development, it is domain-specific, does
not improve its performance with practice, and is blind in the face of
certain sorts of novel situations. Appendix B suggests some preliminary
approaches to these problems.

Sonja does not have a body. It does have a perceptual system, which
is one aspect of embodiment, but it has no real effectors. It does not
have a location in space. (The *amazon* has a location, but the amazon
is no more Sonja's body than it is a human player's body.) Sonja has
no bodily experience. Partly as a consequence it has no real model of
motivations. Research on robotics in frameworks similar to that I took
in Sonja (e. g. by Brooks [28, 29], Connell [46], Mel [179], and Kaelbling
and Rosenschein [141]) suggests direction for research on embodiment.
However, none of these projects have faced issues like the physical dy-

namics of effectors, tactile sensing, or proprioception. I believe that it is time to do so; it may turn out that the implications of problems in motor control will be as far-reaching for central system research as those of problems in perception have been.

9.3   The architecture

Sonja is an *essential connectionist* architecture (section 3.1). This suggests that similar systems could be implemented in neural hardware. Sonja's operation involves no use of some technologies that essential connectionist hardware makes expensive: pointers, variables, inspectable data structures, dynamic storage allocation, or virtual machines. Like many other successful connectionist architectures, it demonstrates that some forms of complex activity are possible without these devices.

Sonja has no modularity in its central system. This lends some credence to the hypothesis of section 3.2.1 that the human central system has no modularity. However, Sonja does not do many of the things the human central system does, and it is possible that other cognitive activities are implemented by separate modules.

In my thesis proposal, I wrote that "I expect the first two stages of Sonja's central network—the aspect registrars and activity proposers—will not be much more code than those of Pengi. Sonja's arbitration network *will* be much more complex." This turned out to be wrong. Sonja's arbitration network is not much more complex; the added complexity is in the registrars and in the visual system itself. It turns out that choosing what to do is easy once you know what's in front of you.

It's not hard to guess why I made this mistake. Several researchers interested in activity (notably Agre, Brooks, Kaelbling, Rosenschein, and myself) realized around 1985 that planning was not an adequate theory of it. Planning is a theory of how to get a system to do the right thing at the right time; we figured we had to provide an alternative. Accordingly, our first papers on activity were about this problem; we came up with ideas like subsumption [25], goals as parallel program specifications [139, 141], dependency networks [3] and action arbitration [5].

Which of these alternatives is best? This turns out to be a non-question. They all work fine; none of them is hard to use, because choosing what to do just isn't difficult. It seems likely that any scheme which is reasonably programmable will work fine. What turns out to be even harder than we expected is perception. (These same conclusions are reported by Flynn and Brooks [88], by Horswill [129], and by Kaelbling (personal communication).) Since our early work there has developed a burgeoning field of work on action selection and complex execution systems. I suspect that this field will exist only so long as it is considered acceptable to test these schemes without a realistic perceptual interface. Workers who have confronted perception have found that on the one hand it is a much harder problem then action selection and that on the other hand once it has been squarely faced most of the difficulties of action selection are eliminated because they arise from inadequate perceptual access in the first place.

There are, of course, some domains and tasks in which choosing what to do is difficult; among these are ones that problem-solving research has focused on. It may be that when we address such domains, research on action selection will become relevant again; but for those who are concerned with embodied activity, there will be several decades of research on more pressing problems.

9.4   Instruction use

9.4.1   General discussion

My primary motivation for implementing Sonja was to illustrate the idea that instructions must be interpreted in terms of their situation of use (section 5.2). Sonja is successful in this; the instructions it uses cannot simply be executed, but must indeed be made sense of. Sonja makes use of two sorts of resources from a situation in interpretation: its perceptual access to the situation and its knowledge of its own current projects. Sonja thereby implements some aspects of the causal theory of reference.

Sonja does not make use of some other resources that are available to people, particularly linguistic context, history more generally, and social interaction. I have suggested some ways these could be incorporated, but much further work is needed. I would like particularly to understand what sort of state one must maintain to engage in extended dialogs and to further understand linguistic repair processes. These could be combined by extending Sonja to participate in negotiated reference, as described by Clark and Wilkes-Gibbs [41].

Sonja uses a wide variety of sorts of instructions (section 5.4.4), suggesting that the approach has broad applicability. On the other hand, there are many sorts of instruction use that are not modeled; section 5.1 explained that Sonja is restricted to the use of immediate, situated, syntactically simple instructions, and is able to make little use of interaction with an instruction giver to clarify instructions it does not understand.

In section 5.4, I argued that two components of making sense of instructions were attention reorientation and activity management. Sonja implements both of these ideas successfully. Implementing the first required incorporating into Sonja a detailed theory of visual attention (section 6.1). Instructions given to Sonja do reorient its attention, and this does result in Sonja acting differently. Implementing sense making in terms of activity management required an extension to Pengi's theory of arbitration, namely discrimination (section 7.2.5), which allows instructions to affect action decisions that Sonja doesn't know enough to make itself. This implementation gives Sonja's instruction use flexibility. Specifically, Sonja can interleave the use of an instruction with other urgent activities, can interpret an instruction in terms of its current projects, and can reject instructions that obviously make no sense.

In section 5.2.4, I argued that instructions must be interpreted *reflexively*, in terms of mutual understanding. I took a passive approach to reflexivity in Sonja: mutual understanding is the result of similarities between the mental machinery of the conversational participants. This approach was successful in Sonja, and seems to be sufficient for the sorts of instructions Sonja is intended to use. This passive approach will certainly not be sufficient in general; a representational approach will be required in many cases.

One way to evaluate Sonja's instruction use is to ask what it is like to be the system's advisor. Does it do the right thing when you tell it to? How often does it need advice? Can you give it the instructions you'd like to, or is the set of instructions it can use too limited?[2] It's hard to answer these questions because so far I am the only person who has acted as the system's advisor, and I understand its operation too well.

---

[2] A test of these questions should involve running the system with intermediate object display (section 6.3) turned off, so that the advisor would have no special access to the system's state.

My impression is that it usually does make the right use of instructions, that it needs advice about as often as a human novice, and that the set of instruction you can give it is indeed annoyingly limited. However, the instructions I find myself wanting to give it are mostly similar to those that it can use, suggesting that no new techniques would be needed to achieve adequate coverage.

Sonja's instruction use is intended to point towards a theory of *plan use*. In [7, 36], Agre and I argue that the plans used by people must also be made situation-specific sense of to be useful. The principal difference between plans and the immediate instructions used by Sonja is that a plan's user must figure out which part of the plan is relevant to the current situation, where as instructions are given at roughly the time they are needed. Some of the instructions given to Sonja, like "Get the potion and set it off," involve temporal sequencing, require that Sonja keep track of which step it is carrying out, and therefore constitute simple plans.

Sonja's instruction use is also intended to point towards new theories of language use generally. Extending the system by incorporating ideas about syntax and semantics would further this extension. Adding a lexicon to the system would motivate inquiry into the pervasive indexicality of individual words and the puzzling phenomenon of *polysemy* [160, 201, 203].

9.4.2   Some specific issues in reference and reflexivity

In many cases, Sonja determines the referent of an indexical noun phrase like "the amulet" by a visual search for the *nearest* object of the given type. It is surprising that such a simple interpretation suffices so often. There are two reasons for this. The first is that in cases in which a simple interpretation will *not* suffice, the advisor can be reflexively counted on to further specify which object is meant. The advisor can be counted on in this way because she will reflexively understand that Sonja (or any other instruction user) is likely to make the simplest interpretation possible. The second reason is a property of Sonja's domain: for the most part, the functional significance of an object is given solely by its type and proximity. In other words, all amulets are functionally equivalent, so if you have to decide which one to get, you might as well get the closest one. Objects wear their function on their sleeves, as it were. This is in contrast with Pengi's domain, Pengo, in which any given ice cube can take on many different functional roles depending on the circumstances: it can be a projectile to kick at a bee, or a projectile a bee has kicked at you, or one a bee might be about to kick at you, or it could be a "stop" which will allow you align another cube to kick it at a bee (see [7, p. 9]), or part of a wall of a corridor you or a bee is going down, it could be used to block what would otherwise be a bee's escape route, or to hold in place a cube that will soon hatch a bee larva unless you kick it to bits. Thus in a domain like Pengo, the functions of objects are mainly determined by their relationships with other objects, rather than by their types. Consequently, domains like Pengo provide more opportunities for interesting methods for determining referents than Amazon does. I originally found Pengo interesting as a domain because of the varied functional significance of ice cubes; unfortunately I forgot this criterion when I chose Amazon as a domain.

Sonja finds a referent for "Go in and get the amulet" by enumerating amulets and checking each to see if it is in a room. This illustrates a more general technique, reference to an entity by way of its relationship with another, unspecified entity. "On your right!" is an example of reference by relating to a specified entity (the amazon in this case). In my studies of collaborative videogame playing, the majority of references are in relation to the two player icons: a player will say "you get this one and I'll go ahead," and "this one" will refer to the thing that is near the speaker, and contrasts with "that one," which refers to the one that is near the hearer. More generally, "this" and "that" refer not simply by proximity but by accessibility; if it is clear that the nearer of two objects is the harder to get, "this" will refer to the further one. (This point has been explored by Fillmore [82] and Hanks [114], and is an illustration of the point that language is grounded not merely in Cartesian space but in lived space: space structured by concrete and social activity.)

A particularly interesting form of indexical interpretation I have not implemented in Sonja is that in which not only the referent but even the method by which the referent is determined depends on the context. When one carpenter says to another "Pass the nail," the hearer looks for nails in the box or on the ladder or whatever. When the speaker says "Give the nail another whack" the hearer looks for a nail in the wall. This reveals another problem with Amazon as a domain: it's spatially uniform. To a first approximation, anything is as likely to be anywhere as anywhere else. This makes it difficult to find cases of this sort of indexicality and difficult to find interesting sorts of visual search. One way this sort of indexicality might show up is if the hearer could be depended on to know the structure of the dungeon (which is constant from game to game) and so where things are found in it. In many videogames, part of getting better is learning the maze, being able to recognize scenes and project where monsters and goodies are going to appear. Since Sonja does not maintain this sort of "cognitive map," it does not provide an opportunity for the sort of indexical interpretation in which the interpretation method depends on the context.

Sonja takes the obstacle referred to in "Go around the top" to be whichever one it has *already* registered. The validity of this and similar interpretations depends on passive reflexivity: the advisor can see which way the amazon is heading and what in the way and almost certainly means to refer to that. Sonja can understand the advisor because the two can depend on their having the same take on the situation. The obstacle that is referred to is the one that *makes sense*. Similarly, Sonja takes the referent of "Get the amulet" to be the amulet it is *already* looking at if there is one; the probable correctness of this interpretation depends on Sonja and the advisor having similar methods for choosing what to look at. In this case, the probability of correctness is quite high, because, as I explained earlier, the domain constraints are such that a very simple strategy for choosing which amulet to look at (the nearest one) is almost always adequate.

9.5 Vision

Sonja's visual system addresses several fundamental but often neglected visual problems: selective application of visual processing to subsets of the image, search for regions of the image with task-relevant properties, and the computation of spatial relationships among parts of the image. These problems arise in most visual tasks. The visual system's design is motivated by psychophysical and neurophysiological evidence. Because this evidence does not constrain all aspects of the design, I have made many interpolations based only on engineering considerations. These interpolations pose new open problems in vision research, many of which could readily be addressed psychophysically.

By connecting visual mechanisms with a natural task domain, Sonja demonstrates that they are in fact useful. Sonja engages in complex, real-time visually-guided activity. Previous work, particularly in robotics, has also connected vision with action. Sonja improves on this work by combining better theories of vision and activity and by tightening the coupling. Sonja's architecture for activity is specifically designed to support task-specific vision, and the book proposes a clean and biologically plausible interface between vision and the central system.

The implementation of Sonja's visual system finesses two hard issues, early vision and object recognition, and raises the question of whether the model could be extended to address these issues. I'll discuss these problems in sections 9.5.1 and 9.5.2. Sonja's domain is two dimensional; section 9.5.3 considers the problem of extending the vision model to three dimensions. Section 9.5.4 evaluates Sonja's VRP according to the set of criteria posed in section 6.4.

9.5.1 Bypassing early vision

Sonja completely bypasses all of the standard difficulties with early vision, such as noise and illumination variations. However, the video game domain would make it hard *not* to bypass these difficulties: video game graphics model uniform illuminance and are themselves noise-free. There are some effects such as the specularity of the face of the CRT screen (which is minimized by the low lighting in game arcades), but these are quite minor. Thus the bypassing does not seem like a major issue once the domain is accepted. It does raise the issue of whether this model of vision can be extended to domains in which early vision is harder. Unfortunately, other research on intermediate vision has similarly failed to address this issue. The relevant psychophysical studies use clean, evenly lit displays with highly discriminable stimuli. Ullman's visual routines paper uses as examples diagram interpretation tasks in which noise issues can be ignored, and this tradition has been continued by other researchers in the area. Noise sensitivity is a serious issue because it is the job of the visual operators to crunch noisy retinotopic arrays down to compact encodings, carrying boolean values in many cases. So unlike the outputs of early vision, which vary continuously, the outputs of visual operators may be *very* wrong if they are not exactly right. Thus, they had better not be sensitive to noise. Is it possible to implement noise-insensitive operators that perform operations similar to those in Sonja? This is an open question on which the plausibility of the model rests. In current research I am constructing a VRP similar to that of Sonja's but based on a real-time early vision constructed by Nishihara [197, 198], and hope to use it in support of a robot system.

9.5.2 Object recognition

Connecting the visual operators directly to the game datastructures gives them segmentation and object recognition for free. This is a serious concern. I offer three mitigating factors: in the Amazon domain it would be hard not to cheat; object types in video games mostly coincide with pop out properties; and Sonja does some object recognition beyond that provided by direct access.

First, it would again be hard *not* to cheat at Amazon object recognition, because the number of types of objects that can appear on the screen is small and because the hard issues in object recognition (occlusion, the rotational instability of features, non-rigid motion, and family resemblance) are not found in the domain. Thus almost any recognition scheme would work fine and nothing would be learned by going to the trouble of implementing one. So it seems reasonable to finesse object recognition once you have accepted the choice of domain.

The second mitigating factor depends on the fact that video games move too quickly for the full object recognition machinery to be brought to bear. Video game designers accordingly exploit tacit understanding of visual search phenomena; they imbue objects which are supposed to be easy to recognize with distinctive combinations of early visual properties. Objects are often actually distinguished by pop out properties. It is rare for video game object recognition to require shape matching or more complex recognition processes.

Giving the visual system access to the icon datastructures does not fully finesse object recognition. What constitutes an object for the Amazon code and what constitutes an object for Sonja differ in some cases, so that Sonja has to do significant work to identify objects. In particular, the game code represents walls in terms of standard square chunks of wall-stuff, and Amazon represents only the positions of these chunks, not their adjacency relationships. Accordingly, Sonja has to cluster the chunks when it recognizes obstacles (section 8.7.3). This non-equivalence of Amazon's objects and Sonja's objects is the third factor mitigating the incompleteness of my implementation.

Sonja does not address shape matching. I've suggested in section

6.6 that shape matching may be a visual channel parallel to the VRP and with complementary functionality, and that Sonja's visual routines model may be compatible with recent shape matching theories. It would be interesting to build a system incorporating both sorts of visual processing.

9.5.3 Three dimensions

The visual routines model as it currently stands makes no provision for three-dimensional scene analysis. This is as true of other work on visual routines as of Sonja; no one has given serious thought to the question of whether the model can be extended to three-dimensional scene analysis. It may be that such an extension is not possible. I'll sketch two possible approaches, however.

We could imagine, first, that early vision reconstructs an accurate depth map from the image, using stereo, shape-from clues, and so forth. Then we could imagine that the VRP uses three-dimensional primitives, rather than two dimensional ones: that it could activate volumes rather than areas, for example. This is not an approach I like, though it seems possible (and even weakly supported by psychophysical evidence from Nakayama and Silverman [194]).

We could imagine, alternatively, that visual operators use two-dimensional data objects, but can access the early depth modalities through them. (This approach seems to be that suggested by Ullman's brief discussion of three dimensional processing in visual routines.) For example, given a retinotopic image position as specified by a visual marker, you could recover the depth information at that point as computed by stereo.

I have argued in section 3.3.1 that the visual system can not and need not produce an accurate three-dimensional model. This is a contentious point; most research in robotics, for example, depends on the existence of such a model. Anecdotal evidence, however, suggests that people are bad at estimating whether particular manipulation tasks can be accomplished in crowded work spaces (such as the guts of a washing machine). While this needs to be tested rigorously, it suggests that accurate three-dimensional representations are unnecessary. Thus I propose that the VRP's depth operators need provide only approximate and relational information. There might, for example, be operators that could answer such questions as "is the location marked by marker 1 nearer or further

from me than the location marked by marker 2?" and "is the location
marked by marker 1 within the range of variation of depth differences
between points contained within activated region 1?" Considerable work
is needed to see whether such a system could support robot manipulation (for example), but this approach does not seem a priori implausible.
(A similar approach has been suggested by Ballard [21].)

9.5.4   Criteria on the set of visual operators

In section 6.4, I proposed a set of criteria on the set of visual operators
in the VRP.

- We want a "spanning" set: that is, a set of operators that together are
sufficient for any task. Here "any task" may mean "any psychologically
plausible task" or, for engineers, "any task in the class of domains of
interest." Thus the set of visual operators, when combined into routines,
are to form a finite means for the realization of an infinite collection of
possible visual processes.

It's hard to formulate this criterion rigorously, but it's clear that Sonja
does not satisfy it. I added operators to the set as needed for particular
tasks. It is not hard to think of other operators of the same general
character that could be added to the set. By the end of the implementation, I found I often had all the operators I needed to implement a new
routine, but not always. This suggests that I may have been approaching an adequate set, but I'm sure that even in the one task of playing
Amazon continued system development would occasionally require new
operators. Mahoney [168] and Romanycia [231] have proposed other sets
of operators extending Ullman's proposal; they involve many operators
which are quite different in character from those I implemented. Because they were addressing quite different tasks than Amazon playing,
it's difficult to evaluate the relative merits of these sets.

   This raises the concern that there is no spanning set, or that it would
too large to implement with the amount of hardware found in the human
brain. The visual routines model is only plausible if a relatively small
spanning set is possible; since operators correspond to innate bits of
hardware, there can be only as many as will fit in the brain. (Given that
we know little about how intermediate vision is actually implemented,
it is hard to say how many this would be. Hundreds might be feasible;

millions probably wouldn't be.) Further research, for example cross-domain studies or formal analysis of the space of spatial reasoning tasks, is required to address this issue.

- A set of operators should not only make it possible to implement any visual task, it ought to make it *easy*. From an engineering standpoint, the VRP should present a nice programming system.

It is hard to evaluate Sonja's VRP on this score for two reasons. First, I never had an opportunity to implement visual routines with with a completed and debugged VRP. This largely negated the visual-system-as-a-programming-language metaphor I was trying to create. Only by the end of the implementation was the VRP relatively complete and reliable; by that time, implementing new routines was fairly straightforward. Further experience with the architecture is needed. Second, there are no alternative implementations of visual routines processors to compare mine with. The only other implementation of visual routines, due to Romanycia [231], has been applied only to abstract geometrical reasoning tasks that are considerably simpler than Amazon playing. Thus it's not clear how hard implementing visual routines *ought* to be.

My feeling, however, is that the set of operators in Sonja is on the whole too *low-level*. Writing routines often seemed to require more work than it felt intuitively like it ought to. It required too much visual "bit diddling"; I wanted to be able to express things more abstractly. Very approximately, I wanted to be able to talk more in terms of topology and less in terms of of geometry. (Section 9.6.5 discusses some examples.) Such abstraction might be provided by higher-level operators. It might also, however, be provided by a "library" of general-purpose parameterized routines which would use low-level operators. Such routines could be implemented using a abstract operations (section 7.2.4).

My feeling also is that the set of operators I implemented is too *top-down*. The central system has to do more directing of the peripheral system than I'd like. There's a good reason for this: bottom-up processing is much more computationally intensive than top-down, and I was not using a parallel machine. Implementing many of the bottom-up operators I would have liked to have had was infeasible given the available hardware.

- A set of operators should also make it easy to *learn* new visual routines.

Lacking good theories of learning, it's hard to evaluate Sonja's operators on this score. In section B.2.4, I'll suggest experiments that might elucidate the problem. In the mean time, I have three guesses about factors that might affect learnability. First, the more top-down a set of visual operators is, the harder it is likely to be to learn to use it. The more central control is needed, the more central control must be learned. The more central control is used, the more difficult it is to interpret the outputs of operators. The outputs of purely bottom-up operators have fixed meanings; the meanings of others depend on the control inputs that were given on the last tick. (Whitehead and Ballard's [293] system which learns visual routines depends on finding configurations of the VRP which make the full state of the world manifest. Such configurations result in VRP outputs that do not require knowledge of previous control inputs to interpret them.) Second, the more state a visual operator depends on, the harder it is likely to be to learn to use it. State, like control inputs, affects the interpretation of the outputs of the operator. Sonja's operator set does not do a good job of satisfying these criteria; it is too top-down and has too much dependence on state. It would be easy to eliminate many control inputs and uses of state if parallel hardware were available. Third, the sheer number of operators might interact with learnability. Learning schemes that serially try combinations of operators would scale exponentially badly with their number. On the other hand, schemes that evaluate combinations in parallel might benefit from larger numbers.

9.6   The system as a whole

9.6.1   Sonja considered as a technology

Sonja effectively exploits aspects of the concrete-situated approach to activity to succeed at a task (playing Amazon) which would be difficult if not impossible to attack with previously existing techniques. Specifically, as detailed in section 4.1, Amazon is complex, uncertain, and real-time; these pose greater difficulties for alternative technologies than for Sonja [7]. Provisionally, then, Sonja vindicates its theory of action; certainly it is an existence proof that the theory works well in some domains.

Other sorts of domains and tasks are beyond the reach of the technologies embodied in Sonja. These technologies are not obviously applicable to writing poetry, for instance; their scope remains to be determined. The approach is more interesting to me than the technologies, however. I believe that the concrete-situated approach is an explanatory framework for all forms of human activity, and not, for instance, applicable only to sensory-motor coordination tasks. This remains to be demonstrated in general.

In the short term, it seems useful to incrementally extend Sonja-like systems to model new forms of activity. One of the motivations for Sonja was to extend the ideas embodied in Pengi to account for some simple forms of language use. Language use is a clearly "cognitive" task, and many had suggested that while Pengi might be a good model for "low-level" control, it wouldn't scale to cognitive abilities.

9.6.2 Quality of play

It's hard to know how to evaluate Sonja's Amazon playing overall. There are some situations in which Sonja clearly plays better than I can, others in which it plays less well but acts sensibly, others in which it makes a clearly bad decision but continues to act sensibly given the decision, others in which it does something that makes no sense, and still others in which it signals a run-time error and dies. Superhuman performance is worrisome from a cognitive modeling point of view; it suggests Sonja has resources people don't. Situations in which Sonja acts sensibly even if not playing very well are non-problematic; they suggest only that the central network must be expanded for better play. Situations in which Sonja acts irrationally are bothersome; they suggest that the existing central network is doing something actively wrong. System crashes may be due to uninteresting bugs or may reflect deeper problems.

The most striking example of superhuman performance is in close combat with many monsters. Sonja is quite a bit better at this than I am. These are situations in which I feel overwhelmed, and watching Sonja in these situations I find it hard to keep track of what it is doing. This probably means that Sonja's visual system has a higher bandwidth for certain operations than mine does. Most likely Sonja can register the right monster to kill more quickly than I can. This is probably attributable to the circuitry for opportunistic shots, because until I implemented opportunistic shooting Sonja played less well in these situations than I do. This implicates scan-along-ray!, which is used to project *the-thing-I-would-hit-if-I-shot-now*. Probably scan-along-ray! should not be a unit-time operator, but should involve a serial scan along the ray, and Sonja should model the time behavior of the equivalent human operation.

Sonja's play could be improved in many situations by implementing routines it currently lacks. (This would help with situations in which Sonja doesn't play as well as it could or in which it makes obviously bad decisions but plays sensibly given the decision.) For example:

- Sonja doesn't know that it should get knifes, keys, and other tools when it needs them.
- The wandering routines could be improved in many ways. For example, Sonja will keep wandering in a particular direction until it actually hits a wall. This looks really stupid. It would be easy to project and avoid collisions.
- Sonja's registrar for the aspect *I-am-under-attack* could be improved in several ways. The most striking one is that currently it never registers as a threat monsters that are behind it. Such monsters are not generally dangerous, but can be when Sonja is shooting and therefore not moving forward.
- Sonja never runs away. It is often wise to do so when confronting a group of monsters too big to tackle at close quarters.
- Sonja doesn't know to dodge fireballs.
- It takes three shuriken hits to kill a ghost. If you can see you've thrown that many at one and that nothing could come between, you might as well stop shooting and do something else; any further shuriken will be wasted. Sonja doesn't know this. This would be a good application of *subitizing* (a fast, innate method for counting small groups of objects [145, 150]), to count the shuriken already in flight. It would also provide a good example of projection, registering the aspect *the-ghost-is-going-to-die*.

I have a file which contains several dozen ideas for extensions of this sort. At my current rate of coding, such routines take half an hour to a few hours each to implement. I expect that continued implementation would decrease this time significantly by continuing to remove bugs in the implementation substrate (particularly the visual system support code). It would be fun to do this, but not much would be learned. A more interesting question to ask is how this process could be automated; see appendix B.

I believe that one reason I can play Amazon better than Sonja can is that I have several redundant ways of parsing the situation and checking that what I am doing makes sense. Although my actions may be triggered directly by a particular registration, I can usually catch myself soon after starting to make a mistake on account of registering the situation a different way. These multiple registrations are probably particularly important in skill acquisition (appendix B); conflicting registrations signal that there's something to be learned.

Bugs in Sonja can be divided into conceptual bugs in the central system and dumb bugs in the visual system. Bugs in the central system cause Sonja to act senselessly. I find few of these; almost all are in the navigation code. Bugs in the vision system sometimes cause Sonja to act senselessly but more often signal run-time errors. These bugs are almost always in the connectivity activation code.

9.6.3   Size of the system

Sonja is among the most complex essential connectionist systems that have been built; perhaps the most complex essential connectionist system for concrete activity constructed to date. (Some other candidates are Connell's mobile robot [46] and Mel's robot learning system [179].) To be fair, however, Sonja's implementation was feasible only because the visual system was *not* implemented as a connectionist network. I have, however, explained how it could in principle be so implemented.

It is difficult to provide meaningful numerical measures of Sonja's complexity. The central system has 2432 primitive machines in it. This corresponds to about 7000 boolean gates if wires carrying nonboolean values are expanded into binary-coded buses. These numbers, however, are meaningless for a number of reasons. Much of the central system is produced by the arbitration compiler, rather than hand-wired, and I have made no attempt to optimize the compiler's output. MACNET does perform some simple optimizations, but with a little work on these two languages it would be possible to cut the amount of central system hardware by a factor of at least two. This may result in a number of gates that seems surprisingly low. The natural comparison to make is with a microprocessor, which has many more than 3500 gates in it.

This comparison is misleading, however; the central system corresponds, loosely, with the control logic of a microprocessor. Most of the circuitry of a microprocessor is in the datapaths, which correspond loosely to Sonja's visual systems. Not surprisingly, the one part of the visual system I implemented in MACNET, the attentional pyramid, requires much more circuitry. Even with only a 16×16 leaf resolution, the attentional pyramid involves more than 10,000 machines. Most of these are devoted to distance comparison circuitry; decomposing the arithmetic machines would yield a circuit of well over 100,000 gates.

The number of proposers in the central system is a somewhat better measure of the system's complexity because it is unaffected by optimizations in MACNET and the arbitration macrology. There are 138 proposers. Another measure of the central system's complexity is the length of the source code (written in the arbitration macrology), a bit more than two thousand lines counting comments.

It is still harder to measure the complexity of the VRP. It is written in another complex (1400-line) macrology I haven't described. The VRP as written in this macrology is about 2300 lines long. Operator definitions vary in length from one line to several pages. Counting duplicates (section 7.2.7), Sonja uses 108 operators.

The system as a whole, including all the support code such as Amazon and the circuit simulator, comprises a bit more than twelve thousand lines of code.

9.6.4   Deictic representation

Objective representation schemes take for granted that the world comes already neatly divided up into objects. A central tenet of the theory of deictic representation is that it is the agent's job to divide the world up, to constitute entities. For the most part, Sonja finesses this job: it is taken care of by the simulated segmentation machinery, which cheats. The exceptions are the constitution of obstacles and rooms, for which Sonja uses the connectivity activation code. Although these examples point the way, the vision issues in constituting objects in domains in which early vision is not trivial are potentially complex, and much work remains.

Sonja's most interesting projection is *the-thing-I'd-hit-if-I-shot-now*. Sonja also projects *this-monster-is-going-to-clobber-me-if-I-don't-get-it-first* by registering the dangerousness of monsters. Projecting the ama-

zon's own motions amounts to path selection, which is what the navigation circuitry is about. I've mentioned earlier that it would be easy to
register *this-ghost-is-going-to-die*, and suggested dodging fireballs, which
would entail projecting their trajectories. Unfortunately, the Amazon
domain makes it difficult to project many other aspects. Monsters always travel directly towards the amazon, so you can project their motion
just by computing how far away they are. All the other changes in the
domain (e. g. monster generation and scroll readying) are random and
thus unprojectable.

9.6.5   Navigation

Navigation took up an unreasonably large fraction of my time implementing Sonja. Understanding why this was might help evaluate Sonja's
architecture. Unfortunately, there were several factors, and it is hard to
determine their relative contributions.

• Navigation is the only activity Sonja engages in that requires activation planes. The marker operators I had already debugged for Pengi
were sufficient for most of the rest of Sonja. The activation operations
were both new and inherently difficult to implement.

• Navigation was the first really complex form of activity I tried to
implement, and so I had to debug the programming framework as I
was implementing it. Implementing equally complex activities would be
much easier now.

• The architecture may have impeded the implementation. It's hard to
evaluate this without more experience.

• I didn't have a strong theory of navigation, or care much about how
it should work. I implemented it by successive addition of *ad hoc* mechanisms.

There is an extensive literature on mobile robot navigation. Mobile
robot navigation is an entirely different problem from Amazon navigation, because a mobile robot sees only a small part of its three-
dimensional surroundings and sees that from a particular perspective.
An Amazon player sees much of the relevant part of the two-dimensional
dungeon from a "God's eye view." Nonetheless, much of the mobile
robot navigation literature is applicable because it assumes that the
robot has an accurate mental map and can reliably find its position on

that map. This simplification reduces the mobile robot navigation problem to one similar to that faced by Sonja. I have not implemented any of the standard proposed solutions because they were not obviously implementable in Sonja's architecture. Because I don't care about navigation for its own sake, I haven't thought about whether or not they could be implemented in a nonobvious way, nor evaluated them on other grounds such as biological plausibility.

Most of the difficulties I encountered in navigation derived from idealizing the amazon as a point. The amazon marker sits on this point; its relationship to obstacles and goals can be determined by simple visual operations. This idealization works well most of the time; it breaks down when the amazon gets close to an obstacle, so that its extent matters. Glitching (section 8.7.3) is the simplest symptom: if the amazon were really a point, drawing a line from the amazon to the goal would suffice to find obstacles.

These difficulties could be solved by application of the *configuration space* approach [166] in which obstacles are enlarged to compensate for shrinking the robot to a point. The set of visual operators I have defined are not sufficient to compute configuration space obstacles. Whether compatible machinery could do so is an interesting open question.

A Collaboration

In this chapter I will describe extensions to Sonja which would allow it to play collaboratively. Besides the intrinsic scientific interest of collaboration, systems that could collaborate are of potential practical importance. Further, I'll suggest in section B.3.1 that the ability to collaborate is a prerequisite for some of the most important skill acquisition dynamics. Finally, conversation is a collaborative process, and I take conversation to be the most important form of language use.

Gauntlet, the arcade game on which Amazon is based, allows up to four players to collaborate in clobbering monsters and collecting goodies. This changes the dynamics of the game considerably; there are many strategies that simply can not be carried off by a single player. Situations that would be fatal for a single player may be easy for several, not merely because of linear additivity of firepower, but because they can operate synergistically. For example, one player can provide covering fire for another when the second is opening a door behind which there are many monsters.

I have implemented a multi-player mode for Amazon; see figure A.1. Sonja can play in multi-player mode; Sonja will play one of the two amazons on the screen and a human can play the other. However, Sonja has no awareness of the other player, and so can not collaborate. If there is any superlinear synergy of effort, it will be due to the human player being able to anticipate and work with Sonja's actions.

Although there may be unforeseen difficulties, I believe that it would be relatively straightforward to add circuitry to Sonja which would allow it to collaborate with a human player in complex, interesting ways. Based on my informal analysis of videotapes of people playing cooperative videogames and engaging in other cooperative activities, I believe that only two extensions to Sonja are required. First, Sonja would need to register the other player's intentions based on her actions. Second, it would need to engage in some situation-specific routines of cooperative action. These abilities would require no architectural extensions, only additional central system circuitry.

In a cooperative situation, each cooperating agent must be able to recognize what the others are up to in order to coordinate its activity with the others'. There is an AI literature on this problem, treated under the rubric of *plan recognition*; for a variety of rather different approaches, see [9, 10, 24, 146, 147, 153, 212, 216]. This literature makes it clear that the problem is very hard in general. However, it is not particularly

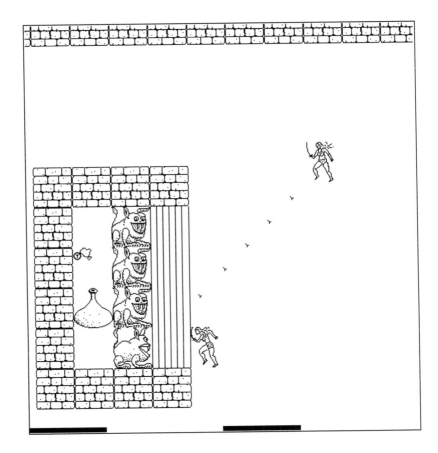

Figure A.1
Two players playing Amazon. The lower left amazon is just about to open the
door. Behind the door are more demons than one amazon could prevail against.
The top right amazon, positioned so that fireballs can not reach her, has laid down
a stream of covering fire which will knock out the bottom two demons before they
have a chance to do much damage to the other amazon.

difficult in playing Amazon. For example, if the other player is heading toward a amulet, it's a good bet, *ceteris paribus*, that she intends to pick it up. I hypothesize that intention recognition is actually pretty easy in most concrete domains. It's easy because once you know what in general someone is doing (such as playing Amazon), the environment constrains what she is up to as strongly as it constrains what you would be up to if you were doing the same thing. So recognizing intentions is easy for the same reason that concrete action is easy: the situation not only tells you what to do, it tells you what someone else is up to. Further, people generally don't recognize *all* or even most of their collaborator's intentions; usually recognizing *some* is quite sufficient to get the job done. So there's no need to find a general solution.

How, more specifically, might intention recognition work in Sonja? Intentions are aspects of the situation which can be registered in just the same way as any other aspects, by visual routines. Continuing our simple example, a visual routine which would register when the other player is heading toward an amulet would be easy to write. To get adequate coverage, a theorist would need to watch a lot of videotape of people playing Amazon cooperatively and figure out what sorts of actions imply what sorts of intentions, and then figure out how to implement visual routines that would register the intentions based on the actions. The reason to register intentions is to collaborate, so only intentions that are relevant to collaboration need be registered.

This account of intention recognition is rather different than those in the existing literature (cited earlier), in that intentions are represented only in the weak sense that Sonja represents everything else. Intentions would not be represented by datastructures. This is consonant with the passive approach to reflexivity taken in section 5.2.4. Registering intentions in this way would, however, permit forms of reflexivity not available to Sonja, in which an interlocutor's utterances are interpreted in the light of her intentions, as registered from her physical actions.

As I said earlier, Amazon permits a variety of specific patterns of collaboration, such as providing covering fire. Extending Sonja to collaborate would require enumerating some of these patterns and implementing routines enabling Sonja to engage in them. For example, if Sonja registered that the other player was heading toward (and therefore probably intended to open) a door behind which there were many dangerous monsters, it could head toward a place from which it would be possible to provide covering fire. Conversely, if Sonja was about to open a dangerous door and noticed the other player situating herself to provide cover, Sonja could pause until the other player was positioned before opening the door.

Collaboration requires communication. In the scenario I've just outlined, Sonja and another player communicate *passively*: they signal their intent by means of actions they would have undertaken for other purposes anyway. No extra circuitry is required for this. Passive communication seems adequate for a lot of collaborative activity. I have sections of videotape several minutes long in which two people engage in intricate collaboration without ever saying anything to each other. Nor do they communicate with gestures or body language; videogame playing requires that both players keep their eyes closely focused on the screen at all times. However, people often do talk with each other as they work together. Although Sonja does not engage in linguistic communication in the course of collaboration, I believe that it would, again, be fairly straightforward to extend it to do so.

In Amazon playing, there are many sorts of cooperation for which linguistic communication is useful. Here are some ways language is used, with examples from my videotapes:

- *Division of labor.* Players often talk about which will take on which monsters, or which will open a door. "I'll clear out that bit." "Ah, *this* thing. I'll take out the main plane deck, you take out the sides if you can." "Aw right, man, you take—I take this dude"
- *Division of spoils.* Players negotiate who gets which goodies. "Hey! That's mine!" "Don't get greedy!"
- *Distribution of risk.* Players negotiate who will bear the brunt of an attack. In one tape, a stronger player repeatedly tells the weaker one "Stay in back of me!". In another, we have the following exchange, which illustrates both this theme and the previous one:

  A: I'm only 30% energy [I.e. I only have 30% energy and so may die soon]

  B: Ah...Just stay with me, and then at the end I'll give you some money, we'll split it evenly

- *Synchronization.* Players may request each other to wait or hurry up in order that they can do something together. "Stop shooting!" "Come on, come on, let's travel!"

- *Long-term plans.* While short-term intentions are usually obvious, longer term, strategical plans more often need to be negotiated explicitly. For example,

> A: Are we gonna go through the time warp again?
>
> B: I wanna see if we can get in through *here*
>
> A: Let's not—I, we *can*, but I *mean*—
>
> B: We're losing energy! [By standing around talking]
>
> A: Let's go this way, take it slowly
>
> B: We'll get there eventually, but, um...

It does not seem difficult to me to imagine how Sonja could engage in dialogues such as these by straightforward applications of the techniques I used in constructing the existing system.

B Skill acquisition

This chapter concerns skill acquisition. It has two main parts. The first is a description of WOMBAT, a system I implemented that tried to acquire skills in the domain of a video game called Robots. WOMBAT combined symbolic search, explanation-based learning, and temporal difference learning in hopes of synergistic performance. WOMBAT didn't work; I explain why, and suggest how to do better. The second part describes various skill acquisition dynamics that future work should model. It suggests that skill acquisition may be a somewhat different problem than has generally been supposed, and indeed an easier one, because various resources are available for the task that have not been exploited by computational work thus far.

There are at least four reasons to study skill acquisition:

• A theory of skill acquisition could address the most serious shortcomings in existing models of activity. For example, numerous criticisms have been made of the theory of activity embodied in Sonja [96]. I believe that I can answer all these criticisms except three: that the central system is domain-specific; that performance does not improve with practice; and that the system is blind in the face of certain sorts of novel situations. Sonja was not designed to address these issues; all three criticisms could be answered by an adequate theory of skill acquisition.

• Skill acquisition is an increasingly pressing engineering problem. Numerous researchers designing situated agents have demonstrated that it is possible to engage in complex activity using quite simple machinery. But as these systems scale up, it seems unlikely that it will be feasible to continue designing this machinery by hand indefinitely.

• Skill acquisition is an interesting scientific problem in its own right, with a substantial psychological literature.

• I believe that a theory of skill acquisition is required before we can study several other cognitive phenomena, because the principal constraint on these phenomena may be the way in which they develop with experience.

The remainder of this appendix is divided into three sections. Section B.1 discusses several existing approaches to skill acquisition; it argues that neither compilation approaches nor purely bottom-up approaches are sufficient. Section B.2 describes and analyzes WOMBAT. WOMBAT combined compilation and bottom-up approaches in hopes of synergy.

Section B.3 describes some skill acquisition dynamics that I think future research should try to model.

B.1   Some existing skill acquisition methods

Existing computational methods for skill acquisition can be loosely divided into two categories: *top-down* and *bottom-up* methods. Top-down methods improve the performance of an agent that reasons from first principles by giving it more knowledge. Bottom-up methods improve performance by empirically comparing the utility of alternative ways of doing something.

Most top-down methods are based on the *planning model* of activity [7]. According to this model, an agent contains (among other things) a *domain theory*, a *planner*, an *executive*, and perhaps a *plan library*. The domain theory specifies the "physics" of the domain: what will happen when particular actions are taken and what things will happen by themselves and when. The planner uses the domain theory to derive *plans* which say what to do in particular situations. The executive uses plans to actually do things. The plan library stores plans for future execution.

The planning model thus involves two types of knowledge: the domain theory and the library of plans. On this model, an agent can improve its skills either by acquiring a better domain theory or by acquiring more plans. The next two sections discuss these possibilities. Section B.1.1 argues that domain theory acquisition can be fruitfully studied only in concert with studies of other forms of skill acquisition. Section B.1.2 argues that *plan compilation* is an inadequate model of skill acquisition. Section B.1.3 then discusses bottom-up skill acquisition.

This overall section (B.1) is not intended as a general survey of the skill acquisition literature, which is immense. It is intended only to set the stage for later sections of this appendix.

B.1.1   Domain theory acquisition

Many skill acquisition systems concentrate on domain theory acquisition [228]. Such systems combine a domain theory learner with a fixed mechanism which computes what to do based only on the theory and the state of the environment.

A domain theory is neither necessary nor sufficient to act intelligently. Empirical methods allow you to acquire skills without a domain theory. People don't fully understand why most of the things they do work. Cooking provides an example: no one could derive successful recipes from first principles. The success of Dan Dan noodles depends on facts about the chemical interactions of its components, on facts about the interactions of various organic molecules with taste buds, on facts about the human nervous system, and on facts about the social construction of the acceptability of foods. Most of these facts are still not known today; few if any were known when the recipe was discovered. The explicit theories cooks have are heuristic, are largely procedural and concrete, and are derived in large part from serendipitous experimentation [112]. Similarly, huge Gothic cathedrals were built before Galileo first began to quantify the relevant mechanics. The skills of cathedral construction were discovered by trial and error, rather than derived from a domain theory.

Acquiring a domain theory is, furthermore, not sufficient for skilled activity. Fully understanding the rules of chess is a negligible fraction of the work of learning to play the game. Skill in chess and many other domains requires much practice.

Since domain theory acquisition is not sufficient for or even the principal factor in skill acquisition, it is probably unwise to address it in isolation. Study of domain theory acquisition would be easier and more useful if it were based on an understanding of *which* facts it's important to learn, *when* they are best learned, and in *what format* they will be useful to a complete agent.

B.1.2   Compilation

The term "compilation" is not precisely defined in the machine learning literature. Approximately, it means caching the results of plan construction by adding plans to a library. If the agent finds itself in a situation for which there is already a plan in the library, it can use that, rather than needing to construct a new plan. (For more sophisticated discussions, see Russell [237] and Ginsberg [96, 97]. Most of the key ideas originate in the MACROPS mechanisms of STRIPS [81].)

Most interesting domains have a state space that is sufficiently large and variable that an agent is unlikely to encounter exactly the same situation twice. This means that plans in the library must apply to many situations in order to be useful. *Explanation-based generalization* [186] is an approach to making plans (and other problem solutions) applicable to situations other than those in which they were originally derived. Various specific techniques are used in explanation-based generalization; the most common one is *dependency analysis* [260]. Dependency analysis traces the history of a problem solving computation to determine which aspects of the problem the solution actually depends on. If the outcome of the computation does not depend on all the aspects of the problem, it can be generalized to allow other aspects to vary freely while retaining correctness. The generalizations produced by this technique are correct only relative to the correctness of the domain theory.

There are roughly two approaches to compilation: *static* and *incremental*. Static compilation systems figure out ahead of time everything that could possibly happen to the agent and what it ought to do in each case and then build the agent as an immutable mechanism that does no planning. Incremental compilation systems maintain a stock of compiled plans for coping with particular eventualities that have occurred in the past. The compiler is called whenever novel situations arise. The difference between static and incremental compilation strategies is *where you put the plan construction time*. The two strategies accordingly have complementary strengths and weaknesses. The advantage of static compilation is that once compilation is complete, the agent will always be able to react quickly to unexpected events. The disadvantage is that static compilation has to compile methods for every eventuality that could ever arise, because the agent can't figure things out later. It seems likely that in many complex domains, there are far too many things that could theoretically happen for there ever to be time for the compiler to consider them all.

In the real world, the same sorts of things happen over and over: a tiny fraction of all the things that could in principle happen. Incremental compilation exploits this dynamic fact. An incremental system gradually builds up ways of acting in those situations that actually occur in practice, and never needs to consider those that don't. Thus, the *total* amount of reasoning an incremental system does may be much less than the amount a static system does. Moreover, reasoning is spread out over a period in which the system is mostly getting useful work done. The problem with incremental compilation is that the system may go catatonic for an unpredictable period whenever it encounters a novel situation. This is dangerous.

Compilation is appealing for the same reason planning is. Building systems the way I built Sonja is hard work; it requires detailed analysis of the domain and of the system's interactions with it. In theory you can just give a domain-independent planner a domain theory and it will figure out what to do for you. Unlike Sonja, which can only do things it was wired up to do, a planner can solve arbitrary problems in the domain. There are two problems: plan construction is combinatorially explosive and adequate domain theories are unavailable for most interesting domains.

Neither static nor incremental compilation is any use if it takes an infeasibly long time to make *each* plan. Current theories of plan construction have superexponential time complexity [33]; in a realistic domain, they would require billions of years to decide what to do in any situation. In practice, planners that work have to be given the domain theory as a carefully crafted set of rules which control inference, often require domain-specific search strategies, and usually depend on a library of hand-written plan fragments. (See the analysis by McDermott [176].)

Compilation depends on a domain theory. A planning-based system can do only as well as its domain theory. People can do much better, as the Dan Dan noodle and cathedral examples show. Almost all existing planning theories further require a *complete* domain theory: one that specifies what will happen in every possible situation. Planning with an incomplete domain theory adds one more layer of exponentiation in the time complexity.

The compilation idea addresses an important observation: people often explicitly work out what to do, and once they have done it a few times it becomes automatic and they don't have to think about it any more. We need a more sophisticated understanding of this phenomenon. We need to understand how people figure out plausible courses of action in complex, incompletely-understood situations and in reasonable amounts of time. We need to discover how people do reasonable things in novel situations when they don't have time to figure out the best thing to do. We need to find out what the product of this figuring-out is. We need to understand how tasks that initially require explicit reasoning become automatic, and how explicit reasoning is integrated with skills that have been acquired inexplicitly. Section B.3 will suggest some starting points.

B.1.3   Bottom-up skill-acquisition methods

Backpropagation   *Backpropagation* [236] is a popular connectionist learning method. It learns to compute a function given sample input/output pairs. Backpropagation can be used as a model of skill acquisition if the input/output pairs are interpreted as situations and actions. Mozer, for instance, has used it as a model of skill acquisition by observing an expert's actions in a video game domain. His system, RAMBOT [190], was presented with thousands of expert input/output pairs from this domain and eventually learned to play tolerably well. Since WOMBAT also operated in this domain, I'll describe it in some detail.

Robots is a video game played on a 20 × 20 rectangular grid. On it are the player (represented by a capital I) and some hostile robots (represented by =). Time is discrete; the player and robots alternate moves. The player and robots can make the eight chess king moves. The robots always march directly toward the player. If a robot reaches the player, the player dies. When two robots collide, they die and leave a junk heap (@). If a robot collides with a junk heap, it dies. The player has one additional move, which is to teleport to a random square of the board. If that square is occupied, the player dies. Here's part of a typical Robots game board:

```
        =
  =

           =
     =    I =      =
          @=
     ==  @=    @
          =
```

The simple rules of Robots generate sufficiently complex interactional dynamics that players continue to improve their performance after playing for hours, not only by speeding their responses, but by discovering new dynamics emergent from the domain.

Some of RAMBOT's weaknesses are instructive. For example, the training set involved two examples in which the player was up against a wall. In one case there was a robot right next to the player. In this case, the only possible move is to teleport, which the expert did. In the other case, the nearest robot was four squares away. In this case, teleporting is a bad strategy because it is risky, and the expert did not teleport. The network was presented with a situation in which the nearest robot was two squares away from the player. Because two is numerically closer to one than to four, RAMBOT teleported. No mechanism which had an understanding of why teleporting was a good idea in the first case (such as a compilation system) would make this mistake. If RAMBOT had been given more examples, it would have eventually learned the right move in the test case; but a skill acquisition system that understands what it is doing and why could learn without that overhead.

Temporal-difference methods   *Temporal-difference (TD) methods*, first used in Samuel's checkers playing program [241], have been studied empirically and analytically by Sutton [22, 266]. TD methods are applicable to *multistep prediction problems*: problems of predicting the outcome of a future event in which data relevant to the prediction are provided gradually up to the point at which the event occurs. For example, your predictions of the weather on Friday will gradually change during the week as new information becomes available. The methods can be made relevant to deciding how to act by using them to predict the eventual success of a course of action, conditional on alternative next actions. TD-based learning systems do not need to be told at every step whether they have acted correctly; they can instead learn by observing the *eventual* outcome of a course of action.

TD methods suppose that a prediction is calculated as a real-valued function of a current *observation vector* and a set of real-valued *weights*. Occasionally the system is also supplied with a real-valued *outcome*. The system performs perfectly if all its predictions between one outcome and the next are equal to the final outcome.

TD methods work by considering the *differences* between successive predictions. As better information is typically available at time $t + 1$ than at time t, typically P_{t+1}, the prediction at time $t + 1$ will be more accurate than P_t. Thus TD methods work by adjusting the weights so that P_t would have been closer to P_{t+1}. When an outcome is discovered, say at time o, the weights are adjusted so that P_o is closer to the actual outcome. In the simplest case, which Sutton calls TD(0) and which seems to work as well as any other, the weights are adjusted according to the formula

$$\Delta w_t = \alpha (P_{t+1} - P_t) \nabla_w P_t,$$

where α is a scalar learning-rate constant and $\nabla_w P_t$ is the gradient of the prediction as a function of the weights.

Sutton's paper on TD methods concerns principally the case in which P is a *linear* function of t. Sutton proves that in these cases TD methods always converge to a correct prediction function. Empirically they also learn quickly. The nonlinear case is less well understood. Sutton proposed using a connectionist network as a nonlinear P and using backpropagation to adjust the weights. Anderson [12] used such a scheme to learn a simulated one-dimensional pole balancing task. I'll explain in section B.2 that I applied the same scheme to video game learning with disappointing results.

B.2   WOMBAT

B.2.1   Motivation

WOMBAT is a skill acquisition system I implemented in 1987 [35]. I hoped to synthesize three dichotomies: top-down and bottom-up learning methods, symbolic and connectionist processing, and phenomenologically articulated and unarticulated learning. I hoped specifically to show that in the Robots domain synthesizing these oppositions would lead to faster and more accurate learning than any of the individual terms.

The analyses of the last section suggest that top-down and bottom-up skill acquisition methods have complementary strengths and weaknesses. Top-down methods suffer from computational intractability and can only do as well as their necessarily limited domain theories let them. Bottom-up methods can be efficient and can empirically discover routines that exploit domain properties not captured in a domain theory. Top-down methods bring a global view to bear and produce justified skills, thereby making the *right* generalizations, whereas bottom-up methods suffer from a local myopia and so are liable to make spurious generalizations.

This makes it seem that combining bottom-up and top-down techniques might lead to synergistic power. Search-intensive top-down techniques could be used only in cases in which they were tractable, by limiting search depth. For example, figuring out that you should teleport only when you are forced to requires a search depth of only one ply.

The usual implementation technologies of top-down and bottom-up methods also show complementary strengths and weaknesses. Top-down methods are usually implemented using symbolic AI techniques, whereas bottom-up methods are often implemented using highly parallel numerical techniques such as connectionist networks. The complementary natures of these technologies have led many to combine them in hopes of synergistic power [55, 119, 246].

Finally, skill acquisition seems phenomenologically to operate in *articulated* and *unarticulated* modes. Most people report that they have little understanding of how they learned to ride a bicycle. They just kept trying until it worked. They didn't make up elaborate theories about how to ride a bicycle and how they were going wrong and how to correct it. In fact few people understand the basic principles which make it possible to ride a bicycle. Most are unaware that in order to turn right you must turn the handlebar slightly left first or you will fall over. They can't say how they balance bicycles; they just do it. This is unarticulated skill acquisition.

Learning other skills requires that you construct or be told numerous stories about how to proceed. The apprentice auto mechanic learns countless specific facts about how engines work and how to diagnose and repair them. Presented with a car that won't start, an expert builds and tests theories of what might be wrong. She can tell you explicitly what her theories are and what the evidence is for them. This is articulated skill acquisition.

Neither mode of skill acquisition occurs in isolation.[1] People probably do make some observations of what is going wrong in learning to ride a bicycle and make relevant corrections. The auto mechanic's skill depends on the "feel" of the bolt she is turning, on inarticulable qualities of the sound of a sick engine, on an apparently ungrounded but reliable hunch about why a particular car might be burning oil. This suggests that there are fruitful synergies in combining the two. It is, further, tempting to identify phenomenologically articulated skill acquisition with top-down symbolic methods and unarticulated skill acquisition with bottom-up connectionist methods.

---

[1]This point has been made by Papert [206].

B.2.2   Implementation

I selected TD methods combined with backpropagation (as discussed
in section B.1.3) as a bottom-up learning method for WOMBAT. I
chose TD because it seemed like the best available bottom-up learning method that does not require presentation of input/output pairs.
Linear situation-action rules don't work in the Robots domain, so I had
to use *some* nonlinear prediction function. A backpropagation network
seemed like the obvious candidate partly because Mozer had shown that
such networks can learn to play Robots given input/output pairs, and
partly because they were the only nonlinear functions Sutton discussed.

I selected brute-force breadth-first search with dependency analysis
generalization as a top-down method. The branching factor in Robots
is sufficiently small (ten), the number of lethal branches sufficiently high,
and the domain rules sufficiently simple that it is practical to do a
complete search in many situations. There are also many situations in
which only a relatively shallow search is possible (because there are few
lethal branches near the root), giving room for the bottom-up method
to be useful. I couldn't think of any domain-independent techniques for
Robots playing that would have done better than breadth-first search.
(Standard planning techniques, for example, do not apply, because the
robots move autonomously.)

Combining the two methods was easy: because search (which I gave
a complete and correct domain theory) always finds correct moves and
because dependency analysis preserves correctness, the dependency networks generated can always override the TD method in case of conflict.

Luckily, I had a connection machine and a connection machine backpropagation implementation available, so I could expect the learning
system to run quickly and I did not have to go to any work to implement backpropagation. TD is so simple that I wrote it in an afternoon.
I connected the pieces together and sat back to watch them learn to play
Robots. An hour later the system was playing no better than chance,
and I began to think something was wrong. I verified that the backpropagation code could learn XOR (the standard test). To test the TD
code, I ran the simple "random walk" example from Sutton's report
with both linear and backpropagation prediction functions. As Sutton
reported, linear TD rapidly and reliably learns to predict in this domain.
However, I found that backpropagation performed much less well, learn-

ing only very slowly and often getting stuck in local minima. Looking carefully at the backpropagation code, I noted with dismay that it contained several global numerical constants, with comments that explained that their values had been empirically chosen for performance in a particular domain. I had naively thought that backpropagation was a fixed algorithm, whereas in fact in practice it is tuned for each application. It might be that I could make the system work much better by tweaking these constants, but that seemed to undermine the points I hoped to make. About this time, I looked more carefully at Mozer's graph of performance vs. trials and noticed that it took several hundred thousand trials for RAMBOT to play at all well. Given that a typical Robots game runs for ten to a hundred moves, it seemed likely that I should expect TD learning to take at least an order of magnitude longer. Even on a connection machine this would mean debugging runs days long. I gave up.

I had, in parallel, been trying to implement the top-down method. Search was an hour's work. Dependency analysis was harder. The search procedure simulated the effects of actions simply by calling the game code, so it always looked at every square of the board. Applied straightforwardly, dependency analysis would say that the situation-action pair learned in a particular situation would apply only to exactly that situation. Since Robots board configurations are generated randomly, there are more than 2^{400} equiprobable situations.

To get any generalization, I'd have to find rules which would find squares whose contents were irrelevant to the outcome of the search and prune them from the dependency set. I repeatedly thought I'd found such rules, tried to prove them correct, failed, and found counterexamples. Eventually I gave up.

It wasn't until a year later that I was able to convince myself that little generalization is possible. Every square on the board is relevant except in cases in which search can show that a teleport is forced in k moves, in which case every square within k of the player icon is relevant. [2] Every robot within these bounds is relevant because it can potentially reach the player; removing a robot can give the player greater freedom to move, or can actually make the situation worse in cases in which, in

---

[2] There are some additional exceptions. For example a long, solid "wall" of junk heaps can shield the I from robots on the far side. However, such walls never arise in practice.

the solution path, that robot crashes into and thereby disables another. Every blank space within these bounds is relevant because introducing a robot at that point can again further constrain the player or save it from forced moves by crashing into another.

This demonstrates rigorously a kind of holism for the Robots domain: the best move depends on every aspect of the situation. Consequently, any general rules for playing Robots can only be heuristic. There are many such rules; some examples are "try to head for the center of mass of the robots when possible" and "try to get aligned pairs of robots to crash into each other by getting between them and running away from them in a direction orthogonal to the axis on which they are aligned." Learning these rules took me a lot of work; it would be interesting indeed to know how I did it. The analysis of the last paragraph shows that it was not by dependency analysis. More generally, this same analysis is likely to apply to any domain in which there are autonomous processes. The correctness of explanation-based generalization in such a domain depends on the *non*-existence of autonomous agencies that were not found in the situation of learning. In many realistic domains there are infinitely many such potentially existing processes, rendering correctness-preserving explanation-based generalization techniques (including dependency analysis) useless.

B.2.3   Related work

Several other researchers have combined top-down with bottom-up learning methods; Schlimmer's thesis [246] reviews some. Drescher's system MARCSYST [58, 59, 60] combines statistical induction of action effects with techniques that synthesize new representations.

The system most similar to WOMBAT is Sutton's DYNA [267] which also combines TD learning with shallow breadth-first search. DYNA uses search somewhat differently, though: like Samuel's checkers program and most subsequent game playing systems, it uses lookahead to apply a static situation evaluator (learned via TD) to hypothetical future situations. This means that more information can be learned from a less deep search, and that a prior domain theory is not required; on the other hand, it does not permit dependency analysis.

In an empirical test in a toy domain, Sutton has shown that adding search to TD dramatically improved its performance. This result is encouraging, though it will need to be confirmed by tests in more realistic domains. DYNA's test domain also allowed a linear predictor, which eliminates the problems WOMBAT had with nonlinear prediction. More research on combining TD with nonlinear prediction functions is needed.

B.2.4 Analysis

WOMBAT didn't work. Backpropagation TD methods learned slowly and poorly (at least without tuning), and I couldn't make dependency analysis apply. What can we learn from this failure?

A first observation is that my problems with these techniques are ones that were well-known to experts in connectionism and explanation-based generalization respectively.

• It is by now common knowledge that backpropagation is too slow and unreliable for many tasks [72]; this was less widely known in 1987 when I tried to use it. Since that time a host of improved connectionist learning algorithms have been demonstrated, many of which perform better than backpropagation on standard benchmarks (see, for instance, [72]).

• It was naive of me not to realize that backpropagation requires tuning. The existence of various learning-rate parameters is stated clearly in papers on the subject [236].

• Experiments with combining backpropagation and TD methods had only begun in 1987; since then other workers (e. g. Kaelbling [140] and Shepanski and Macy [251]) have reported similarly disappointing results.

• The inapplicability of dependency analysis in many domains is well-understood by researchers in explanation-based learning, though this is not a point which has been widely publicized.

It is, however, a poor worker who blames his tools. There are reasons to think that even had they worked, the system as a whole would not have addressed the skill acquisition problem as deeply as I had hoped. I believe that future research in this area must examine in greater detail the *situating* of the learning machinery, both in terms of its relationships with other modules and in terms of the dynamics of its interaction with the physical and social environment of the agent.

For example, it is broadly recognized that the efficiency and often success of most learning algorithms depends crucially on the input representation. This implies that productive research on learning depends on finding input representations that allow the system to learn quickly but which are also efficiently computable by other modules. Similarly, the outputs of a learning module must be useful to some other module. In the case of skill acquisition, perception gives some of the most important inputs and action takes some of the most important outputs. This means that useful theories of skill acquisition will depend, among other things, on adequate theories of perception and action.

Mozer, in RAMBOT, observed that a purely retinotopic representation of Robots situations would not allow efficient learning. The problem is that correct moves do not generally depend on where on the board the player icon is, but only its position relative to the robots. A retinotopic representation does not allow generalization of learned responses to situations that are identical but shifted, rotated, or scaled on the board. Mozer solved this problem by applying a sequence of *ad hoc* normalizing transformations to the board before retinotopic encoding.

Sonja solves this problem by means of visual markers, which give position-independence to the visual representation, and by means of visual operators which compute properties such as alignment directly, thus giving orientation and scale independence when appropriate. I had hoped to use WOMBAT to quantitatively test my argument (in section 3.3.3) that the visual routines model allows faster task-dependent vision learning than a retinotopic model. It would have been interesting to run WOMBAT with an unmodified retinotopic visual system, with Mozer's modified retinotopic visual system, and with a Sonja-like visual routines processor, and to compare learning rates. This would also provide a means of observing the effects on learning rates of alternative choices for specific visual operators. (Whitehead and Ballard's [293] successful use of TD with a VRP inspired by that of Pengi is encouraging.) Unfortunately, backpropagation wasn't up to the job. I hope to conduct similar experiments with a better prediction function implementation [39].

B.3   The phenomenology and dynamics of skill acquisition

An easy mistake is to formalize a phenomenon too soon, and then to seek technical solutions to a problem which has little relationship with reality. The planning model of activity grew out of such a premature formalization. WOMBAT probably made the same mistake. We need to understand more about the dynamics of skill acquisition; more about what a skill acquisition system is actually called on to do, and what external resources are available to it. This is a big job, though fortunately one on which considerable work has already done in several fields outside of AI. This section describes both some of my work on these problems and some work by others. Much of this work is phenomenological; it describes what acquiring skills seems like to the learner. I will describe things that happened to me while acquiring particular skills. Converting such phenomenological descriptions into computational theories will take considerable future research, but it gives some ideas of what such theories ought to account for.

Section B.3.1 describes some resources for skill acquisition, such as routineness and situatedness, that are emphasized by the concrete-situated view of activity. I particularly discuss social situatedness and apprenticeship.

Section B.3.2 describes some phenomenology of unarticulated skill acquisition. I identify two unarticulated skill acquisition dynamics, routine optimization and scene individuation.

Section B.3.3 describes some interactions between unarticulated skill acquisition and articulation. I discuss a dynamic of articulating skills acquired inarticulately and suggest that inarticulate acquisition is partly cognitively penetrable and that articulation is in part directed by inarticulate processes.

Section B.3.4 describes some abilities for which a skill acquisition system should be held accountable: formation of deictic representations, acquisition of specifically visual routines, and learning to collaborate.

Section B.3.5 describes some phenomenology of articulation. I suggest that articulated representations consist at least in part of internal natural language utterances.

B.3.1 Resources for skill acquisition

Chapter 2 described a variety of resources which are both necessary for and generally available to an agent engaged in concrete activity. Routineness, situatedness, and deictic representation are examples. I believe these resources are also key to skill acquisition.

Because activity is ongoing, an agent can choose when to learn. Life continues whether you learn from an event or not. Because activity is

mostly routine, the same events will occur over and over, so if you can't
learn from them now, you'll have another chance later. The events that
are easy to learn from are those that almost make sense but not quite;
situations in which you can almost do the right thing but not quite. If
the lesson of a novel experience is not clear, it was probably well beyond
your understanding, and you can just forget about it. Thus, an agent
can choose its own training set, one that it optimized for its particular
abilities. This dynamic of selecting events to learn from becomes clear
in watching people learning to play video games. In a well-designed
game, even a novice can survive for a while by taking actions that are
obvious from looking at the screen. Yet for even an expert player, much
of what happens is surprising. A video game gets you to feed it quarters
for a long time by providing you with continuing opportunities to learn
regardless of your skill level.

Because activity is situated and mostly routine, you face similar situations over and over again. This gives you an opportunity to try alternative ways of doing things to see which work best.

Because activity is physically situated, you can often look at a situation to see what to do. I have argued earlier that vision is primarily
task dependent. Nevertheless, when people are shown a novel situation,
they are able to engage in a different sort of looking that forms some
sort of description of it in task-independent terms—geometrically, for
example. Ullman hypothesizes that this sort of looking is implemented
by *universal visual routines*. Probably these routines take a lot more
visual work than task-dependent vision, because task-dependent visual
routines already know what aspects of the situation to look at to extract the information you need for action, whereas universal routines
may have to examine a scene exhaustively.

Universal visual routines probably do not play a major role in skilled
performance, but are probably important in skill acquisition. When you
first encounter a novel situation, you can get *some* information about it,
which will probably give you *some* idea of what to do. Trying that idea
out will give you better ideas, and gradually you'll come to understand
what means what in the situation and so how to look at it in the usual
task-dependent way.

Because deictic representations do not represent identity and because
they are acquired, they frequently represent the same object in several ways. In section B.3.4 I hypothesize that deictic representations

are created largely by bottom-up mechanisms which don't have enough global understanding to avoid redundant representation. (Sonja rarely has more than one representation of an object, because I had to wire its representations by hand.) These redundant representations are a resource in skill acquisition because conflicts between them signal opportunities to learn. Because deictic representation is in task-dependent terms, these opportunities are also phrased in task-dependent terms.

Human learning always takes place in a social, as well as physical, context. Much of it, particularly in childhood, takes place in the presence of others who are more skilled in the task at hand; even when this is not the case, one can always find others to call on for help when necessary. The social context also facilitates learning by providing tools and institutions that make skill acquisition easier.

These effects, which may be of overwhelming importance to skill acquisition, have been largely neglected by computational study. (For one exception, see Siegler and Shrager [253].) One good reason for this neglect is that participating in a social context is a prerequisite to learning from one, and AI systems do not yet really do this. One of my motivations in studying instruction use was to lay part of the groundwork for such participation. The relationship between human instruction givers and users is a social one. The proposed collaborative extension of Sonja discussed in appendix A would be a further step towards social participation by machines.

Fortunately, some ways in which a social context potentiates skill acquisition have been studied in detail by social scientists, e. g. Hutchins [126], Kaye [148], Lave [161], and Rogoff [230]. I'll give just few examples; all are apprenticeship dynamics, though social support for skill acquisition is a broader phenomenon.

The first I've already described briefly in section 2.4. If two people of different skill levels are collaborating on a task, it will get done most efficiently if the more skilled participant takes on the more difficult bits. For example, in my video tapes of collaborative video game playing, the more skilled player usually fights the nastier monsters. This has the often unintended side-effect that the more skilled participant demonstrates competent performance of the more difficult parts of the task for the less skilled participant. This make learning by imitation easier.

In my tapes of collaborative video game playing, curses form a substantial fraction of the talk. Curses (and other interjections) probably have numerous functions; some are particularly relevant for skill acquisition. When the more skilled player yells "Fuck!", it signals two things to the less skilled player: that what has just happened was *important* and that it was *bad*. Neither of these things may be obvious otherwise. Knowing these things is important for directing the attention of skill acquisition processes (see section B.3.3) and as an input to routine optimization (see section B.3.2) which (like TD methods) probably require an estimate of the desirability of situations and events.

B.3.2   The phenomenology of unarticulated skill acquisition

There are many tasks at which you simply get better with practice without being able to say why. It is (by definition) hard to study this phenomenologically. It seems to encompass two different phenomena, however: *routine optimization*, which compares alternative ways of doing things, and *scene individuation*, which discovers recurring configurations of the world.

Routine optimization   Here's a story which suggests that at least one way you get better is by doing something in different ways and comparing them to see which works better.

> The video game Xybots has several kinds of robots that shoot at you. The different types of robots have different firing patterns; it is hard to figure out what rules underlie them. At some point in the course of learning to play the game, I found that it was best to dance back and forth in front of some types of robots (so that their bullets would mostly miss me) while shooting at them, whereas it was best to stand my ground while shooting at other types and absorb whatever bullets came by. I had no idea at the time why this was, nor did I think to question it.

The next story suggests that routine optimization exploits *accidentally* discovered alternatives:

> For the first time today I drove with a shift and an open can of coke. It wasn't real clear what to do with the can. Putting it between my legs was losing—not because there was anything obviously wrong, but because it somehow felt

like if I had to brake suddenly it would get in the way. One time I had to turn suddenly and didn't have time to put the can back between my legs, so I just grabbed the wheel as well as the can (using my right hand, where the can had been). The can then mostly stayed in my hand, but this was really awkward, especially when it came time to shift. So the can shuttled back and forth between my legs and right hand. Then one time I was about to shift and by reflex passed the can to my left hand. I think there must be a general-purpose get-rid-of-this-thing-in-my-right-hand reflex that transfers what's in it to your left hand automatically when you suddenly need to use your right. Keeping the can in my left hand worked better, because the can didn't interfere with my right hand. When I wanted to take a swig I'd pass the can from my left to my right hand, drink, and pass it back. Finally it occurred to me that I could use my left hand to drink with instead.

Most of this was minimally conscious. I did do some thinking; I noted that the between-the-legs strategy didn't work well. I noted that holding the can in my hands interfered with shifting. And the use-left-hand-to-drink optimization was fully conscious. But the rest just happened. Random circumstances (e. g. needing to shift suddenly) caused perturbations in my routine, some of which happened to make it work better, so they stuck.

When I was learning to play Pengo, there came a point at which I found I could predict moderately accurately the partially random motions of bees. I found then that I didn't need to be as cautious about approaching them. This led to my playing a more offensive game: rather than running away a lot, I'd swoop in on a bee and clobber it before it knew what had hit it. (Bees get actively hostile when you get within a certain radius of them; otherwise they just wander around randomly.) This in turn altered the way I approached other tasks in the domain. A wave of change propagated through all my routines; changing the way I did each thing altered the dynamics of my interactions with the game in ways that enabled me to accomplish other tasks quite differently.

Here again changes external to various routines resulted in my doing things differently, which led to new routines.

These stories and others like them make me believe in a mechanism whose job it is to compare alternate ways of doing things. It suggests that this mechanism is not responsible for *generating* alternatives, but merely for comparing them. TD methods have something of this character.

Scene individuation   Part of getting good at an activity is learning to recognize particular recurring configurations of the domain. In section B.3.4, I'll suggest one of the reasons this is important is that having learned to recognize these configurations, you can assign functional significances to them, thereby forming deictic representations.

Much of the work of learning to play certain video games is in learning to find your way about in the simulated space. These games have fixed dungeons or terrains in which you can navigate, and particular events tend to occur in particular places. Eventually you may get a complete mental map of the world, but in intermediate stages you find instead that you come to recognize particular places that you have been before without necessarily remembering connectivity information. At first the terrain is an undifferentiated background to continuous combat, but then you come to be able to say "Oh, this is the bit of graveyard where all the skeletons come to life and at the end there's the guy with a pig's head." Often you come to recognize scenes before you are able to use the recognition for anything. Later you may be able to say ". . . so I should use the magic potion at the end."

Situations that are individuated may not correspond to places but to configurations of objects.

It took me a while to realize that in this configuration:

    = I=

there is no possible move. I kept trying to move diagonally leftward and up or down, but the robot on the left prevents that.

In order to make this articulation, I had to have a vocabulary item, that in which the I is between two robots, one adjacent and another one unit away, all colinear. That is, I had to recognize many different instances of this situation as similar in order to notice that I was consistently losing in it.

B.3.3 Interactions between articulated and unarticulated skill acquisition

Articulating the Stumbled Upon *Stumbling upon* is a dynamic whereby an agent is pursuing a dumb strategy S_1 in a situation s, and in s it turns out that applying S_1 amounts to the same thing as applying S_2, which is a smart strategy for s, and next time the agent gets into a situation like s, the agent does S_2. This is an instance of the dynamic (discussed in section B.3.1) whereby an agent is always able to engage in an activity at some level and so can choose when to learn. Good opportunities to learn are provided by circumstances in which things go unexpectedly well; stumbling-upon is one reason they might.

Here is an example which will illustrate other themes as well. It comes from learning to play Gauntlet (the commercial game Amazon is based on).

I was in a tall, narrow room with a door at the top. On the other side of the door there were a zillion ghosts. There was nothing I could do except open the door, nowhere else to go. So I opened the door and was confronted with more ghosts than I could possibly deal with. I did the only thing possible, which was to run away. There was no reason to think that this would be especially effective, as there was nowhere to run to, really; there was no other way out. But I soon got to be at the bottom of the screen, which panned down with me, and since I could run faster than the ghosts, most of them fell behind and dropped off the top of the screen. Since ghosts don't chase you when they are off the screen, there were only a couple left pursuing me, and I could pick them off easily. Then I went back up and the ghosts that had been sitting just beyond the edge of the screen were revealed, and they chased me, and this looped. Eventually I picked off all the ghosts this way.

This quite subtle strategy, which I could not easily have thought up by myself, fell out completely passively from doing at every step the only possible thing, even when it didn't seem especially justified. Here S_1 is "run away" and S_2 is "repeatedly lure small numbers of ghosts away from the pack and pick them off".

Presently, I articulated what I was doing. Once I'd done that, I could and did do it consistently whenever I got into a situation in which it was appropriate. Then I stumbled upon further optimizations of the routine. This is a common dynamic of *alternation* of inarticulate and articulate learning. A useful routine is passively stumbled upon; inarticulate mechanisms make you start doing it more often; articulation notices that you are *already* doing a clever thing and explains it; this allows you to do it better and more consistently; that results in new patterns of interaction in which there are new phenomena to be stumbled upon.

The second half of alternation, in which a new articulated understanding gives rise to dynamics which are optimized inarticulately, has been termed *cognitive mediation* by Shrager [254]. Piaget has used the term *reflecting abstraction* for the first half (articulating what you already know how to do) [92]. Papert [206] has described some of their interactions.

In many cases *understanding precedes representation*. You do something a few times by stumbling on it; your routine optimization machinery makes you do it more frequently; only then do you notice and articulate what you were doing. Another example of this dynamic comes from learning to drive with a stick shift:

> About three weeks ago I noticed that I'd started leaving my hand on the stick for longish periods, which I hadn't done before. It turns out that I was doing it when I "knew" (that is, when perceivable context conditions implied) that I was going to have to shift several times in the next minute or two (typically, accelerating up to > 35 from first or second) and that I was on the straight (so I didn't need the hand on the wheel for steering). Once I realized that this was why I was doing it, I was able to exploit this articulation to do it better, more reliably, and more often.

Articulation directed by inarticulate mechanisms How do you know when to articulate a phenomenon? How do you notice that you are doing something new? What makes you explicitly wonder about why something happens? Articulation is triggered at least in part by inarticulate mechanisms.

In learning to play Robots, I noticed at some point that sometimes when you move it doesn't change the configuration of the robots at all, they just translate, so it's a no-op. Then I noticed that once this happens, it keeps happening. Then I noticed that this happens always on a diagonal move. For a bit I overgeneralized and supposed that all diagonal moves have this property. But they don't. It seemed that the ones that did were ones when I was running away. Then in thinking about it it occurred to me that it seemed to happen only when all the robots were in one quadrant and I was moving away from that quadrant. Observation confirmed this. Later I figured out why this had to be the case.

This sequence of discoveries resulted from first noticing that moving is sometimes a no-op. How did that happen? Well, because there are usually robots marching toward you from every direction, the game board usually looks like a whirlpool converging on the player. Under the conditions I discovered, the contents of the game board translate as a block instead. Convergence on a point and global translation are two of the half-dozen characteristic optical flow patterns that are primitively detected primitively by the human visual system [174]. The discovered condition stood out so well because it is the only time the global optical flow pattern changes.

More generally, we may suppose that certain events are detected as *interesting* by the sensory systems. Other plausible examples are sudden motions, looming, and loud noises. Detecting such phenomena and flagging them as interesting must have strong evolutionary value.

Directing unarticulated mechanisms The unarticulated skill acquisition mechanisms seem to be partly cognitively penetrable. The phenomenology is that you note some interesting occurrence and think "I wonder how that happened!" And you find yourself paying a bit more attention to things like that in the future, and then later the answer to your wondering just pops out, becomes obvious. Presumably you directed the focus of attention of some mechanism which figured it out for you. Here is an example from learning to play Robots:

This interesting thing just happened: I was hoping two non-aligned robots would somehow align and collide, but they didn't. However, another robot collided with one of the two, and then the last one crashed into that pile, and then the remaining ten or so robots elegantly crashed into it too. I need to figure out how that happened.

Half an hour later, I wrote:

Here's the thing I was looking for:

```
 =  I
 =           -m->    ==  I   -j->   =@ I   -j->   @ I
                      =
 =
```

[This shows a sequence of four situations with arrows between them. The letters in the arrows are keystrokes used to move the I; m is down and right and j is standing in place.]

I guess the point is that I was looking for the upper two robots to collide, and so not seeing that the outer two could— I had some implicit, incorrect notion of *the-robot-this-robot-will-collide-with-if-it's-gonna-collide-with-anything*.

The result of seeing what was going on was the development of a new visual routine, based on alignment, for registering *the-robot-this-robot-will-collide-with*.

B.3.4 Tasks for a skill acquisition system

The formation of deictic representations If domain-specific deictic representations are as important in activity as I believe, learning them must be one of the major skill-acquisition tasks. Here is an example:

One day I cooked four hundred pancakes in a few hours, having cooked perhaps a dozen of them before in my life.
Plan for pancakes:

1. Pour some batter

2. Turn it over when it is done on the first side
3. Take it off when it is done on the second side

This is a nonoperational plan; it takes a lot of work to apply. As my pancake-making routine developed, I got better and better at each step.

The hard thing about step 2 is that the obvious operationalization is to lift the edge of the pancake to see if it is brown enough yet. This is inefficient. After making fifty pancakes I was pretty good at estimating roughly how long it ought to take, which made it more efficient. But not efficient enough.

After making a hundred or so pancakes I noticed that bubbles formed in the batter as they cooked. After another fifty I noticed that the number of bubbles increased more or less monotonically with time. After another fifty pancakes it occurred to me that this meant that there might be a threshold number of bubbles that would tell me when the pancake was done. This would be a good thing, because the bubbles are visible from the top, so I wouldn't have to lift the edge of a pancake to know when it was done. So I started actively experimenting to find the right number of bubbles and rapidly discovered the correct answer.

When I tell this story, I'm told that this is in fact standard pancake cooking wisdom (which I didn't know), except that the correct criterion goes according to the distribution of bubbles, rather than the number. I'd probably have figured this out in a few hundred more pancakes.

In this example learning proceeded bottom-up. I individuated particular scenes in the pancake-cooking routine before I knew what they were good for. Later I attached a functional significance to one of these scenes and thereby formed a new deictic representation of the aspect *the-pancake-I'm-looking-at-is-ready*.

Acquiring visual routines Visual routines are presumably built by the same machinery that builds other routines, and gradually improve. Here's a Robots example:

> As I get better and better at the game, my eyes look at a
> less and less local area around the I character. Presumably
> that's because I know what to look for. I couldn't project
> all the movements of all the robots in even a five-by-five
> area—or, if I could, it would slow things way way down—
> but I don't need to, because I know which ones are relevant.
> I'm probably looking at the same number of robots as I did
> before, but now I know which ones are interesting.

There are some difficulties and resources that are specific to learning
visual routines. I've argued that a principal resource for skill acquisition
in general is the ability to look at a situation and make sense of it.
This resource is not directly available in learning visual routines; you
can't look directly at the state of your visual operators, because those
are your machinery for looking with. This argues for minimizing such
hidden state and for making as much information as possible about the
operation of the visual system available to the central system (see also
section 9.5.4).

On the other hand, the existence of universal routines is probably
a principal resource in constructing task-specific routines. If you can
always fall back on universal routines, you can use them when first engaging in a novel task, and gradually optimize out the operations that
turn out to be irrelevant. A probable phenomenological correlate of this
in learning to play video games is the sensation that, as you get better
at the game, you need to look at less and less, can find things on the
screen more quickly, and see more and more out of the corner of your
eye.

It's hard to study visual routine optimization, because visual routines
are not externally observable and have little or no introspective corre-
lates. One exception is foveation, which is externally observable (with
an eye tracker) and cognitively penetrable (you can tell which way you
are looking and you can move your eyes to wherever you want). Stories
in Sudnow's book on learning to play video games [265] suggest that
learning patterns of foveation is crucial in acquiring visual skills. He
describes learning to play Breakout, a ping-pong inspired video game in
which you use a paddle to bat a ball against a row of bricks. Much of
the difficulty in playing the game is that you have to somehow attend to
the paddle, the ball, and the bricks simultaneously. Much of his learning

consisted of trying alternative patterns of foveation on these objects and saccades between them. Eventually, he found he could play competently without foveating on any of these objects. This suggests that skills that initially require foveation eventually come instead to use covert visual attention without foveation. I hypothesize that a learning dynamic systematically turns foveation routines into covert attentional routines. It is possible to do this because once a skill becomes routine, less visual acuity is required; you don't have to keep checking the identity of a tracked object because you know from experience what must be there.

Learning to collaborate A social agent must acquire collaborative skills as well as solitary ones. This means in part learning specific collaborative routines, such as providing covering fire (as described in appendix A). It also means learning broader patterns of collaboration: learning general schemes for dividing up labor, for example. Still more broadly, a social agent must acquire the interactive skills that constitute being a member of its culture. An agent must learn how to walk the walk and talk the talk that make it an American or a Yanomamo or a member of the cheerleading clique or a Rotarian or a psychotherapist.

Much is known about such enculturation. Perhaps it can provide guidance for the study of skill acquisition generally.

B.3.5 The phenomenology of articulation

In WOMBAT, I implicitly modeled articulations as the premise sets extracted by dependency analysis. This is not psychologically plausible; nor, as I showed, is it adequate technically. What are articulations, really?

I think that the insight of explanation-based learning, that you learn by understanding what is going on in a particular situation and apply this understanding in later situations, is right. But, as Schank has argued [242], existing accounts of explanation are simplistic. Proofs, plans (in the sense of the AI planning literature) and problem-solver traces are impoverished and psychologically implausible substitutes for explanations. Schank argues instead that "a human being is a bunch of stories" [243]. People convert interesting experiences into stories. They store them away, regurgitate them, and use them under appropriate circumstances. They swap stories with others. Their actions are guided by stories they made up or heard from someone else. But what is a "story"? Schank imagines that it's a network of mentalese. I take the metaphor more literally: I take it that many articulations are *internal natural language utterances*. I've explored this idea further elsewhere [34].

Bibliography

[1] Norihiro Abe, Itsuya Soga, Saburo Tsuji, "A plot understanding system on reference to both image and language." IJCAI-81, pp. 77–84.

[2] G. Adorni, A. Boccalatte, and M. DiManzo, "Cognitive Models for Computer Vision." In J. Horecký, ed., *COLING82* (proceedings), North-Holland Publishing Company, Amsterdam, 1982, pp. 7–12.

[3] Philip E. Agre, "Routines." MIT AI Memo 828, 1985.

[4] Philip E. Agre, *The Dynamic Structure of Everyday Life*. Cambridge University Press, forthcoming.

[5] Philip E. Agre and David Chapman, "Pengi: An Implementation of a Theory of Activity," AAAI-87.

[6] Philip E. Agre and David Chapman, "Indexicality and the Binding Problem." *Proceedings of the AAAI Symposium "How can slow components think so fast?"*, 1988.

[7] Philip E. Agre and David Chapman, "What are Plans For?" To appear in Pattie Maes, ed., *New Architectures for Autonomous Agents: Task-level Decomposition and Emergent Functionality*. MIT Press, Cambridge, Massachusetts, 1991. Also in *Robotics and Autonomous Systems* **6** (1990), pp. 17–34. Also printed as MIT AI Memo 1050a, October 1989.

[8] Subutai Ahmad and Stephen Omohundro, "Equilateral Triangles: A Challenge for Connectionist Vision." *Proceedings of the 12th Annual Meeting of the Cognitive Science Society*, MIT, 1990.

[9] James F. Allen, *A Plan Based Approach to Speech Act Recognition*. University of Toronto Technical Report TR 121/79, 1979.

[10] James Allen, "Recognizing intentions from natural language utterances." In Michael Brady and Robert C. Berwick, eds., *Computational Models of Discourse*, MIT Press, Cambridge, MA, 1983, pp. 107–166.

[11] James F. Allen, "Towards a General Model of Action and Time." *Artificial Intelligence* 23/2 (1984), pp. 123–154.

[12] Charles W. Anderson, "Strategy Learning with Multilayer Connectionist Representations." *Proceedings of the Fourth International Workshop on Machine Learning*, Morgan Kaufmann, 1987, pp. 103–114.

[13] C. H. Anderson and D. C. Van Essen, "Shifter circuits: A computational strategy for dynamic aspects of visual processing." *Proceedings of the National Academy of Sciences, USA*, Vol. 84, pp. 6297–6301, September 1987.

[14] Douglas Appelt, "Planning English Referring Expressions." *Artificial Intelligence* **26** (1985), pp. 1–33.

[15] Douglas Appelt, "Planning English Sentences." Cambridge University Press, Cambridge, 1985.

[16] Doug Appelt, "Reference and Pragmatic Identification." TINLAP-3, 1987.

[17] Douglas Appelt and Amichai Kronfeld, "A Computational Model of Referring." IJCAI-87 pp. 640–7.

[18] N. I. Badler, *Temporal Scene Analysis: Conceptual Description of Object Movements*. Technical Report TR-80, Department of Computer Science, University of Toronto, 1975.

[19] Dana H. Ballard, "Cortical connections and parallel processing: structure and function." *The Behavioral and Brian Sciences* **9** (1986) pp. 67–120.

[20] Dana H. Ballard, *Eye Movements and Spatial Cognition.* University of Rochester Department of Computer Science TR 218, 1987.

[21] Dana H. Ballard, "Reference Frames for Animate Vision." IJCAI-89, pp. 1635–1641.

[22] A. G. Barto, R. S. Sutton, and C. J. C. H. Watkins, *Learning and Sequential Decision Making.* University of Massachusetts at Amherst COINS Technical Report 89-95. Also, to appear as a chapter in M. Gabriel and J. W. Moore, *Learning and Computational Neuroscience*, MIT Press, Cambridge, MA.

[23] Barwise and Perry, *Situations and Attitudes.* MIT Press, Cambridge Massachusetts and London England, 1983.

[24] Astrid   Brietzmann   and   Guenther   Go-erz, "Pragmatics in Speech Understanding—Revisited." In J. Horecký, ed., *COLING82* (proceedings), North-Holland Publishing Company, Amsterdam, 1982, pp. 49-54.

[25] Rodney A. Brooks, "A Robust Layered Control System for a Mobile Robot." *IEEE Journal of Robotics and Automation*, RA-2 (1986), April, 14–23.

[26] Rodney A. Brooks, "Achieving Artificial Intelligence Through Building Robots." MIT AI Memo 899, May, 1986.

[27] Rodney A. Brooks, "Intelligence Without Representation." *Preprints of the Workshop on Foundations of Artificial Intelligence*, June, 1987. Revised version to appear in *Artificial Intelligence.*

[28] Rodney A. Brooks, "A Robot that Walks: Emergent Behavior from a Carefully Evolved Network." *Neural Computation* **1:2**, Summer, 1989.

[29] Rodney A. Brooks and Anita M. Flynn, "A Robot Being." *Proceedings of the NATO Workshop on Robotics and Biological Systems*, Tuscany, Italy, June, 1989.

[30] John Seely Brown, Allan Collins and Paul Duguid, *Situated Cognition and the Culture of Learning.* Institute for Reasearch on Learning Report IRL88-0008, December, 1988. A shortened version also appeared in *Educational Researcher*, February 1989.

[31] David Chapman, "Naive Mathematics and Naive Problem Solving." MIT AI Working Paper 249, June, 1983.

[32] David Chapman, "Cognitive Cliches." MIT AI Working Paper 286, April, 1986.

[33] David Chapman, "Planning for Conjunctive Goals." *Artificial Intelligence*, **32** (1987) pp. 333-377.

[34] David Chapman, "Connections, Encodings, and Descriptions." Unpublished area exam, Department of Computer Science, MIT, 1987.

[35] David Chapman, "Articulation and Experience: Notes towards a Thesis Proposal." Unpublished ms., 1987.

[36] David Chapman, "From Planning to Instruction Use." *Proceedings of The Rochester Planning Workshop: From Formal Systems to Practical Systems*, University of Rochester Computer Science Technical Report 284, April, 1989.

[37] David Chapman, "Penguins Can Make Cake." *AI Magazine*, Vol. 10, No. 4 (Winter 1989), pp. 45–50.

[38] David Chapman and Philip E. Agre, "Abstract Reasoning as Emergent From Concrete Activity." In M. P. Georgeff and A. L. Lansky (editors), *Reasoning about Actions and Plans*, Proceedings of the 1986 Workshop at Timberline, Oregon, Morgan Kaufmann, Los Altos CA, 1987, pp. 411–424.

[39] David Chapman and Leslie Pack Kaelbling, *Learning from Delayed Reinforcement in a Complex Domain*. Teleos Research Technical Report 90-11, December 1990.

[40] Herbert H. Clark and Catherine R. Marshall, "Definite reference and mutual knowledge." Chapter 1 in Aravind K. Joshi, Bonnie L. Webber, and Ivan A. Sag, *Elements of Discourse Understanding*, Cambridge University Press, Cambridge, 1981.

[41] Herbert H. Clark and Deanna Wilkes-Gibbs, "Referring as a collaborative process." *Cognition* **22** (1986) pp. 1–39.

[42] P. R. Cohen, "The need for identification as a planned action." IJCAI-81, pp. 31-36.

[43] Philip R. Cohen, "The Pragmatics of Referring and the Modality of Communication." *Computational Linguistics* 10:2, April–June 1984, pp. 97–125.

[44] *Computational Linguistics*, Special Issue on Tense and Aspect, 14:2 (June, 1988).

[45] Jonathan H. Connell, *A Behavior-Based Arm Controller*. MIT AI Memo 1025, June, 1988.

[46] Jonathan Hudson Connell, *A Colony Architecture for an Artificial Creature*. MIT AI TR 1151, 1989. Also, Academic Press, in publication.

[47] Francis Crick, "Function of the thalamic reticular complex: The searchlight hypothesis." *Proceedings of the National Academy of Science*, Vol. 81, pp. 4586–4590, July 1984.

[48] Francis Crick, "The recent excitement about neural networks." *Nature* Vol. 337 (12 January 1989) pp. 129–132.

[49] Francis Crick and Chisato Asanuma, "Certain Aspects of the Anatomy and Physiology of the Cerebral Cortex." Chapter 20 in James L. McClelland, David E. Rumelhart, and the PDP Research Group, *Parallel Distributed Processing: Explorations in the Microstructure of Cognition*, MIT Press, Cambridge, MA, 1986.

[50] Nigel Cross, "Designerly ways of knowing." *Design Studies* vol. 3 no. 4 (October 1982), pp. 221–227.

[51] Anthony Davey, "The Formalisation of Discourse Production." PhD Thesis, University of Edinburgh, 1974.

[52] Anthony Davey, *Discourse Production—A Computational Model of Some Aspects of a Speaker*. Edinburgh University Press, Edinburgh, 1978.

[53] Donald Davidson, "The Logical Form of Action Sentences." In Nicholas Rescher, ed., *The Logic of Decision and Action*, University of Pittsburgh Press, 1966.

[54] James Raymond Davis, "Back Seat Driver: voice assisted automobile navigation." PhD Dissertation, Media Arts and Sciences Section, MIT, 1989.

[55] David S. Day, "JANUS: An Architecture for Integrating Automatic and Controlled Problem Solving." *Program of the Ninth Annual Conference of the Cognitive Science Society*, 1987, Seattle, LEA, Hillsdale, NJ, pp. 655–662.

[56] David R. Dowty, *Word Meaning and Montague Grammar.* D. Reidel, Dordrecht, 1979.

[57] Jon Doyle, *A Model For Deliberation, Action, and Introspection.* MIT AI Technical Report 581, 1980.

[58] Gary Drescher, "A mechanism for early Piagetian learning." AAAI87.

[59] Gary Drescher, "Learning from experience without prior knowledge in a complicated world." *Proceedings of the 1988 Spring Symposium: Parallel Models of Intelligence.*

[60] Gary Drescher, "Made-up minds: a constructivist approach to artificial intelligence." PhD Thesis, Department of Electrical Engineering and Computer Science, MIT, 1989.

[61] Hubert Dreyfus, *Being-in-the-world: A commentary on Heidegger's Being and Time, Division I.* MIT Press, forthcoming.

[62] Jon Driver and Gordon C. Baylis, "Movement and Visual Attention: The Spotlight Metaphor Breaks Down." *Journal of Experimental Psychology: Human Perception and Performance.* 15:3 (1989) pp. 448–456.

[63] Starkey Duncan, Jr. and Donald W. Fiske, *Interaction Structure and Strategy,* Cambridge University Press, 1985.

[64] Shimon Edelman, Heinrich Bulthoff, and Daphna Weinshall, "Stimulus familiarity determines recognition strategy for novel 3D objects." MIT AI Memo 1138, July 1989.

[65] Shimon Edelman and Tomaso Poggio, "Representations in High-Level Vision: Reassessing the Inverse Optics Paradigm." *Proceedings of the 1989 Image Understanding Workshop,* 1989.

[66] H. Eichenbaum and N. J. Cohen, "Representation in the Hippocampus: What do Hippocampal Neurons Code?" *Trends in Neuroscience,* Vol. 11, No. 6, 1988.

[67] Mürvet Enç, "Tense Without Scope: An Analysis of Nouns as Indexicals." PhD Thesis, Department of Linguistics, University of Wisconsin–Madison, 1981.

[68] F. L. Engel, "Visual Conspicuity, Directed Attention, and Retinal Locus." *Vision Research* Vol. 11 (1971) pp. 563–576.

[69] F. L. Engel, "Visual Conspicuity and Selective Background Interference in Eccentric Vision." *Vision Research* Vol. 14 (1974) pp. 459–471.

[70] C. W. Eriksen and J. D. St. James, "Visual attention within and around the field of focal attention: a zoom lens model." *Perception and Psychophysics* **40** (1986) pp. 225–240.

[71] Gareth Evans, *The Varieties of Reference.* Oxford University Press, Oxford, 1982.

[72] Scott E. Fahlman, "An Empirical Study of Learning Speed in Back-Propagation Networks." Carnegie Mellon University Computer Science Department Report CMU-CS-88-162, 1988.

[73] Martha J. Farah, "Mechanisms of Imagery-Perception Interaction." *Journal of Experimental Psychology: Human Perception and Performance* 15:2 (1989), pp. 203–211.

[74] M. J. Farah, J. L. Brunn, M. A. Wallace, and N. Madigan, "Structure of Objects in Central Vision Affects the Distribution of Visual Attention In Neglect." *Society for Neuroscience Abstracts* 15:1 (1989), p. 481.

[75] Jerome A. Feldman, *Memory and change in connection networks.* University of Rochester Computer Science Department Technical Report 96, 1981.

[76] Jerome A. Feldman, "Dynamic connections in neural networks." *Biological Cybernetics* **46** (1982), pp. 27–39.

[77] Jerome A. Feldman, "Four frames suffice: A provisional model of vision and space." *The Behavioral and Brain Sciences* 8:2 (1985) pp. 265–313. With commentary from various authors.

[78] Jerome A. Feldman, "Connectionist Models and Parallelism in High Level Vision." *Computer Vision, Graphics, and Image Processing* **31** pp. 178–200.

[79] Jerome A. Feldman, *Neural Representation of Conceptual Knowledge.* Rochester Computer Science Department TR189, 1986.

[80] Jerome A. Feldman and Dana Ballard, "Connectionist Models and their Properties." *Cognitive Science* **6** (1982) pp. 205–254.

[81] Richard E. Fikes, Peter E. Hart, and Nils J. Nilsson, "Learning and Executing Generalized Robot Plans." *Artificial Intelligence* **3** (1972) pp. 251–288.

[82] Charles Fillmore, *Santa Cruz Lectures on Deixis: 1971.* Indiana University Linguistics Club, 1975.

[83] Charles J. Fillmore, "Frames and the Semantics of Understanding." *Quaderni Di Semantica*, Vol. VI, no. 2, December 1985.

[84] R. James Firby, "An investigation into reactive planning in complex domains." AAAI-87.

[85] Martin A. Fischler, "On the Representation of Natural Scenes." In Allen R. Hanson and Edward M. Riseman, eds., *Computer Vision Systems*, Academic Press, New York, 1978, pp. 47–52.

[86] J. A. Fisher, "Very Long Instruction Word Architectures and the ELI-512." *Proceedings of the Tenth Annual Symposium on Computer Architecture*, 1983, pp. 140–150.

[87] Margaret Morrison Fleck, "Local Rotational Symmetries." MIT AI Technical Report 852, 1985.

[88] Anita M. Flynn and Rodney A. Brooks, "Building Robots: Expectations and Experiences." *Proceedings of the IEEE Intelligent Robots and Systems Conference*, Tsukuba, Japan, September, 1989. Also published as "Battling Reality," MIT AI Memo 1148, October, 1989.

[89] Jerry A. Fodor, *The Modularity of Mind.* MIT Press, Cambridge, MA, 1983.

[90] Jerry A. Fodor and Zenon W. Pylyshyn, "Connectionism and Cognitive Architecture: A Critical Analysis." *Cognition* **28** (1988) pp. 3–71.

[91] Kunihiko Fukushima, "A Neural Network Model for Selective Attention in Visual Pattern Recognition." *Biological Cybernetics* **55** (1986) pp. 5–15.

[92] Hans G. Furth, *Piaget and Knowledge: Theoretical Foundations.* Prentice-Hall, Englewood Cliffs, NJ, 1969.

[93] C. R. Gallistel, *The organization of action: A new synthesis.* Erlbaum, 1980.

[94] Michael P. Georgeff, "Planning." In Joseph F. Traub, Barbara J. Grosz, Butler W. Lampson, and Nils J. Nilsson, eds, *Annual Review of Computer Science* **2**, Annual Reviews Inc., Palo Alto, CA, 1987, pp. 359–400.

[95] Michael Georgeff and Amy Lansky, "Reactive reasoning and planning." AAAI-87, pp. 677–682.

[96] Matthew L. Ginsberg, "Universal Planning: An (Almost) Universally Bad Idea." *AI Magazine*, Vol. 10, No. 4 (Winter 1989), pp. 40–44.

[97] Matthew L. Ginsberg, "Ginsberg Replies to Chapman and Schoppers: Universal Planning Research: A Good or Bad Idea?" *AI Magazine*, Vol. 10, No. 4 (Winter 1989), pp. 61-62.

[98] Andrew Golding, Paul S. Rosenbloom, and John E. Laird, "Learning Search Control from Outside Guidance." IJCAI-87, pp. 334–337.

[99] Bradley A. Goodman, "Reference and Reference Failures." *TINLAP-3: Theoretical Issues in Natural Language Processing–3, Position Papers*, New Mexico State University, 1987, pp. 150–154.

[100] Peter Gouras, "Oculomotor System." Chapter 34 in E. R. Kandel and J. H. Schwartz, *Principles of Neural Science*, Elsevier North-Holland, New York, 1981, pp. 394–405.

[101] W. E. L. Grimson and Daniel P. Huttenlocher "On the Verification of Hypothesized Matches in Model-Based Recognition." MIT Artificial Intelligence Laboratory Memo 1110, 1989.

[102] W. E. L. Grimson and Tomaás Lozano-Pérez, "Model-Based Recognition and Localization from Sparse Range or Tactile Data." *International Journal of Robotics Research* 3(3), pp. 3–35.

[103] Barbara J. Grosz, "The representation and use of focus in a system for understanding dialogs." IJCAI-77, pp. 67–76. Reprinted in Barbara J. Grosz, Karen Sparck Jones, and Bonnie Lynn Webber, eds., *Readings in Natural Language*, Morgan-Kauffman, Los Altos, 1986, pp. 353–362.

[104] Barbara J. Grosz, "Discourse Knowledge." Section 4 in Donald E. Walker, ed., *Understanding Spoken Language*, Elsevier North Holland, New York, 1978, pp. 229–344.

[105] Barbara J. Grosz, "Utterance and Objective: Issues in Natural Language Communication." IJCAI-79, pp. 1067–1076.

[106] Barbara J. Grosz, "Focusing and Description in Natural Language Dialogues." Chapter 3 in Aravind K. Joshi, Bonnie L. Webber, and Ivan A. Sag, *Elements of Discourse Understanding,* Cambridge University Press, Cambridge, 1981.

[107] Barbara J. Grosz, Gary G. Hendrix, and Ann E. Robinson, "Using Process Knowledge in Understanding Task-Oriented Dialogs." IJCAI-77, p. 90.

[108] Barbara J. Grosz, Aravind K. Joshi, and Scott Weinstein, "Providing a Unified Account of Definite Noun Phrases in Discourse." ACL-83, pp. 44–50.

[109] Barbara J. Grosz, Martha E. Pollack, and Candace L. Sidner, "Computational Models of Discourse." In M. Posner, ed., *Foundations of Cognitive Science*, MIT Press, Cambridge, MA, 1989.

[110] Barbara J. Grosz and Candace L. Sidner, "Attention, Intentions, and the Structure of Discourse." *Computational Linguistics* 12:3, July-September 1986, pp. 175–204.

[111] Barbara J. Grosz and Candace L. Sidner, "Plans for Discourse." In P. Cohen, J. Morgan, and M. Pollack, eds., *Intentions in Communication*. MIT Press, Cambridge, MA, to appear.

[112] Kristian J. Hammond, *Case-Based Planning: Viewing Planning as a Memory Task*. Academic Press, 1989.

[113] Jorge Hankamer and Ivan Sag, "Deep and Surface Anaphora." *Linguistic Inquiry* **7** no. 3 (Summer, 1976) pp. 391–426.

[114] William F. Hanks, *Referential Practice: Language and Lived Space Among the Maya*. University of Chicago Press, Chicago, in press.

[115] Patrick J. Hayes, "The Naive Physics Manifesto." In Donald Michie, ed., *Expert Systems in the Micro-Electronic Age* , Edinburgh University Press, 1978.

[116] Patrick J. Hayes, *The Second Naive Physics Manifesto*. Rochester University Cognitive Science Technical Report URCS-10, 1983.

[117] Patrick J. Hayes, *Naive Physics 1: Ontology for Liquids*. Manuscript, University of Essex, 1978.

[118] Martin Heidegger, *Being and Time*. Harper and Row, 1927/1961.

[119] James Hendler, *Integrating Marker-Passing and Problem-Solving: A Spreading Activation Approach to Improved Choices in Planning*. University of Maryland Department of Computer Science TR-1624, 1986.

[120] John Heritage, *Garfinkel and Ethnomethodology*, Polity Press, Cambridge, England, 1984.

[121] Annette Herskovits, *Language and Spatial Cognition: An interdisciplinary study of the preposition in English*. Cambridge University Press, Cambridge, 1986.

[122] W. Daniel Hillis, *The Connection Machine*. MIT Press, Cambridge, MA, 1985.

[123] J. Hirschberg, D. Litman, J. Pierrehumbert, and G. Ward, "Intonation and the Intentional Structure of Discourse." IJCAI-87 pp. 636–9.

[124] B. K. P. Horn, *Robot Vision*. MIT Press, Cambridge MA, 1986.

[125] Edward Hendrik Hovy, *Generating Natural Language Under Pragmatic Constraints*. Yale CSD RR 521, March 1987.

[126] Edwin Hutchins, "Leaning to Navigate in Context." Manuscript prepared for the Workshop on Context, Cognition, and Activity, Stenungsund, Sweden, August 6–9, 1987.

[127] Daniel P. Huttenlocher, *Three-Dimensional Recognition of Solid Objects from a Two-Dimensional Image*. MIT AI TR 1045, October, 1988.

[128] Daniel P. Huttenlocher and Shimon Ullman, "Recognizing Solid Objects by Alignment", *Proceedings of the 1988 DARPA Image Understanding Workshop*, pp. 1114–1124.

[129] Ian Douglas Horswill, *Reactive Navigation for Mobile Robots*. MS Thesis, MIT Department of Electrical Engineering and Computer Science, May, 1988.

[130] Ian Douglas Horswill and Rodney Allen Brooks, "Situated Vision in a Dynamic World: Chasing Objects." *AAAI-88*.

[131] Ray Jackendoff, *Semantics and Cognition*. MIT Press, Cambridge, MA, 1983.

[132] Robert J. Jarvella and Wolfang Klein, eds., *Speech, Place, and Action: Studies in Deixis and Related Topics*. John Wiley & Sons, Ltd., Cichester, 1982.

[133] Pierre Jolicoeur, Shimon Ullman, and Marilynn Mackay, "Curve tracing: A possible basic operation in the perception of spatial relations." *Memory and Cognition* 1986, 14 (2), pp. 129–140.

[134] Brigitte Jordan and Nancy Fuller, "On the non-fatal nature of trouble: Sense-making and trouble-managing in Lingua Franca talk." *Semiotica* **13** (1975), pp. 1–31.

[135] Aravind K. Joshi, Bonnie L. Webber, and Ivan A. Sag, *Elements of Discourse Understanding*, Cambridge University Press, Cambridge, 1981.

[136] Bela Julesz, "A brief outline of the texton theory of human vision." *Trends in NeuroScience*, February, 1984, pp. 41–45.

[137] B. Julesz and J. R. Bergen, "Textons, the fundamental elements in preattentive vision and perception of textures." *Bell Systems Technical Journal* **62** (1983), pp. 1619–1645.

[138] Leslie Pack Kaelbling, "Rex: A Symbolic Language for the Design and Parallel Implementation of Embedded Systems." *Proceedings of the AIAA Conference on Computers in Aerospace*, Wakefield, Massachusetts, 1987.

[139] Leslie Pack Kaelbling, "Goals as Parallel Program Specifications." *Proceedings of the Seventh National Conference on Artificial Intelligence*, Minneapolis-St. Paul, Minnesota, 1988.

[140] Leslie Pack Kaelbling, *Learning in Embedded Systems*. Teleos Research TR-90-04, June 1990.

[141] Leslie Pack Kaelbling and Stanley J. Rosenchein, "Action and Planning in Embedded Agents." To appear in Pattie Maes, ed., *New Architectures for Autonomous Agents: Task-level Decomposition and Emergent Functionality*, MIT Press, Cambridge, Massachusetts, 1991.

[142] Leslie Pack Kaelbling and Nathan J. Wilson, *Rex Programmer's Manual*. SRI International Artificial Intelligence Center TR 381R, Menlo Park, California, 1988.

[143] Eric R. Kandel and James H. Schwartz, *Principles of Neural Science*. Elsevier, New York, 1985 (second edition).

[144] Jerrold Katz and Jerry Fodor, "The structure of a semantic theory." *Language* **39** (1963), pp. 170–210.

[145] E. L. Kaufman, M. W. Lord, T. W. Reese, and J. Volkmann, "The Discrimination of Visual Number." *American Journal of Psychology*, **62** (1949), pp. 498–525.

[146] Henry A. Kautz, *A Formal Theory of Plan Recognition*. University of Rochester Department of Computer Science TR 215, 1987.

[147] H. A. Kautz and J. F. Allen, "Generalized plan recognition." AAAI-86.

[148] Kenneth Kaye, *The Mental and Social Life of Babies: How Parents Create Persons*. University of Chicago Press, 1982.

[149] Maxine Hong Kingston, *The Woman Warrior: memoirs of a girlhood among ghosts*. Knopf, New York, 1977.

[150] D. Klahr and J. G. Wallace, "The Role of Quantification Operators in the Development of Conservation of Quantity." *Cognitive Psychology* **4** (1973) pp. 301–327.

[151] Raymond Klein, "Inhibitory tagging system facilitates visual search." *Nature* vol. 334 (4 August 1988) pp. 430–431.

[152] Christof Koch and Shimon Ullman, "Selecting One Among the Many: A Simple Network Implementing Shifts in Selective Visual Attention." *Human Neurobiology* **4** (1985) pp. 219–227. Also published as MIT AI Memo 770/C.B.I.P. Paper 003, January, 1984.

[153] Kurt Konolige and Martha E. Pollack, "Ascribing Plans To Agents." *IJCAI-89*.

[154] Saul A. Kripke, *Naming and Necessity*. Harvard University Press, Cambridge, MA, 1980 (second edition). Originally printed in Donald Davidson and Gilbert Harman, eds., *Semantics of Natural Language*, Reidel, Dordrecht, 1972, pp. 253–355.

[155] Amichai Kronfeld, "Donnellan's Distinction and a Computational Model of Reference." ACL-86, pp. 186–191.

[156] Amichai Kronfeld, "Goals of Referring Acts." *TINLAP-3: Theoretical Issues in Natural Language Processing–3, Position Papers*, New Mexico State University, 1987, pp. 143–149.

[157] Ben J. A. Kröse, "Local structure analyzers as determinants of preattentive pattern discrimination." *Biological Cybernetics* **55** (1987), pp. 289–298.

[158] Ben J. A. Kröse and Bela Julesz, "The Control and Speed of Shifts of Attention." *Vision Research* Vol. 29 No. 11 (1989), pp. 1607–1619.

[159] John E. Laird, Eric S. Yager, Christopher M. Tuck, and Michael Hucka, "Learning in Tele-autonomous Systems using Soar." *Proceedings of the 1989 NASA Conference on Space Telerobotics*.

[160] George Lakoff, *Women, Fire, and Dangerous Things: What Categories Reveal about the Mind*. University of Chicago Press, Chicago, 1987.

[161] Jean Lave, *Tailored Learning: Apprenticeship and everyday practice among craftsmen in West Africa*. In preparation.

[162] Douglas B. Lenat, "EURISKO: A Program That Learns New Heuristics and Domain Concepts." *Artificial Intelligence* **21** (1983) pp. 61-98.

[163] Douglas B. Lenat and John Seely Brown, "Why AM and Eurisko Appear to Work." *Artificial Intelligence* **23** (1984) pp. 269-294. An earlier, shorter version of this paper also appeared in *AAAI-83*, pp. 236-240.

[164] Stephen C. Levinson, *Pragmatics*. Cambridge University Press, Cambridge, 1983.

[165] Long-Ji Lin, Reid Simmons, and Christopher Fedor, *Experience with a Task Control Architecture for Mobile Robots*. Carnegie Mellon University Robotics Institute Technical Report 89-29, 1989.

[166] Tomas Lozano-Perez, "Spatial Planning: A Configuration Space Approach." *IEEE Transactions on Computers*, Vol. C-32, No. 2, February 1983, pp. 108–120.

[167] D. G. Lowe, *Perceptual Organization and Visual Recognition*. Kluwer, 1985.

[168] Jim Mahoney, "Proposal for a system for spatial analysis of schematic drawings by visual routines." Unpublished M.S. thesis proposal, MIT AI Lab, June, 1985.

[169] James V. Mahoney, *Image Chunking: Defining Spatial Building Blocks for Scene Analysis*. MIT AI Lab TR-980, August, 1987.

[170] Heinz Marburger, Bernd Neumann, and Hans-Joachim Novak, "Natural Language Dialogue about Moving Objects in an Automatically Analyzed Traffic Scene." IJCAI-81, pp. 49–51.

[171] D. Marr, "Early Processing of Visual Information." *Philosophical Transactions of the Royal Society, Series B*, Vol. 275 B 942. 47 (19 October 1976) pp. 483–519.

[172] David Marr, *Vision*. W. H. Freeman and Company, San Francisco, 1982.

[173] Matthew T. Mason, "Compliance and Force Control for Computer Controlled Manipulators." *IEEE Transactions on Systems, Man, and Cybernetics*, Vol. SMC-11, No. 6, June 1981, pp 418–432.

[174] John H. R. Maunsell and William T. Newsome, "Visual Processing in Monkey Extrastriate Cortex." *Ann. Rev. Neurosci. 1987* **10** (1987) 363–401.

[175] John McCarthy, "The Advice Taker." Originally published 1958, reprinted in Marvin Minsky, ed., *Semantic Information Processing*, MIT Press, Cambridge, Massachusetts and London, England, 1968.

[176] Drew McDermott, *Regression Planning*. Yale CSD RR 752, November, 1989. Also submitted to the *International Journal of Intelligent Systems*, special issue on Temporal Representation and Reasoning.

[177] J. McDermott and C. Forgy, *Production System Conflict Resolution Strategies*. CMU Department of Computer Science, Technical Report (no number), December 1976.

[178] David McNeil, "Iconic gestures of children and adults." *Semiotica* **62** (1986) pp. 107–128.

[179] Bartlett W. Mel, *MURPHY: A Neurally-Inspired Connectionist Approach to Learning and Performance in Vision-Based Robot Motion Planning*. University of Illinois Center for Complex Systems Research report CCSR-89-17A, 1989.

[180] David P. Miller, "Execution monitoring for a mobile robot system." *Proceedings of the SPIE 1989 Conference on Intelligent Control and Adaptive Systems*, Philadelphia, 1989.

[181] George A. Miller and Philip N. Johnson-Laird, *Language and Perception*. Harvard University Press, Cambridge, Massachusetts, 1976.

[182] Ruth Garret Millikan, *Language, Thought, and Other Biological Categories: New Foundations for Realism*. MIT Press, Cambridge, MA, 1984.

[183] Marvin Minsky, *Computation: Finite and Infinite Machines*. Prentice-Hall, Inc., Englewood Cliffs, N. J., 1967.

[184] Marvin Minsky, "A Framework for Representing Knowledge." MIT AI Memo 306, 1974. Condensed version in P. H. Winston, *The Psychology of Computer Vision*, McGraw-Hill, New York, 1975.

[185] Marvin Minsky, *The Society of Mind*. Simon and Schuster, New York, 1986.

[186] Tom M. Mitchell, Richard M. Keller, and Smadar T. Kedar-Cabelli, "Explanation-Based Generalization: A Unifying View." *Machine Learning* **1** (1986), pp. 47–80.

[187] Marc Moens and Mark Steedman, "Temporal Ontology and Temporal Reference." *Computational Linguistics*, Special Issue on Tense and Aspect, 14:2 (June, 1988), pp. 15–28.

[188] Jefferey Moran and Robert Desimone, "Selective attention gates visual processing in the extrastriate cortex." *Science* **229** (1985), pp. 782–784.

[189] David J. Mostow, *Mechanical Transformation of Task Heuristics into Operational Procedures*. PhD Thesis, Computer Science Deparment, Carnegie-Mellon University, 14 April 1981. CMU-CS-81-113.

[190] Michael C. Mozer, "RAMBOT: A Connectionist Expert System that Learns by Example." Institute for Cognitive Science Report 8610, University of California at San Diego, La Jolla, August, 1986.

[191] Michael C. Mozer, "A connectionist model of selective attention in visual perception." *Program of the Tenth Annual Conference of the Cognitive Science Society*, Montreal, 1988, pp. 195–201.

[192] Michael C. Mozer, *The Perception of Multiple Objects: A Connectionist Approach*. MIT Press, Cambridge, MA, forthcoming.

[193] V. B. Mountcastle, B. C. Motter, M. A. Steinmetz, and A. K. Sestokas, "Common and Differential Effects of Attentive Fixation on the Excitability of Parietal and Prestriate (V4) Cortical Visual Neurons in the Macaque Monkey." *The Journal of Neuroscience*, July 1987, 7(7), pp. 2239–2255.

[194] K. Nakayama and G. H. Silverman, "Serial and parallel processing of visual feature conjunctions." *Nature* **320** (1986), pp. 264-265.

[195] Ken Nakayama and Manfred Mackeben, "Sustained and Transient Components of Focal Visual Attention." *Vision Research* 29:11 (1989), pp. 1631—1647.

[196] Allen Newell and Herbert A. Simon, *Human Problem Solving*. Prentice-Hall, 1972.

[197] H. K. Nishihara, "Practical Real-Time Imaging Stereo Matcher," *Optical Engineering* **23**, 5, 536–545, Sept.–Oct. 1984. Also in *Readings in Computer Vision: Issues, Problems, Principles, and Paradigms*, edited by M. A. Fischler and O. Firschein, Morgan Kaufmann, Los Altos, 1987.

[198] H. Keith Nishihara, "RTVS-3 Real-Time Binocular Stereo and Optical Flow Measurement System System Description." Teleos Research internal document.

[199] H. Novak, "Strategies for Generating Coherent Descriptions of Object Motions in Street Scenes." In G. Kempen, ed., *Natural Language Generation: New Results in Artificial Intelligence, Psychology, and Linguistics*, pp. 117–132. Martinus Nijhoff Publishers, 1987.

[200] Donald A. Norman, "Reflections on Cognition and Parallel Distributed Processing." Chapter 26 in James L. McClelland, David E. Rumelhart, and the PDP Research Group, *Parallel Distributed Processing: Explorations in the Microstructure of Cognition*, MIT Press, Cambridge, MA, 1986.

[201] Geoffrey D. Nunberg, *The Pragmatics of Reference*. PhD Thesis, University of California, Berkeley. Reproduced by the Indiana University Linguistics Club. June, 1978.

[202] Geoffrey Nunberg, "Validating Pragmatic Explanations." In Peter Cole, ed., *Radical Pragmatics*, Academic Press, New York, 1981.

[203] Geoffrey Nunberg, "The Non-Uniqueness of Semantic Solutions: Polysemy." *Linguistics and Philosophy* **3** (1979), pp. 143–184.

[204] Naoyuki Okada, "SUPP: Understanding Moving Picture Patterns Based on Linguistic Knowledge." IJCAI-79, pp. 690–692.

[205] John Howard Palevich, "Dandy—an Expandable Real Time Adventure." Bachelor's Thesis, MIT, 1982.

[206] Seymour Papert, *Mindstorms: Children, Computers, and Powerful Ideas*. Basic Books, New York, 1980.

[207] Barbara Hall Partee, "Opacity, coreference, and pronouns." In Donald Davidson and Gilbert Harman, eds., *Semantics of Natural Language*, Reidel, Dordrecht, 1972, pp. 415–441.

[208] Barbara H. Partee, ed., *Montague Grammar*. Academic Press, New York, 1976.

[209] Barbara H. Partee, "Nominal and Temporal Anaphora." *Linguistics and Philosophy* 7 (1984), pp. 243–286.

[210] David W. Payton, "Internalized Plans: a representation for action resources." To appear in Pattie Maes, ed., *New Architectures for Autonomous Agents: Task-level Decomposition and Emergent Functionality*, MIT Press, Cambridge, Massachusetts, 1991.

[211] Alex P. Pentland, ed., *From Pixels to Predicates: Recent Advances in Computational and Robotic Vision*. Ablex, Norwood, NJ, 1986.

[212] C. R. Perrault and P. R. Allen, "A Plan-Based Analysis of Indirect Speech Acts." *American Journal of Computational Linguistics* 6(3) (1980), pp. 167–182.

[213] D. I. Perrett, E. T. Rolls, and W. Cann, "Visual Neurones Responsive to Faces in the Monkey Temporal Cortex." *Exp. Brain Res.* (1982) 47:329–342.

[214] J. Pierrehumbert and J. Hirschberg, "The Meaning of Intonational Contours in the Interpretation of Discourse." In Philip R. Cohen, Jerry Morgan, and Martha E. Pollack, eds., *Intentions in Communication*, MIT Press, Cambridge MA, to appear.

[215] Livia Polanyi, Remko Scha, and Andras Kornai, "A Computational Model of the Linguistic Structure of Discourse." Manuscript, 1988.

[216] Martha E. Pollack, "A Model of Plan Inference that Distinguishes Between the Beliefs of Actors and Observers." In M. P. Georgeff and A. L. Lansky (editors), *Reasoning about Actions and Plans*, Proceedings of the 1986 Workshop at Timberline, Oregon, Morgan Kaufmann, Los Altos CA, 1987, pp. 279–295.

[217] Martha E. Pollack, "Plans as complex mental attitudes." In Philip R. Cohen, Jerry Morgan, and Martha E. Pollack, eds., *Intentions in Communication*, MIT Press, Cambridge MA, to appear.

[218] Michael I. Posner, Charles R. R. Snyder, and Brian J. Davidson, "Attention and Detection of Signals." *Journal of Experimental Psychology: General*, 1980, Vol. 109, No. 2, pp. 160–174.

[219] M. I. Posner, Y. Cohen and R. D. Rafal, "Neural systems control of spatial orienting." *Philosophical Transactions of the Royal Society of London, Series B* **298** (1982) pp. 187–198.

[220] Mary C. Potter, "Representational Buffers: The Eye-Mind Hypothesis in Picture Perception, Reading, and Visual Search." Chapter 24 in *Eye Movements in Reading: Perceptual and Language Processes*. Academic Press, New York, 1983.

[221] Elizabeth F. Preston, "Representational and Non-Representational Intentionality: Husserl, Heidegger, and Artificial Intelligence." PhD Dissertation, Department of Philosophy, Boston University, 1988.

[222] Beth Preston, "Heidegger and Artificial Intelligence," presented at the Western Division American Philosophical Association Conference, 1989.

[223] Zenon Pylyshyn, "The Role of Location Indexes in Spatial Perception: A Sketch of the FINST Spatial-Index Model." *Cognition*, 32:1 (June, 1989), pp. 65–96.

[224] Zenon W. Pylyshyn and R. Storm, "Tracking multiple independent targets: Evidence for a parallel tracking mechanism." *Spatial Vision* 3:1-19.

[225] Gudula Retz-Schmidt, "Various Views on Spatial Prepositions." *AI Magazine*, Summer 1988, pp. 95-105.

[226] Gudula Retz-Schmidt, "Deictic and Intrinsic Use of Spatial Prepositions: A Multidisciplinary Comparison." VITRA Memo 13, Universität des Saarlandes, Saarbrüken, December 1986.

[227] Martin H. Ringle and Bertram C. Bruce, "Conversation Failure." Chapter 7 in Wendy G. Lehnert and Martin H. Ringle, eds., *Strategies for Natural Language Processing*, Lawrence Earlbaum Associates, Hillsdale, NJ, 1982, pp. 203-221.

[228] Ronald L. Rivest and Robert E. Schapire, "A New Approach to Unsupervised Learning in Deterministic Environments." In P. Langley, ed., *Proceedings of the Fourth International Workshop on Machine Learning*, pp. 78–87.

[229] Ann E. Robinson, "Determining Verb Phrase Referents in Dialogs." *American Journal of Computational Linguistics*, vol. 7, no. 1, January-March 1981, pp. 1–16.

[230] Barbara Rogoff, *Apprenticeship in Thinking: Cognitive Development in Social Context*. Oxford University Press, Oxford, 1989.

[231] Marc H. J. Romanycia, "The Design and Control of Visual Routines for the Computation of Simple Geometric Properties and Relations." University of British Columbia Department of Computer Science Technical Report 87-34, 1987.

[232] Ragnar Rommetveit, *On Message Structure: A framework for the study of language and communication*. John Wiley and Sons, London, 1974.

[233] Stanley J. Rosenschein, "Formal Theories of Knowledge in AI and Robotics." SRI International AI Center Technical Note 362, 1985.

[234] Stan Rosenschein, "Synthesizing Information-Tracking Automata from Environment Descriptions." *Proceedings of the First International Conference on Principles of Knowledge Representation and Reasoning*. Toronto, 1989.

[235] Stanley J. Rosenschein and Leslie Pack Kaelbling, "The Synthesis of Digital Machines with Provable Epistemic Properties." In Joseph Y. Halpern, editor, *Theoretical Aspects of Reasoning about Knowlege*. Proceedings of the 1986 Conference, pages 83–98. Morgan Kauffman Publishers, 1986.

[236] David E. Rumelhart, Geoffrey E. Hinton, and Ronald J. Williams, "Learning Internal Representations by Error Propagation." Chapter 8 in James L. McClelland, David E. Rumelhart, and the PDP Research Group, *Parallel Distributed Processing: Explorations in the Microstructure of Cognition*, MIT Press, Cambridge, MA, 1986.

[237] Stuart J. Russell, "Execution architectures and compilation." IJCAI-89, pp. 15–20.

[238] Sacerdoti, Earl D., *A Structure for Plans and Behavior*. American Elsevier, New York, 1977. Also SRI AI Technical Note 109, August, 1975.

[239] H. Sakata, H. Shibutani, and K. Kawano, "Functional properties of visual tracking neurons in posterior parietal association cortext of the monkey." *Journal of Neurophysiology* 49 (1983) pp. 1364–1380.

[240] Hanan Samet, "The quadtree and related hierarchical data structures." *ACM Computing Surveys* 16:2 (1984) pp. 187–260.

[241] Arthur L. Samuel, "Some studies in machine learning using the game of checkers." *IBM Journal on Research and Development*, 3 (1959), pp. 210–229. Reprinted in Edward A. Feigenbaum and Jerome Feldman, eds., *Computers and Thought*, McGraw-Hill, New York, 1963, pp. 71–105.

[242] Roger C. Schank, Gregg C. Collins, and Lawrence E. Hunter, "Transcending inductive category formation in learning." *The Behavioral and Brain Sciences* **9** (1986), pp. 639–686.

[243] Roger C. Schank, "That reminds me of a story." Forthcoming.

[244] Emanuel Schegloff, Gail Jefferson, and Harvey Sacks, "The preference for self-repair in the organization of repair in conversation." *Language* Vol. 53 No. 2 (1977), pp. 361–382.

[245] J. R. J. Schirra, G. Bosch, C. K. Sung, G. Zimmermann, "From Image Sequences to Natural Language: A First Step Towards Automatic Perception and Description of Motions." VITRA Memo 26, December 1987.

[246] Jeffrey Curtis Schlimmer, *Concept Acquisition Through Representational Adjustment.* University of California at Irvine Technical Report 87-19, 1987.

[247] J. R. Searle, "Indirect Speech Acts." In P. Cole and J. L. Morgan, eds., *Syntax and Semantics, Vol. 3: Speech Acts,* Academic Press, New York, 1975, pp. 59–82.

[248] A. Shafrir, "Fast region coloring and computation of inside/outside relations," M. Sc. Thesis, Department of Applied Mathematics, Feinberg Graduate School, Weizmann Institute of Science, Rehevot, Israel.

[249] Mary L. Shaw, "A capacity allocation model for reaction time." *Journal of Experimental Psychology: Human Perception and Performance,* **4** (1978), pp. 586–598.

[250] M. L. Shaw and P. Shaw, "Optimal allocation of cognitive resources to spatial locations." *Journal of Experimental Psychology: Human Perception and Performance,* **3** (1977), pp. 201–211.

[251] J. F. Shepansky and S. A. Macy, "Teaching Artificial Neural Systems to Drive: Manual Training Techniques for Autonomous Systems." *Proceedings of the First Annual International Conference on Neural Networks,* San Diego, CA, June 21–24, 1987.

[252] Lokendra Shastri and Jerome A. Feldman, *Semantic Networks and Neural Nets.* University of Rochester Computer Science Department TR131, 1984.

[253] Robert S. Siegler and Jeffrey Shrager, "Strategy Choices in Addition and Subtraction: How Do Children Know What to Do?" Chapter 9 in Catherine Sophian, ed., *Origins of Cognitive Skills: The Eighteenth Annual Carnegie Symposium on Cognition,* Lawrence Earlbaum Associates, Hillsdale, NJ, 1984, pp. 229–287.

[254] Jeff Shrager, "(Cognitive) Mediation Theory: An Addition to Models of Skill Acquisition." Unpublished, Xerox PARC, 1986.

[255] J. Shrager, D. Klahr, and W. G. Chase, "Segmentation and Quantification of Random Dot Patterns." *Proceedings of the 23rd Annual Meeting of the Psychonomics Society,* 1982.

[256] Candace Lee Sidner, *Towards a Computational Theory of Definite Anaphora Comprehension in English Discourse.* MIT AI TR 537, June 1979.

[257] Candace L. Sidner, "Focusing in the comprehension of definite anaphora." In Michael Brady and Robert C. Berwick, eds., *Computational Models of Discourse,* MIT Press, Cambridge, MA, 1983, pp. 267–330.

[258] C. L. Sidner, "The Pragmatics of Non-Anaphoric Noun Phrases." Section 9 in *Research in Knowledge Representation for Natural Language Understanding,* Bolt Beranek and Newman Inc. Report No. 5421, 1983.

[259] Herbert Simon, *The Sciences of the Artificial*. MIT Press, Cambridge, MA, 1970.

[260] Richard M. Stallman and Gerald J. Sussman, "Forward Reasoning and Dependency Directed Backtracking in a System for Computer-Aided Circuit Analysis." *Artificial Intelligence* 9 (1977) pp. 135–196.

[261] Lawrence Stark and Stephen R. Ellis, "Scanpaths Revisited: Cognitive Models Direct Active Looking." In Fisher, Monty, and Senders, eds., *Eye Movements: Cognition and Visual Perception*, Erlbaum Press, New Jersey, 1981, pp. 193–226.

[262] Gary W. Strong and Bruce A. Whitehead, "A solution to the tag-assignment problem for neural networks." *Behavioral and Brain Sciences* (1989) 12, pp. 381–433.

[263] Susan U. Stucky, "The Situated Processing of Situated Language." *Linguistics and Philosphy* 12, pp. 347–357. Also published as Center for the Study of Language and Information Report No. CSLI-87-80, March, 1987.

[264] Lucy A. Suchman, *Plans and Situated Actions: The problem of human-machine communication*. Cambridge University Press, Cambridge, 1987.

[265] David Sudnow, *Pilgrim In the Microworld*. Warner Books, New York, 1983.

[266] Richard S. Sutton, "Learning to Predict by the Methods of Temporal Differences." *Machine Learning* 3:1 (August 1988), pp. 9–44. Also published as GTE Computer and Intelligent Systems Laboratory TR87-509.1, January 1987.

[267] Richard S. Sutton, "First Results with Dyna, an Integrated Architecture for Learning, Planning, and Reacting." Submitted to the 1990 Stanford Spring Symposium on Planning.

[268] Leonard Talmy, "How language structures space." In Herbert Pick and Linda Acredolo, eds., *Spatial Orientation: Theory, Research, and Application*, Plenum Press, 1983.

[269] Alfred Tarski, "The Semantic Conception of Truth." *Philosophy and Phenomenological Research*, 4 (1944), pp. 341–376.

[270] Christopher J. Terman, *Simulation Tools for Digital Design*. MIT Laboratory for Computer Science TR-304, 1983.

[271] William B. Thompson and Ting-Chuen Pong, "Detecting Moving Objects." *Proceedings of the First International Conference on Computer Vision*, 1987, pp. 201–208.

[272] David S. Touretzky, "BoltzCONS: Reconciling Connectionism with the Recursive Nature of Stacks and Trees." *Proceedings of the Eighth Annual Conference of the Cognitive Science Society*, Amberst, Massachussets, August, 1986.

[273] David S. Touretzky and Geoffrey E. Hinton, "Symbols Among the Neurons: Details of a Connectionist Inference Architecture." *IJCAI-85*.

[274] David S. Touretzky and Geoffrey E. Hinton, *A Distributed Connectionist Production System*. CMU CS TR 86-172, Pittsburgh, 1986.

[275] Anne Treisman, "Perceptual Grouping and Attention in Visual Search for Features and Objects." *Journal of Experimental Psychology: Human Perception and Performance*, Vol. 8 No. 2 (1982) pp. 194–214.

[276] Anne M. Treisman and Garry Gelade, "A Feature-Integration Theory of Attention." *Cognitive Psychology* 12 (1980), pp. 97–136.

[277] Anne Treisman and Janet Souther, "Search Asymmetry: A Diagnostic for Preattentive Processing of Separable Features." *Journal of Experimental Psychology: General*, Vol. 114, No. 3 (September 1985), pp. 285–310.

[278] Anne Treisman and Stephen Gormican, "Feature Analysis in Early Vision: Evidence From Search Asymmetries." *Psychological Review* Vol. 95 (1988), No. 1, pp. 15–48.

[279] Yehoshua Tsal, "Do Illusory Conjunctions Support the Feature Integration Theory? A Critical Review of Theory and Findings." *Journal of Experimental Psychology: Human Perception and Performance* 15:2 (1989), pp. 394–400.

[280] John Tsotsos, "A Framework for Visual Motion Understanding." *IEEE Transactions on Pattern Analysis and Machine Intelligence,* vol. PAMI-2, no. 6, November, 1980, pp. 563–573.

[281] John K. Tsotsos, "Analyzing vision at the complexity level." *Behavioral and Brain Sciences* 13:3 (1990), pp. 423–469.

[282] Shimon Ullman, "Filling in the Gaps: The Shape of Subjective Contours and a Model for their Generation." *Biological Cybernetics* 25:1 (1976), pp. 1–6.

[283] Shimon Ullman, "Visual Routines." *Cognition* 18 (1984), pp. 97–159. Also published as MIT A.I. Memo 723, June 1983.

[284] L. G. Ungerleider and M. Mishkin, "Two cortical visual systems." In D. J. Ingle, M. A. Goodale, and R. J. W. Mansfield, *Analysis of Visual Behavior,* MIT Press, Cambridge, MA, 1982.

[285] Steven Vere and Timothy Bickmore, "A Basic Agent." Manuscript, Lockheed AI Center, Palo Alto, California, 1989.

[286] Kathryn J. Waddell and Barbara Rogoff, "Contextual Organization and Intentionality in Adult's Spatial Memory." *Developmental Psychology* Vol. 23, No. 4 (1987).

[287] Donald E. Walker, ed., *Understanding Spoken Language.* Elsevier North Holland, New York, 1978.

[288] David L. Waltz, "Generating and Understanding Scene Descriptions." Chapter 12 in Aravind K. Joshi, Bonnie L. Webber, and Ivan A. Sag, *Elements of Discourse Understanding,* Cambridge University Press, Cambridge, 1981.

[289] David L. Waltz, "Toward a Detailed Model of Processing for Language Describing the Physical World." IJCAI-81, pp. 1–6.

[290] David L. Waltz and Lois C. Boggess, "Visual Analog Representations for Natural Language Understanding." IJCAI-79, pp. 926–934.

[291] Bonnie Lynn Webber, "Discourse model synthesis: preliminaries to reference." Chapter 13 in Aravind K. Joshi, Bonnie L. Webber, and Ivan A. Sag, *Elements of Discourse Understanding,* Cambridge University Press, Cambridge, 1981.

[292] Bonnie Lynn Webber, "Tense as discourse anaphor." *Computational Linguistics,* Special Issue on Tense and Aspect, 14:2 (June, 1988), pp. 61–73.

[293] Steven D. Whitehead and Dana H. Ballard, "Active Perception and Reinforcement Learning." University of Rochester Computer Science Department Technical Report 331, 1990.

[294] David E. Wilkins, *Practical Planning: Extending the Classical AI Planning Paradigm.* Morgan Kaufmann Publishers, Los Altos CA, 1988.

[295] Terry Winograd, *Procedures as a Representation for Data in a Computer Program for Understanding Natural Language.* MAC-TR-84, MIT, Cambridge, Mass., January 1971.

[296] Terry Winograd and Fernando Flores, *Understanding Computers and Cognition: A New Foundation for Design.* Addison-Wesley, Reading, Massachusetts, 1987.

[297] Erich Woisetschlaeger, "A Semantic Theory of the English Auxiliary System." PhD Thesis, Department of Linguistics and Philosophy, Massachussetts Institute of Technology, 1976. Distributed by the Indiana University Linguistics Club.

[298] Jeremy M. Wolfe, Kyle R. Cave, and Susan L. Franzel, "Guided Search: An Alternative to the Feature Integration Model for Visual Search." *Journal of Experimental Psychology: Human Perception and Performance* 15:3 (1989), pp. 419–433.

[299] S. M. Zeki, "The functional organization of projections from striate to prestriate visual cortex in the rhesus monkey." *Cold Spring Harbor Symposium on Quantitative Biology* **40** (1975), pp. 591–600.

[300] S. M. Zeki, "Uniformity and Diversity of Structure and Function in Rhesus Monkey Prestriate Visual Cortex." *Journal of Physiology* **277** (1978), pp. 273–290.

[301] David Zipser, "Biologically Plausible Models of Place Recognition and Goal Location." Chapter 23 in James L. McClelland, David E. Rumelhart, and the PDP Research Group, *Parallel Distributed Processing: Explorations in the Microstructure of Cognition*, MIT Press, Cambridge, MA, 1986.

Index

Artificial Intelligence
Patrick Henry Winston, founding editor
J. Michael Brady, Daniel G. Bobrow, and Randall Davis, current editors

Model-Based Control of a Robot Manipulator, Chae H. An, Christopher G. Atkeson, and John M. Hollerbach, 1988

A Robot Ping-Pong Player: Experiment in Real-Time Intelligent Control, Russell L. Andersson, 1988

Robotics Research: The Fourth International Symposium, edited by Robert C. Bolles and Bernard Roth, 1988

The Paralation Model: Architecture-Independent Parallel Programming, Gary Sabot, 1988

Concurrent System for Knowledge Processing: An Actor Perspective, edited by Carl Hewitt and Gul Agha, 1989

Automated Deduction in Nonclassical Logics: Efficient Matrix Proof Methods for Modal and Intuitionistic Logics, Lincoln Wallen, 1989

Shape from Shading, edited by Berthold K.P. Horn and Michael J. Brooks, 1989

Ontic: A Knowledge Representation System for Mathematics, David A. McAllester, 1989

Solid Shape, Jan J. Koenderink, 1990

Expert Systems: Human Issues, edited by Dianne Berry and Anna Hart, 1990

Artificial Intelligence: Concepts and Applications, edited by A. R. Mirzai, 1990

Robotics Research: The Fifth International Symposium, edited by Hirofumi Miura and Suguru Arimoto, 1990

Theories of Comparative Analysis, Daniel S. Weld, 1990

Artificial Intelligence at MIT: Expanding Frontiers, edited by Patrick Henry Winston and Sarah Alexandra Shellard, 1990

Vector Models for Data-Parallel Computing, Guy E. Blelloch, 1990

Experiments in the Machine Interpretation of Visual Motion, David W. Murray and Bernard F. Buxton, 1990

Object Recognition by Computer: The Role of Geometric Constraints, W. Eric L. Grimson, 1990

Representing and Reasoning With Probabilistic Knowledge: A Logical Approach to Probabilities, Fahiem Bacchus, 1990

3D Model Recognition from Stereoscopic Cues, edited by John E.W. Mayhew and John P. Frisby, 1991

Artificial Vision for Mobile Robots: Stereo Vision and Multisensory Perception, Nicholas Ayache, 1991

Truth and Modality for Knowledge Representation, Raymond Turner, 1991

Made-Up Minds: A Constructivist Approach to Artificial Intelligence, Gary L. Drescher, 1991

Vision, Instruction, and Action, David Chapman, 1991

The MIT Press, with Peter Denning as general consulting editor, publishes computer science books in the following series:

ACM Doctoral Dissertation Award and Distinguished Dissertation Series

Artificial Intelligence
Patrick Winston, founding editor
J. Michael Brady, Daniel G. Bobrow, and Randall Davis, editors

Charles Babbage Institute Reprint Series for the History of Computing
Martin Campbell-Kelly, editor

Computer Systems
Herb Schwetman, editor

Explorations with Logo
E. Paul Goldenberg, editor

Foundations of Computing
Michael Garey and Albert Meyer, editors

History of Computing
I. Bernard Cohen and William Aspray, editors

Information Systems
Michael Lesk, editor

Logic Programming
Ehud Shapiro, editor; Fernando Pereira, Koichi Furukawa, Jean-Louis Lassez, and David H. D. Warren, associate editors

The MIT Press Electrical Engineering and Computer Science Series

Research Monographs in Parallel and Distributed Processing
Christopher Jesshope and David Klappholz, editors

Scientific and Engineering Computation
Janusz Kowalik, editor

Technical Communication and Information Systems
Ed Barrett, editor